ISO 9000 and the
Service Sector

Also available from ASQC Quality Press

LearnerFirst™ How to Implement ISO 9000 (software)
with Dr. Lawrence A. Wilson

ISO 9000: Preparing for Registration
James L. Lamprecht

Documenting Quality for ISO 9000 and Other Industry Standards
Gary E. MacLean

At the Service Quality Frontier
Mary M. LoSardo and Norma M. Rossi

A Guidebook to ISO 9000 and ANSI/ASQC Q90
Ronald J. Cottman

To receive a complimentary catalog of publications,
call 800-248-1946.

ISO 9000 and the Service Sector

A Critical Interpretation of the 1994 Revisions

James L. Lamprecht

ASQC Quality Press
Milwaukee, Wisconsin

ISO 9000 and the Service Sector: A Critical Interpretation of the 1994 Revisions
James L. Lamprecht

Library of Congress Cataloging-in-Publication Data

Lamprecht, James L., 1947–
    ISO 9000 and the service sector: a critical interpretation of the
    1994 revisions / James L. Lamprecht.
        p.   cm.
    Includes bibliographical references and index.
    ISBN 0-87389-313-1
    1. Service industries—Quality control.   2. Quality assurance—
Management.   3. Quality control—Management.   I. Title.
HD9980.5.L3   1994
658.5'.62—dc20   94-27380
                                                     CIP

10 9 8 7 6 5 4 3 2 1

ISBN 0-87389-313-1

Acquisitions Editor: Susan Westergard
Project Editor: Kelley Cardinal
Production Editor: Annette Wall
Marketing Administrator: Mark Olson
Set in Avant Garde and Janson Text by Linda J. Shepherd.
Cover design by Shannon Eglinton.
Printed and bound by BookCrafters, Inc.

ASQC Mission: To facilitate continuous improvement and increase customer satisfaction by identifying, communicating, and promoting the use of quality principles, concepts, and technologies; and thereby be recognized throughout the world as the leading authority on, and champion for, quality.

For a free copy of the ASQC Quality Press Publications Catalog, including ASQC membership information, call 800-248-1946.

Printed in the United States of America

  Printed on acid-free recycled paper

ASQC
Quality Press
611 East Wisconsin Avenue
Milwaukee, Wisconsin 53202

Contents

Preface

Ever since 1989, when the first U.S. firms began to achieve registration to one of the three international quality assurance standards found within the ISO 9000 series, interest in ISO 9000 registration has continued to grow at a phenomenal rate.[1] As of December 1993, nearly 1900 firms had achieved registration. Of these, only a handful belong to the service industry. Thus, although few U.S. and European firms have already registered their services, these international standards are still relatively unknown within the various sectors of the service industry. This is hardly surprising when one considers that the generic nature of the ISO 9000 series (which primarily has been implemented by the manufacturing, processing, and assembly sectors) has caused great interpretive confusion among its adopters. Surely, if the series is causing difficulties in the manufacturing, processing, and assembly world, the phenomenon could only be worse within the service industry where processes and procedures are not always as well defined or documented.

The ISO 9000 Series and the Service Sector: Does It Make Sense?

The adaptability of the ISO 9000 series to the service industry has already been demonstrated in Europe, Asia, and the United States. The

ISO 9001, ISO 9002 and, to a lesser extent, ISO 9003 standards have been adopted by airlines (Swissair), hospitals, restaurants, temporary help placement agencies, consulting firms, law firms, a port authority (Tilbury, London), and many other services in the United Kingdom. Butchery outlets of supermarket chains have been registered to the ISO 9002 model in the Netherlands and Denmark. In Belgium, one terminal of the port of Antwerp has completed the recertification process. In the United Sates, examples include software distributors, warehouses, transportation and delivery industries, software developers, software translation agencies, and a stevedore agency (no terminal operators, yet). In France, examples of service industries already registered to ISO 9002 include slaughterhouses, organizations responsible for the maintenance of equipment, dealerships, various enterprises within the transportation sector (particularly with regard to the shipment of hazardous chemicals), ski resorts and spas, hotels, the French government printing office, consulting services, and catering services. No doubt, additional examples could be cited for other regions of the world.

The application of the ISO 9000 series to the service industry is further substantiated when one recognizes that the 1994 revision expands the definition of the term *product* to include hardware, software, processed material, and service "or a combination thereof and shall apply to 'intended product' only."[2]

Despite evidence of successful applications, the question remains as to how well the (updated) standards will translate to the service industry. Indeed, in early 1991 when the author was first asked about the application of the ISO 9000 series to the service sector, difficult issues were more often raised than solved. The challenge continued as I began writing. It soon became apparent that, although most of the standards' clauses translated easily to the service world, some clauses did not transpose well (this will become evident in chapters 4 and 6). Moreover, in the case of some service industries (explored in chapters 5 and 6), the application was sometimes tedious yet, more often than not, relevant. Consequently, I found myself oscillating back and forth between two divergent conclusions: sometimes the application of the standard made perfect sense; sometimes it felt artificially contrived and, hence, convoluted and of dubious value.

My dilemma was resolved when I came across a statement made by Edward De Bono in his latest book, *Surpetition*. Crediting Rosabeth Moss Kanter, De Bono observes that "all products are ways of providing a service."[3] Indeed, the argument could be made that whenever a manufacturer supplies a product, a service is rendered. Products such as toasters, lawn mowers, microwave ovens, televisions, and so on, provide services to their users. Similarly, one can argue that in many cases, whenever a manufacturer launches a product, the company's customer support-service group and/or field service representatives are affected instantly. I would therefore agree with De Bono's conclusion, when he proposes that there are no conceptual differences between a product and a service.[4]

Objectives and Purpose

My intention is not to duplicate the efforts of the many authors who have produced a variety of books on the service industry.[5] Rather, my purpose is

• To present a *critical* review of the ISO 9000 series (with emphasis on the 9001 standard) to service organizations in general. I have emphasized "critical" because the book is not just a description of how each and every clause can apply to the service industry. On several occasions throughout the book (especially in chapter 6), a critical analysis is offered regarding some of the more challenging requirements of the standards, particularly as they relate to some industries within the service sector. While achieving this task, it will become evident that my purpose is not to convince the reader that she or he must adopt the ISO 9000 series. There is very little, if any, preaching within these pages. The decision as to whether or not the ISO 9000 series standards should be adopted rests solely with the reader or his or her customers. It is my hope that this book will provide information that will enable the reader to reach a more rational decision and facilitate an eventual implementation.

• To demonstrate that the service industry can, in most cases and with some thoughtful adaptations, adopt the ISO 9000 series standards.

• To explain and reflect on how the ISO 9000 series needs to be smartly applied to suit the type of industry.

- To provide some industry specific examples on how each paragraph of the ISO 9000 series models (specifically ISO 9001) can be interpreted.

- To alleviate the considerable frustration experienced by the service sector when faced with the task of interpreting, applying, and implementing the ISO 9000 series to their particular industry.

- To help skeptics decide whether or not the ISO 9000 series can be of any value to them.

- To attempt to redirect the rigid interpretation of the standards occasionally demonstrated by some third-party auditors who seem oblivious to the subtle but fundamental differences between certain sectors of the service industry, as well as differences between regulated and nonregulated industries.

Opinions vary as to whether or not the 1994 revisions are to be considered minor or substantial. They certainly are more verbose, and that is not always for the best. For instance, in some cases the contributors felt they had to expand on certain themes in order to clarify a point. On more than one occasion, however, the contributors rely on redundancy to drive home a point. Since little can now be done about the revisions, one might as well adopt and adapt them.

My selection of service industries is limited to a little over half a dozen industries (restaurants, hospitals, banks, consulting firms, landscaping contractors, higher education (with many caveats), food processors, warehouses/distributors, and a few other cases). I realize that someone, somewhere, is likely to object because I did not cover her or his industry. I hope that most readers will recognize that no book can cover all industries. To do so would require writing thousands of books each tailored for a particular industry (there are over 1700 types of services in the Seattle area alone). Even if such a task could be accomplished, a book written for distributors would not satisfy all distributors. Certainly, distributors in general serve one basic function—to distribute goods—but there are some basic differences between a distributor of software and a distributor of valves and pipes to the petrochemical industry. One of the fundamental differences is the type of customers they both serve. The distributor of valves and pipes has a much narrower customer base than the distributor of software who must serve thousands of customers nationwide.

I should also point out that this book does not duplicate many of the ancillary topics already addressed by the author in previous works. For example, regarding implementation, little has been added to what has already been said in my previous two books: *ISO 9000: Preparing for Registration* and *Implementing the ISO 9000 Series.*[6] I see no reason to assume that the implementation process should be any different than the one found in the manufacturing/assembling world (see chapter 7 for additional comments). Although written for a different purpose, I have found the following quotation from E. F. Schumacher's *Small Is Beautiful,* to be the most concise, relevant, and timeless advice regarding implementation strategy.[7]

> The best formulation of the necessary interplay of theory and practice, that I know of, comes from Mao Tse-Tung. Go to practical people, he says, and learn from them: then synthesize their experience into principles and theories; and then return to the practical people and call upon them to put these principles and methods into practice so as to solve their problems and achieve freedom and happiness.

Although I cannot promise you that achieving ISO 9000 registration will bring freedom and happiness to all, I can assure you that employee participation is required if the documentation of your quality assurance system is to resemble the working reality.

Organization

The book is subdivided into two major parts: Part I (chapters 1–3) and Part II (chapters 4–8). The primary purpose of chapter 1 is to (1) review cases of inefficiencies within selected services and (2) demonstrate how the standards could be applied to improve performance. In chapter 2, several themes are presented. The scope, hierarchy, and structure of the series is first reviewed. Differences between the standards are then explained and a brief critical analysis of the ISO 9004-2 guidelines follows. The chapter concludes with an overview as to the applicability of the standards to the service industry (the very leitmotif of this book). Chapter 3 introduces the reader to topics generally not considered by quality professionals. After a review of previous works, the chapter explores concepts of central place theory and economic geography and how they relate to the implementation of the ISO 9000 series. Applications of TQM to the service industry are also covered and some comparisons are made to determine if lessons can be learned.

Part II consists of a detailed critical analysis of how the standards may be applied to the service sector. Chapter 4 introduces the reader to the ISO 9001 standard by analyzing how each clause and subclause could apply to a restaurant. Chapter 5 examines the suitability of the standards when applied to other services. Chapter 6 focuses on some paragraphs, particularly Design Control, that might lead to difficulties or require some careful interpretation for certain types of services. Chapter 7 offers some suggestions on how to approach the challenge of implementation as well as selecting a registrar. Chapter 8 concludes by asking two important questions: is the ISO 9000 series for everyone, and what should one look for in years to come? Appendix A provides the reader with an example of a quality manual. Appendix B is written for software developers and offers an overview of the ISO 9000-3 standard. Limitations of the ISO 9000-3 guidelines are outlined and the guidelines are compared to the Software Engineering Institute's maturity model. Some suggestions and guidance are offered to facilitate implementation. Appendix C addresses some of the current interest expressed by the construction industry in the ISO 9000 series. Appendix D is a glossary of terms used throughout the standard. Since the glossary includes more than a simple definition of terms, the reader is urged to constantly refer to it.

What This Book Is Not

This book does not attempt to apply ISO 9004-2, *Quality Management and Quality System Elements: Guidelines for Services*, to the service industry. This fact should be of no consequence whatsoever to most readers, so why mention it? I have addressed myself to the subpopulation of consultants or ISO 9000 experts who might object to the fact that I have chosen to essentially ignore the ISO 9004-2 guidelines. My primary reason for not selecting the ISO 9004-2 guidelines is that, although well written, the guidelines do not offer any significant improvement to the ISO 9001, ISO 9002, and ISO 9003 standards. Also, as demonstrated in chapter 2, the guidelines are vague and offer few suggestions as to how one might apply the standards. It is important to note that all current worldwide applications of the ISO 9000 series mentioned previously have adopted either the ISO 9001, ISO 9002, or (rarely) the ISO 9003 model for quality assurance. Finally, and most importantly, one must recognize that the ISO 9004-2 guidelines are not enforceable as standards (one can presently only obtain a certificate of registration for ISO 9001, ISO 9002, or ISO 9003). Consequently, given the current importance and hype surrounding the ISO 9000 movement, it is unlikely that anyone would want to adopt a standard for which no recognition (in other words, official registration) would be granted. Such is human nature.

The book does not paraphrase the standards, rather it should be used with the standards. At a minimum, I strongly suggest that the reader purchase the ISO 9001, ISO 9002, or ISO 9003 standard and use the book as an interpretive guide. Purchase of ISO 9000-1 and ISO 9004-1 also is recommended.

Finally, I should reiterate that I do not attempt to find applications where none can be found. In other words, my purpose is not to suggest that the standards can benefit or should be applied to every sector of the service industry. Hence, the use of the word *critical* in the subtitle.

Overall Philosophy

Since the publication of my first book, *ISO 9000: Preparing for Registration*, a host of ISO 9000 books have appeared on the market. Unlike some other authors, I have deliberately shied away from what could be referred to as the prescriptive style of advice. This style consists of specifically telling the reader what must be done to address each clause of the standards and I believe it is contradictory to the standards' intent. Indeed, the ISO 9000 series provides generic models for quality management and quality assurance. In other words, the standards do not specifically prescribe how the user must satisfy a clause, it merely states that a clause and its associated subclauses must be satisfied somehow.

Naturally, the temptation is to ask, "What must I specifically do to satisfy that clause?" There really is not one answer to that question.

My approach is different. Although I recognize the importance of providing examples, and will do so throughout the book (including a quality manual in Appendix A), I do not believe that examples from one industry are necessarily relevant to another except to provide suggestions upon which one can build a customized system. I would even go as far as stating that solely relying on examples might have a detrimental effect. Indeed, this approach might lead the reader into thinking that she or he has to adopt a similar style or method when, in fact, the suggested approach would be inappropriate or ineffective. In order to avoid misleading the reader, I prefer to present the standards from different perspectives (in other words, industries). The objective is to let the reader learn, question, and understand how ISO 9001 and ISO 9002 (the two are now essentially the same with the exception of one paragraph) can be interpreted and applied from a variety of points of view. Then, and only then, can the reader effectively apply the standards to his or her particular set of requirements (see chapters 4 through 6).

Intended Audience

As was the case with my previous two books, my primary focus is on the broad base of ISO 9000 implementers. Nevertheless, many of my comments also are addressed to the population of auditors, consultants, and students of the ISO 9000 series. I hope that they find the book of value. As for the implementers, they can be grouped into three major factions: (1) those who are simply curious as to what the ISO 9000 series is all about, (2) those who are considering implementing an ISO 9000-type quality assurance system simply because their competition recently has achieved registration, and (3) those who recently have been asked by one or more of their major accounts to look into ISO 9000 registration. Although I assume that the reader has some familiarity with the basic principles of quality assurance, all of the chapters should be accessible to the most novice of readers.

By necessity, the focus is targeted for the service industries. Since I am relying on the 1994 updates to the ISO 9000 series, however, I believe that anyone within the manufacturing/assembly world who is either considering ISO 9000 registration or is about to upgrade his or her current system (to the 1994 version) would also benefit. The one major difference from my previous two books is that I am also addressing myself to the population of auditors (and indirectly to the registrars they represent) and consultants. I hope that some of the thoughts and opinions expressed in the following pages will stimulate reflections and debates. The ensuing discussions should lead to corrective and preventive actions. I know of no better way to introduce change.

James Lamprecht
1420 N.W. Gilman Blvd, #2576
Issaquah, WA 98027-7001
Ph: 206-644-9504
Fax: 206-644-9524

Notes

1. Over the past couple of years, the ISO 9000 series of document has grown considerably. Several guidelines have now been added or are in the process of being added to the series. My focus in this book will not be to review all of these guidelines. Rather, when I refer to the ISO 9000 series of documents, I am referring to the five documents ISO 9000-1, ISO 9001, ISO 9002, ISO 9003, and ISO 9004-1 revised in 1994. More specifically, the primary focus of the book will be on the ISO 9001 standard, which encompasses the other two standards (namely, ISO 9002 and ISO 9003).

2. ANSI/ASQC Q9001, 1994, paragraph 3.1, notes 2 and 4.

3. Edward De Bono, *Surpetition* (New York: Harper Business, 1993), 155. Philip B. Crosby in his *Quality Without Tears* (New York: Plume, 1984) proposes a very similar argument on pages 121–124 (Service vs. Manufacturing).

4. There are, of course, differences between the type of processes and services rendered by service organizations (for example, a library and a publisher who provides the library with books.

5. See for example, R. Lee Harris, *The Customer Is King* (Milwaukee, Wis.: ASQC Quality Press, 1991); Linda M. Lash, *The Complete Guide to Customer Service* (New York: John Wiley & Sons, 1989); Ron Willingham, *Hey! I'm the Customer* (New York: Prentice Hall, 1992); Laura A. Liswood, *Servicing Them Right* (New York: Harper Business, 1990); Karl Albrecht and Ron Zemke, *Service in America* (New York: Warner Books, 1985); Jacques H. Horowitz, *The Quality of Service, Towards the Conquest of the Customer* (Paris: InterEditions, 1987); Valerie A. Zeithaml, A. Parasuraman, and Leonard L. Berry, *Delivering Quality Service* (New York: The Free Press, 1990); Thomas F. Wallace, *Customer Driven Strategy* (Essex Junction, Vt.: Oliver Wright Publications, 1992); and Lionel Stebbing, *Quality Management in the Service Industry* (New York: Ellis Horwood, 1990). This last book relies heavily on the ISO 9000 series without really informing the reader except in the bibliography.

6. Both books are published by Marcel Dekker. The first book also is available from ASQC Quality Press.

7. E. F. Schumacher, *Small Is Beautiful* (New York: Perennial Library, Harper & Row, 1973), 253.

Acknowledgments

I wish to thank the reviewers and editors for providing me with their valuable time and comments. Naturally, I could not satisfy all requests without running the risk of contradicting myself. Nevertheless, there is no doubt that their critical comments have helped me significantly improve the contents. My thanks to them. I also would like to express special thanks to Michael Stanick for his technical assistance regarding landscaping. My appreciation also is extended to the many managers who have graciously allowed me to interview them. As always, I would like to thank my wife, Shirley, for patiently enduring more ISO stories.

Part I

The Meaning of Quality in the Service Sector

1 The Veneer of Quality in the Service Industry

The purpose of this opening chapter is threefold: (1) to demonstrate that the service industry, as any other industry, is not immune to problems of quality, (2) to illustrate that in many cases (after some allowances are made) there are striking similarities between the service industry and the manufacturing/assembly world, and (3) to introduce the reader to a cursory interpretation of the ISO 9001 standard while simultaneously demonstrating its suitability to the service industry.

What Do You Mean by Quality?

I always have managed to resist the temptation to define quality. Finding flaws in the myriad of definitions was so much easier. While searching for the all-encompassing perfect definition of quality, I have avoided referring to the ISO 8402 (1986) quality vocabulary document because I found the definitions listed in ISO 8402 to be occasionally disappointing.

The current definition of quality: "The totality of features and characteristics of a product or service that bear on its ability to satisfy stated or implied needs," is no exception. Although the seven notes attached to the definition provide some valuable insights, my principal objection concerns the reference to implied needs. I believe "perceived need" would have been more accurate but, equally difficult to satisfy.

As a customer of goods and services, I often am unable to clearly explain to a salesperson the nature of my implied needs. In many cases, customers have great difficulties stating their needs. In other cases, particularly in the service sector, customers have little or no input in the definition/requirements of quality (of service). For example, some hotels seem to be designed with little, if any, customer input. Little emphasis seems to be placed on internal (in other words, hotel-generated) noise reduction. Carefully structured surveys could provide design engineers with valuable input information that would help them focus on such internal noise generators as slamming doors, noisy plumbing, loud televisions, and so on. Other examples could be cited (see John McKnight's review of service and need in chapter 3).

Among the many definitions of quality provided throughout the decades, I find the following by J. Sittig to be most practical.[1]

> The problem of quality then is a problem of adjustment of the properties of a product to the situation of demand. *This adjustment is made all the more difficult by the fact that the same product has to comply with the demands of potential customers, whose requirements differ.*

I believe Sittig's definition captures the essence of the daily challenges faced by thousands of suppliers as they attempt to satisfy their myriad of customer requirements. The challenge to have the same product comply with a variety of demands also is experienced by the ISO 9000 series standards. Indeed, in this case, there are three standards (ISO 9001, ISO 9002, ISO 9003) that are applied to a great variety of business environments. As Sittig observes in the case of quality, in order to ensure reasonable longevity and overall customer satisfaction, the ISO 9000 series (or rather its interpretation) will have to adapt and expand to satisfy the varied needs of its broad customer bases. Failure to do so will surely produce irate customers.

What Is Meant by Service?

In an attempt to define what is meant by the words *service industry*, I read through a few books on the subject. Most were not helpful. One definition proposed that the service sector consisted of "industries whose output is intangible."[2] Although one could argue that certain services such as consulting or educational services may be categorized as *intangible* services, the definition is unnecessarily limiting because it eliminates many entrepreneurs from the service industry. Indeed, warehousing facilities, distributors, delivery services, cleaning and maintenance services, as well as countless others, do provide *tangible* services. Frustrated, I picked up my dictionary and looked up the word *service*. After reading through some 17 definitions of service I was left with the notion that a service was

- The occupation or duties of a servant
- Employment in duties or work for another, especially for a government
- Work done for others as an occupation or business
- One of 14 other definitions[3]

So much for a concise definition.

Although most people might have a good idea as to what is meant by the service industry, defining what it is and what it represents is a much more difficult task. Part of the difficulty is that the word *service* covers a very broad range of activities (as a cursory look through your local Yellow Pages will confirm). The corner convenience store, the gas station, the barber shop, the supermarket, the local bank, your favorite restaurant, the regional cable service, the regional utility company, the local hospital, and the Internal Revenue Service all provide services. As will be explored further in chapter 3, however, these services vary not only in their nature, but in a crucial dimension that to date has been ignored by service experts and quality gurus alike—the geographical extent of their sphere of influence. In other words, each of the aforementioned services requires a different population density threshold in order to survive. Consequently, the ensuing hierarchical spatial relationship between services will play an important role when one tries to adapt the ISO 9000 series standards to various sectors of the service industry.

Although chapter 3 provides a more careful analysis and definition of the service industry, this chapter proposes that the service industry consists of all those public or private industries (invariably listed in the Yellow Pages) whose activities range from abrasives to zoning consultants.[4] Having defined the bounds of the service industry, let us explore what is meant by *the veneer of quality in the service industry*.

Our Service Industry from a Foreigner's Point of View

Some time ago, I was having a conversation with a British friend. I no longer remember how or why but the topic eventually drifted toward the quality of service in the United States. To my surprise, my friend suggested that the quality of service in the United States left something to be desired. Having lived in the United Kingdom and France I have had countless contacts with a great variety of British and French service industries. Contrary to the many stories one hears about the typically rude waiter in Paris, my experience in both the United Kingdom and France was positive. Naturally, I also had my share (few as they were) of frustrating experiences. For example, I recall the seemingly endless telephone rings and long pauses listening to recorded messages while waiting for someone at British Rail or Air France to pick up the phone. It seems that (at least in the United Kingdom and France) most employees have a propensity to perceive the phone as a nuisance rather than an opportunity to serve a customer.

I also recall how difficult it was to obtain general information regarding the service industry. When the time came to rent a television (a rather routine act in most U.S. towns), my wife and I discovered that the process of finding a store that would rent televisions was more difficult than anticipated. Naturally, part of our difficulties concerned the fact that we were unfamiliar with the culture. Nonetheless, obtaining information relating to the service industry in general (particularly leasing) appeared to be generally more difficult than in the United States.

So, how could my friend claim that the service industry in the United States left a lot to be desired? What did he mean? His reply was, "You have a fine veneer of quality, you know, the have-a-nice-day–type of comments, but beyond that there is not as much follow-through as in the U.K." After initially rejecting his explanation, probably more on nationalistic principles than on reason, I began to reflect on his comments and asked myself: "Could he be right?" If so, what was the evidence. Reviewing some of my recent frustrating experiences with various sectors of the service industry, I had to rescind my original thought.

Perhaps the service industry could benefit from an ISO 9000–type quality assurance system; perhaps my British friend was right after all.

The following examples (all based on personal experiences, but probably shared by many) will help illustrate how the service industry routinely violates some of the basic tenets of quality assurance modeled in the ISO 9000 series. I first will present the cases and then review the specific nonconformances that would likely be uncovered should the service in question apply for registration.

"All of Our Agents Are Busy, Please Stay on the Line," or the Curse of the 800 Number

At one time or another everyone has had to dial an 800 number. It is very likely that most people have had to listen to the following messages (or variety thereof).

> All our agents are busy. Your call is important to us.
> Please stay on the line for the next available agent. Do
> not hang up as this will cause further delays.

On more than one occasion, I have had to listen to the above message for as much as *12* minutes. This compares favorably with the 14 minutes for Air France and the 12 to 14 minutes for British Rail. Having had to wait several times, I decided to write a letter, which, to this day, remains unanswered.[5]

"We Are Doing the Best We Can"

This example relates to my experience with a Pacific Northwest utility company. The area I used to live in is very forested and hilly; 90-foot trees surround most of the properties. These bucolic surroundings have their unfortunate drawbacks whenever strong winds start blowing. Fortunately, strong winds do not blow every day, but they do blow every winter. When they do, branches (up to 18 to 20 feet), and occasionally trees, come crashing down. Naturally, power shortages are never too far behind. This happens every year. In December 1992 the winds were gusting stronger than usual and we lost power. What was unusual was the duration of the power shortage.

As an expert in power shortages, I decided to wait a couple of hours before calling the emergency number. As usual, the number was busy. There was not even a recording to inform customers as to the maintenance status. Four hours later (around midnight) the number was still busy. Repeated dialing within the next 10 minutes proved to be futile. At 3:30 A.M. I finally got through. When I politely explained my problem I was told: "We are doing the best we can, sir." I could not resist replying: "Obviously, that is not good enough since I have now been waiting for nearly eight hours." When I suggested that a tree trimming program should be considered since the problem was recurring every year, the reply was: "That would cost money, and we don't have the staff to keep all year." Of course, I had not suggested that a special staff be maintained all year, only during the high wind season. Eighteen and a half hours later power was restored. They finally had done all that they could.

The Case of the Uninformed Clerk

This account relates to an incident I experienced with an automotive service center. I had lost one of the gold-plated emblems on the trunk of my car. I am not sure if the emblem fell off or was deliberately snapped off by some overzealous collector. At any rate, I decided that the missing part had to be replaced. Calling the service department of my nearest dealer, I was confident that the matter could be resolved rather quickly. The following (abbreviated) conversation ensued.

Lamprecht: "I'd like to replace the gold-plated emblem for the trunk."

Service: "You'll have to purchase the whole set."

Lamprecht: "How much?"

Service: "$450."

Lamprecht: "$450! But I only need one of the pieces, not the whole set."

Service: "Sorry, for the gold-plated emblems, you'll have to buy the set. Perhaps you could buy the regular silver set and have it plated."

Lamprecht: "How much?"

Service: "$25 plus plating."

Lamprecht: "Where is it plated?"

Service: "I don't really know. I'll transfer you to sales."

(I repeat the entire story to the salesperson.)

Sales: "Oh no, that's not right. You don't have to buy the whole set and you don't have to worry about gold plating. We have the gold-plated item you need for $45. Let me transfer you to service."

Lamprecht: "But service told me. . . ."

Sales: "You'll have to talk to Ed. I'll transfer you."

Lamprecht: "May I speak with Ed?"

(I tell Ed my story for the third time.)

Ed: "Yeah, that is right. We have the item in stock. Do you want to pick it up this afternoon?"

Lamprecht: "Yes, thank you."

[*Note:* When I purchased the item, I noticed that the $45 emblem was made of plastic!]

"The Check Is in the Mail"

As a consultant, I often subcontract with various organizations. This next story is very dear to me because it deals with an aspect of quality assurance that often is neglected even by serious practitioners of total quality management. In this particular instance there is an ironic twist to the story: the company in question is a major accounting firm that prides itself in practicing total quality management.

I had completed an ISO 9000 consulting assignment on behalf of the accounting firm some time in late September. It was now late November and I still had not been paid despite repeated reassurances that I would be paid within 30 days. After numerous phone calls, during which I was given wonderful excuses such as "The check was cut yesterday, but we can't mail it until next week," I was on the verge of giving up. By late December, I was still waiting. I then decided to call accounting and find out what was happening. As one might expect, it took the customary three phone calls before I finally was connected with someone who knew what I was talking about. I eventually found out that the person responsible for the account was Eric X. Naturally, I could not reach Eric, but I did leave a message on his voice mail. Meanwhile (the matter was now approaching 90 days), I decided that it was time to talk to someone in upper management. Recounting my story for the nth time, I was told that accounting "does not have its act together," and I was assured that an answer would be provided within a couple of days. Sure enough, the next day the manager explained that my check was found on Eric's desk (Eric, by the way, had not bothered to return my phone call). The check would be mailed within the next couple of days. I received it one week later, nearly 100 days after the completion of the assignment.

"Where Are My Test Results?"

Similar problems undoubtedly have been experienced by thousands of individuals. When my wife and I applied for a new insurance policy (a case study in itself, but I will spare you the details), we had to have blood tests. When we requested that the test results be mailed to us, we were informed that although test results normally were not mailed, we could request them and expect them within four to six weeks.[6] Six weeks later we still did not have our test results. More phone calls (some placed directly to the laboratory performing the tests), more excuses/explanations/apologies, and nine weeks later we still did not have our test results. One day, the test results arrived. I no longer recall exactly how long it took, but it was more than eight months later.

"When Can I Expect My Bank Cards?"

A similar incident occurred with our local bank when we ordered our bank (cash withdrawal) cards. Once again we were told the wait would be three to four weeks for the cards. Five weeks later there still were no cards. When we explained that we really needed the cards, we were told that we should reapply for a new set, which would take another three to four weeks to arrive. We filled out the second set of forms and waited. About a week later (a total of six weeks) the first set appeared. The second set was mailed four weeks later.[7]

"I'd Like to Correct My Address"

Over the past three years I have moved four times. Certainly that is more than the average person. Every move requires a change of address. Invariably, the process went smoothly except for one minor problem: remnants of the old address somehow were transferred to the new address. This problem has occurred more than once and I often have wondered how the error could happen since I always call in the agency in question and read my address to the operator in charge of address correction. In addition, I always mark the new address on the back of all the envelopes and make sure I tick off the change of address box.

"You Can't Order That!"

This last example epitomizes what my British friend meant by the "Have a nice day" type of quality. I was having breakfast in a hotel near San Francisco where I was giving a seminar. It was early and there were few customers. A gentleman sat at a table near mine and began studying the menu. The waitress arrived and greeted him with the usual "Hi, coffee?", which he declined. When she came back the following conversation took place.

Gentleman: "I'd like to order this" (pointing at the menu).

Waitress: "You can't have that."

Gentleman: "Why not? It's perfect—I am not too hungry."

Waitress: "I'm sorry, that is a child's breakfast. It is half-price."

Gentleman: "I'll pay the difference, but that is exactly what I would like."

Waitress: "I'm sorry, I can't give it to you."

Gentleman: "Is that management's policy?"

Waitress: "Yes, I'm sorry."

Gentleman: "That is a bad policy. Well, all right, give me this" (pointing at the menu).

Obviously, not all policies are good policies. A better policy would have been to allow the waitress to deviate from the procedure. Of course, maybe another waitress, more willing to please the customer rather than the policy, would have accepted the order.

ISO 9000 and the Service Industry

What the previous accounts reveal is that procedures could have been improved in the majority of cases, along with customer satisfaction, if a quality assurance system modeled after the ISO 9000 series had been in place. Most of the cases reveal clear deficiencies in one or more paragraphs of ISO 9001 or ISO 9002.[8] For example, the following *apparent* deficiencies or weaknesses are evident (I have emphasized apparent because an audit is necessary to fully investigate if there are deficiencies).

- Management responsibility
- Verification resources and personnel
- The quality system
- Contract review
- Purchasing (policy)
- Process control
- Product identification and traceability
- In-process inspection
- Control of nonconforming product
- Corrective action
- Training

A review of each of the items follows.

Management Responsibility

Most of the case histories exhibit a range of problems centered around management responsibility issues. For example, regarding the 12-minute wait on the 800 line, one can only assume that this is a deliberate policy on the part of management. I do not mean to suggest that management sets the waiting time at 12 minutes, but that it does not provide enough resources (in other words, operators), which directly affects the length of the queue. From the customer's point of view the message coming from the supplier seems to be: "Since we are providing you with access to a free 800 number, you should be willing to wait a certain amount of time, and we will determine how long is too long." In this particular case, recall that my letter to customer relations never was answered.[9]

Similarly, the utility company appears to be saying to its customers, "It is all right if you are inconvenienced a few hours out of the year. Besides, we could not possibly cut all the trees along the lines." This argument is almost convincing. After all, one might argue that a power outage of 24 hours per year is equivalent to a 99.997 efficiency rate. Not bad, except when you consider that a few thousand angry customers are affected by the outage.

In each of these cases it is difficult, but not impossible, for customers to negotiate with the supplier for better services. Nevertheless, these suppliers, although regulated by various state and government agencies, are at a significant advantage since they benefit from an enviable monopolistic position.

In both cases, the supplier had not addressed one or more of the following criteria specified by paragraph 4.1.2.1 (Responsibility and Authority) of the standards.[10]

1. Initiate action to prevent the occurrence of any nonconformities relating to the product/service, process, and quality system.

2. Identify and record any problems relating to the product/service, process, and quality system.

3. Initiate, recommend, or provide solutions through designated channels.

4. Verify the implementation of solutions.

5. Control further processing, delivery, or installation of nonconforming product/service until the deficiency or unsatisfactory condition has been corrected.

The phone company could probably argue that the 12-minute wait is not a nonconformity. Moreover, because of limited resources (imposed by difficult economic conditions), customers should be expected to wait a certain amount of time.[11] Therein lies one of the major difficulties with many service companies—the responsibility, authority, and the interrelation of all personnel who manage, perform, and verify work affecting quality is not always defined.[12] Obviously, some organizations within the service sector know something about management responsibility and quality of service. When I called another carrier to ask the same question I was immediately transferred to someone in charge of quality. I had similar success when I called a local Seattle bank (and a hospital) and was transferred to the vice president in charge of service quality (see chapter 5).

Contract Review, Nonconformity, and Process Control

Within certain sectors of the service industry, contracts tend to be verbal and/or ill-defined (a characteristic also found in the manufacturing world). In such cases, poorly or vaguely stated contracts, which assume or presume an understanding of services rendered, can lead to difficulties and occasional ill feelings between a customer and the supplier. Even if the verbal instructions are precise and apparently well understood, surprises can occur. One such example was illustrated in the the-check-is-in-the-mail anecdote. The subject of payment within net thirty days had been specified more than once. Nonetheless, because of certain management/accounting policies that specifically allowed for, or tolerated delays, the 30-day policy is violated repeatedly. In this particular instance several clauses of the standards could be invoked for possible noncompliance. Besides contract review, one could also cite management responsibility, process control, control of nonconforming service, lack of corrective actions, and no internal verification/audit activities. The system is allowed to operate at its current level of inefficiency.

Beginning with contract review, it appears that the supplier (in other words, the accounting firm) does not maintain, or perhaps does not follow, its own procedures for contract review. In this particular case, one of the root causes was the firm's client who was delinquent by as much as 70 days. Not receiving its payment, the firm did what was predictable—it delayed payment to its subcontractor (in other words, me). A clear policy statement could have helped, although not necessarily resolved, the problem. Guided by requirements imposed by the ISO 9001 or ISO 9002 standards, the following action could have been formalized.

> Ensure that contract reviews are maintained and that
> the contractual requirements are adequately defined
> and documented.

Specific statements stating payment policy, as well as penalties, could be included. Naturally, the reality of everyday operations dictates that carefully specified contractual requirements do not guarantee compliance. If some customers choose to take longer than agreed upon to pay their suppliers, one cannot always rely on the (costly) legal system to enforce contracts.

The best contract procedure does not amount to anything if management is willing to accept a risky customer, that is, a customer whose financial status is poorly rated. We are back to management responsibility and quality policy issues. One would therefore question operational procedures. Certain unwritten procedures do exist, but one wonders if other equally pertinent procedures should not be implemented. For example, in an effort to monitor customer satisfaction, project status, and overall cost maintenance, consultants are routinely monitored (much to their annoyance) by the firm's partners. Rather than monitor their consultants, the firm should also monitor its clients, a delicate situation in the consulting service industry.

Finally, since these incidences of delayed payments were repeated once more, it is evident that no nonconforming procedures were in place or, if they were, they were not followed. Procedures to ensure that service that does not conform to specified requirements is prevented from inadvertent recurrence were absent.[13]

Inspection and Verification Activities and Training

When an address correction is not correctly filled out, a process known as *verification activity* does not take place. Yet, given the millions of orders that are placed over the phone every day by hundreds of mail order service organizations, the process of mail ordering and credit payment has reached a very high level of sophistication and accuracy. Surely someone is doing something right most of the time. If so, why is address correction prone to a higher frequency of error? The answer may be that the transaction is not considered a purchase and therefore is not subject to the same scrutiny. Consequently, the operator in charge of address corrections may not be trained to verify (read back to the user) the new address as it appears on his or her screen; hence the opportunity for error.

Poorly defined processes, few corrective actions to redress customer complaints, inadequate or nonexistent formal procedures to resolve recurring nonconforming activities, failure to verify purchasing orders, management's failure to audit its quality assurance system, and inadequate or poorly defined operational parameters are some examples of typical everyday problems faced by the service industry. In most cases, customers walk away frustrated by their experiences. In other cases, failure to implement an effective quality assurance system can lead to deadly consequences.

Case Study: *E. Coli* O157.H7 and the Importance of Traceability and Other Related Quality Assurance Issues

In January 1993 when four children died as a result of *E. coli* infection contracted in a Seattle fast-food restaurant, USDA officials worked frantically to upgrade their current inspection system. Investigation revealed the deadly infection had been caused by tainted meat that had not been cooked long enough. To avoid recurrence of such an unfortunate incidence, the following new rules have been proposed.[14]

- Animals must be identified by place of origin, so that tainted meat can be traced back to the farm where the livestock was raised.

- Rapid testing for contamination.

- More detailed records on meat sales and transfers, to help trace bad meat to its origins.

- New labeling designed to educate the public on how to handle and cook meat safely.

- Tighter safety controls at slaughter and meat processing plants.

- Proposed new methods to slaughter and cut up beef to reduce feces contamination.

All of these recommendations closely parallel ISO 9002 requirements. In fact, many of the paragraphs are particularly relevant. To help illustrate some of the virtues of the ISO 9000 series, let us review some of the questions that could have been raised by an ISO 9000 auditor had the fast-food restaurant applied for 9002 certification.[15] Figure 1.1 shows a schematic of the customer-supplier relationship. (*Note:* Comments and/or questions are listed according to the relevant ISO paragraphs and subparagraphs.)

1. *Purchasing: assessment of subcontractors (4.6.2)*–As an auditor I would like to know how the fast-food restaurant places orders with its suppliers. Particularly, I would like to know the selection process and the quality requirements upon which the selection process is based. I also

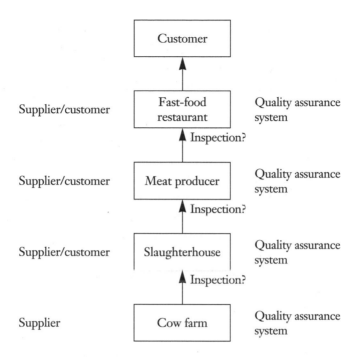

Figure 1.1. Supplier/customer chain.

would like to see the list of *approved* suppliers. In this case this is important because it appears that the contaminated meat came from a California supplier. One would therefore like to know, as required by the standard, what was the selection process for suppliers. Finally, I would like to know how the fast-food restaurant ensures that the supplier's quality assurance system is effective. We now know that USDA inspection/approval was inadequate.

2. *Verification of purchased product*–Paragraph 4.6.4.2, only required if specified in the contract, often is not applicable in the manufacturing world; however in this instance it is relevant. Users of the standards often are confused by the clause because the paragraph refers to the purchaser and the *supplier.* In the slightly confusing parlance of ISO (1987) (updated in 1994), the purchaser is the customer and the supplier is the user of the standard. Thus, if the fast-food firm is applying for ISO 9002

registration, it is the supplier. Its customers would then be referred to as the purchasers (of hamburgers). If, however, the company supplying the meat patties to the fast-food chain is applying for ISO 9002 registration, it now becomes the supplier and the fast-food chain is the purchaser (of meat patties).

The paragraph requires that, when specified in the contract, the purchaser (in other words, the fast-food restaurant) or its representative "shall be afforded the right to verify at the subcontractor premises and the supplier's premises that subcontracted product conforms to specified requirements."[16] Such a requirement should be very important. Interpreting the standard from the fast-food restaurant's point of view, an ISO 9000 auditor would like to know if its contract with the supplier of meat calls for verification at the source (if not, why not). If verification is called for, one also would like to know the specific requirements (for example, type of laboratory analysis). If the paragraph is to be applied, records would have to be maintained by the purchasing department.

3. *Product identification and traceability*–Until recently this apparently was not an important criterion. However, as shown, improvement in methods would require animal traceability to the farm. Such a requirement is in direct agreement with the Product Identification and Traceability clause (4.8), which requires that, where appropriate, the supplier shall establish and maintain procedures and records for identifying the product during all stages of production, delivery, and installation.

An auditor would like to know how batches or lots of meat are identified and traced throughout the various processes. The nature and extent of traceability would have to be determined and enforced by the USDA. The ISO 9000 auditor would only verify that the procedures are called for, in place, and followed.

4. *Process control*–Since it appears that the meat was not cooked long enough at a high enough temperature, the auditor would like to review the cooking procedures for meat. Specifically, and following the Process Control clause (4.9) of the ISO 9001 or 9002 standard, the auditor would look for evidence that the various processes and work instructions are documented and compliant with specific standards/codes. In addition, the auditor would investigate what characteristics (for example,

temperature) are monitored during cooking or other processes. Additionally, since the standard speaks of criteria for workmanship, the auditor would like to know how said workmanship is monitored/controlled for effectiveness. Are representative samples (for example, photographs) used to determine criteria of acceptability. In most cases, the customer decides if the workmanship is appropriate; if it isn't, the meal is returned for reprocessing.

5. *Inspection and testing* (4.10)–Although relevant, these paragraphs would have to be adapted to the fast-food industry. Clauses 4.10.1 through 4.10.5 refer to incoming, in-process, and final inspection. Although one could imagine an incoming inspection plan for meat patties (but not at the restaurant site), it is more difficult to envision an in-process and final inspection and testing procedure. Certainly, the cook does perform some form of visual in-process and final inspection to ensure that the order conforms to customer specifications. Chapter 4 will elaborate on these issues.

6. *Inspection, measuring, and test equipment*–This is one of the longest clauses (known as paragraph 4.11). Although it might appear not to be applicable at first sight, it is pertinent. Since meat must be cooked at certain temperatures (140° Fahrenheit in many states), it is important to ensure that all thermometers and timer devices are properly calibrated and accurate within a certain acceptable tolerance. These are some of the issues addressed by the Inspection, Measuring, and Test Equipment clause. The auditor would like to verify when the instruments (in other words, ovens) were last tested, how frequently thermometers are calibrated, accuracy of the thermometers, and other important related questions.

7. *Other important questions*–The auditor also would like to know how often the quality assurance system is audited, location of the records, and corrective actions implemented during the last audit. Also, the issue of training is important. What sort of training, if any, is in place, and are records of said training maintained.

Naturally, a host of other questions could be asked, but the purpose of this anecdote was not to present all possible scenarios. Rather, the objective was to demonstrate that, with some adaptation, creativity, and interpretation, the ISO 9000 series can be effectively applied to various service industries.

Of particular relevance to this case is the successful application in the Netherlands and Denmark of the ISO 9002 model to butchery outlets. In the Netherlands, a consumer group led by the Product Board for Livestock and Meat (PVV) has pressured the Dutch meat and livestock industry to develop the *Integrale Keting Beheersing* (IKB or integral chain management), a system of integrated quality control for the meat industry. The system is partly based on the ISO 9000 series of quality assurance, and it is estimated that by the year 2000, "the entire Dutch meat sector will conform to ISO 9000 quality standards: from the animal geneticists to breeders, pig fatteners, slaughterhouses, cutting plants, retailers, butchers, and supermarkets—all the way along the supply chain to the consumer's shopping bag."[17] Perhaps a similar scenario could be envisaged in the United States in the near future.

Some Do It Right!

There are many organizations within the service industry that do provide excellent services. Most of us have experienced excellent service, courtesy, and friendliness on the part of staff members. My dentist and his staff have developed a series of procedures that certainly have little to do with dentistry, but always are appreciated. Every year my wife and I receive a birthday card. When we check in the staff always seem to remember our last conversation. They always ask us about our last trip, which may have been six to 12 months earlier.

Puzzled as to how they could remember the vacation schedules of hundreds of clients and other various tidbits of information, I asked Dr. J., "How do you do it?"

"Simple," he replied, "we keep a personal file on all of our customers where we enter not only dental records, but other information such as where you lived last year." Impressive. Now if only I did not have to wait 15 to 20 minutes after arriving on time, everything would be perfect.

My second positive experience relates to a restaurant in Houston where the food is excellent and the service efficient. One of the usual features of that restaurant is that customers are assigned a waiter/wait-ress, but any waiter/waitress can bring drinks, food, or refill glasses. Intrigued by the process, I asked the manager if the tips were also shared by all waiters. "No," she replied, "each waiter is responsible for his or her table, but we emphasize teamwork."

Further questioning revealed that each waiter and waitress follows a two-day training session at the company's headquarters. The training program emphasizes the general operation procedures of the restaurant as well as lectures on the etiquette of waiting on customers. The train-ing session is then followed up with two additional days of on-the-job training, where the trainee shadows a graduate and learns how the sys-tem works. That is a pretty good quality policy for a restaurant where the staff is 100 percent part-time students.

Conclusion

This chapter's intent was to illustrate how standards could not only be applied to the service industry, but also could be beneficial to many sectors of the service industry. As is the case with the manufacturing/assembly world, the application of a quality assurance model will not guarantee zero defects. The personal frustrating experiences described herein will not disappear the minute an ISO 9000–type quality assurance system is implemented. Nonetheless, there are advantages for adopting a quality assurance system modeled after the ISO 9000 series. At a minimum, the formalization of a quality system into a concise and thoughtful set of documented procedures is a worthy exercise that should benefit the user. If one is to rely on testimonials from the manufacturing world, imple-mentation of an ISO 9000 quality assurance model usually shows divi-dends within the first few months. Even if operational costs are not significantly reduced, improvement in system efficiency (brought about by teamwork) invariably leads to increased customer satisfaction. The remaining chapters should prove that point.

Before demonstrating how the ISO 9000 series can be adapted to the service industry, the origin, structure, and contents of the ISO 9000 series must be explained.

Notes

1. J. Sittig, "Defining Quality Costs," *Quality Engineering* 28 (1964): 105, emphasis added. I find Marianne Murdock's one-page definition of quality to be very good in *On Q 8* (October 1993): 3. Perhaps quality cannot be concisely defined.

2. K. Albrecht and R. Zemke, *Service in America* (New York: Warner Books, 1985).

3. *American Heritage Dictionary*, 2d ed., s.v. "service."

4. These are the first and last entries listed in the yellow pages of the city I currently live in (Bellevue, Washington).

5. I am not suggesting that all 800 numbers require much patience. Some companies do answer their 800 line after the first ring. It has been my experience, however, that in the majority of cases, 800 numbers are tantamount to waiting.

6. Have you ever wondered why in today's world of express mail some services (except billing), still take four to six weeks to be delivered. For example, most airlines claim they require a three- to four-week notice in order to deliver mileage award tickets free of charge. Of course, for an administrative fee ranging from $35 to $60 they can miraculously arrange for those same tickets to be delivered the next day.

7. The three to four weeks delivery for bank cards is not unique to the United States. When we lived in France, we ordered bank cards with the BNP in Paris. After filling out a few forms (French banks are much more conservative than American banks when it comes to issuing bank cards), we were told: "About four weeks before delivery." Sure enough, four weeks later to the day, we received our cards packed in a protective sleeve. Within two weeks of using our cards, we discovered that they no longer worked. Explaining my problem to the bank clerk, I was told that the bank had problems with the card supplier. "You must make sure you protect your card. Always store your card in the sleeve."

    "But, I do!" I replied.

    "Well, I don't know what to tell you. Would you like to order new cards?"

8. These deficiencies also are typical in the manufacturing and assembly industries.

9. The irony is that the company in question is spending quite a few dollars advertising how wonderful their service is. Certainly, one could not argue that their employees are most helpful, however, if you do not have enough patience, you will never know how helpful they might be.

10. ANSI/ASQC Q9001, 1994, paragraph 4.1.2.1 Responsibility and Authority, with the following modification by the author: the word *service* has been appended to the word *product*. I should add that in the case of the utility company, an intensive tree trimming program was recently implemented; perhaps too many customers finally complained! Due to its more limited scope, the ISO 9003 standard has less demands.

11. Such delays are acceptable, particularly when they are announced. For example, some companies do inform their customers that "your expected wait will be three minutes," and it is.

12. ANSI/ASQC Q9001, 1994, paragraph 4.1.2.1.

13. An informal/undocumented corrective action was implemented when I eventually was allowed to directly bill the client. Naturally, the client paid within 30 days.

14. Extracted from the *Seattle Post-Intelligencer*, 17 March 1993.

15. The comments that follow would apply to every one of the suppliers listed in Figure 1.1. Certainly, the slaughterhouse could use ISO 9002 registration.

16. ANSI/ASQC Q9001, 1994, paragraph 4.6.4.2.

17. F. Van Rossem, "Piggybacking on ISO 9000," *ISO 9000 News 2* (November/December 1993): 7–8.

2   The ISO 9000 Series Standards

Introduction

The purpose of this chapter is to (1) provide the reader with an overview of the ISO 9000 series: its structure, hierarchy, and interpretation of its contents, (2) to review the updates made to the series, and (3) comment on some of the issues relating to the practicality of applying the standards to services. Specific examples will be introduced for various industries in Part II. The focus will be on the ISO 9001 model, the most inclusive quality assurance system. This is done as a necessity and convenience. To devote three chapters for three standards that are nested within one another would be a futile exercise. Users wishing to focus on ISO 9002 or ISO 9003 can ignore the appropriate paragraphs.

Preamble to the ISO 9000 Series

Leaders of the European community have long recognized that different technical regulations and national standards in the individual member states were a real obstacle impeding the development of Europe's full competitive potential. To alleviate the problem, the council responded on May 7, 1985, with a resolution setting out a new approach to technical harmonization and standards. The resolution outlined four basic principles.[1]

1. Legislative harmonization is limited to the adoption, by means of Directives based on Article 100 of the European Economic Community (EEC) Treaty, of the essential safety requirements (or other requirements in the general interest) with which products put on the market must conform in order to enjoy free movement throughout the Community;

2. The task of drawing up the technical specifications needed for the production and placing on the market of products conforming to the essential requirements established by the Directives, while taking into account the current stage of technology, is entrusted to the competent standardized bodies;

3. *The technical specifications are not mandatory and maintain their status as voluntary standards;*

4. Nevertheless, at the same time national authorities are obliged to recognize that products manufactured in conformity with the harmonized standards (or, provisionally, with national standards) are presumed to conform to the "essential requirements" established in the Directives. *This leaves the producer the choice of not manufacturing in conformity with the standards, in which case however, he has an obligation to prove that his products conform to the essential requirements of the Directives.*

What Are Directives?

A directive is an EEC law binding on the Member States as to the result to be achieved, but the choice of method is their own. In practice, national implementation legislation in the form deemed appropriate in each

Member State is necessary in most cases. *This is an important point as businesses affected by a directive have to take account of the national implementing legislation as well as the directive.*[2]

Of the 282 directives currently available, only a few apply to so-called regulated products. The main categories of regulated products are

- Pressure vessels
- Toy safety
- Machine safety
- Mobile machinery and lifting and loading appliances
- Electromagnetic compatibility
- Nonautomatic weighing instruments
- Active implantable medical devices
- Gas appliances
- Personal protective equipment
- Testing and certification: conformity assessment procedures
- Lifts
- Electrical equipment for use in potential explosive atmospheres

Although the European directives cover a broad range of topics from "Duty free admission of fuel contained in the fuel tank of commercial motor vehicles, lorries and coaches," (Directive 1) to "Proposal for a Third Council Directive Life Insurance amending," (Directive 320); few, if any of the directives are specifically written for the service sector. Directive 109, entitled "Recommendation on standardized information in existing hotels," is one of the few directives that may indirectly affect a service industry. Even in this case, it is doubtful that the directive would require some form of ISO 9000 registration. Nevertheless, although few if any directives directly affect the service sector, one should not conclude that the service sector is immune to the ISO 9000 series. Indeed, *it is not* immune to ISO 9000, as more service industries are finding out.

The ISO 9000 Series

The ISO 9000 series officially came into existence in 1987 when the following five documents were published by the International Organization for Standardization in Geneva.[3]

1. ISO 9000-1 (ANSI/ASQC Q9000-1)
   Quality Management and Quality Assurance Standards: Guidelines for Selection and Use

2. ISO 9001 (ANSI/ASQC Q9001)
   Quality Systems—Model for Quality Assurance in Design/ Development, Production, Installation, and Servicing

3. ISO 9002 (ANSI/ASQC Q9002)
   Quality Systems—Model for Quality Assurance in Production and Installation

4. ISO 9003 (ANSI/ASQC Q9003)
   Quality Systems—Model for Quality Assurance in Final Inspection and Test

5. ISO 9004-1 (ANSI/ASQC Q9004-1)
   Quality Management and Quality System Elements—Guidelines

Although not immediately accepted by the world community, since 1989 the standards' popularity have increased exponentially. In the United States, where the standards have been adopted as the ANSI/ASQC Q-9000-1–Q9004-1 series, nearly 1800 sites had achieved registration as of December 1993. Perhaps the single most important driving force that has led to today's guarded acceptance of the ISO 9000 series has been the fear of being locked out of the European market once economic unification is completed. This fear, exaggerated as it may be, can be attributed partially to occasional inaccurate press coverage.[4] Since much has already been written about the ISO 9000 series, I see no need to add to the already overabundant literature, except to provide the reader with some key references found in the bibliography.

Scope of the ISO 9000 Series of Quality Assurance Models

It is important to remember that although the ISO 9000 series was written for all industries, its contents and structure favor the manufacturing world.

This has led to the greatest source of confusion among those wishing to implement an ISO 9000–type quality assurance system.[5] Part of the difficulty experienced by many is that the standards are not as prescriptive as some users would like them to be. Although the standards do dictate that the user (in other words, supplier) shall have procedures for a variety of processes, not one sentence specifies how anyone should implement a particular clause. This deliberate approach (considered frustrating by some and infinitely wise by others) is exemplified by the following paragraph of ISO 9001, ISO 9002, and ISO 9003 (all three paragraphs are identical).[6]

> It is intended that these Standards will normally be adopted in their present form, *but on occasions they may need to be tailored by adding or deleting certain quality system requirements for specific contractual situations.*

As for the scope, it is still broad but not as eloquently stated as the 1987 edition, which follows.[7]

> This Standard specifies quality-system requirements for use *where a supplier's* [needs to demonstrate] his *capability to:*
>
> - design and supply conforming product (ISO 9001).
> - supply conforming product to an established design (ISO 9002).
> - detect and control the disposition of any product nonconformity during final inspection and test (ISO 9003).

The scope of the 1994 updates seems to regress slightly by stating: "the requirements specified are aimed primarily at achieving customer satisfaction by preventing nonconformity at all stages. . . ."[8]

Before proceeding, it must be emphasized that as far as the standards are concerned, the term *product* is now defined as "The result of activities or processes." Product includes hardware, software, processed material, and service, or a combination thereof and shall apply to *intended product* only.[9] Consequently, although the standards have been implemented overwhelmingly by organizations within the manufacturing, processing, and assembly world, they certainly apply, with some interpretation (the very purpose of this book) to the service sector. We shall return to this point later.

From a global perspective, the standards represent

- A generic set of quality systems requirements designed as a baseline model for quality assurance, which could be used by any industry that is in the business of providing a product/service

- The reference to quality systems implies an organizational structure made up of several interconnected and interrelated components (in other words, processes and departments)

- The importance of contractual agreement between two parties: a customer and his or her supplier (who may be contractually required to achieve ISO 9000 registration)

The Structure of the ISO 9000 Series

The five documents making up the ISO 9000 series are structured as shown in Figure 2.1. The two documents entitled ISO 9000-1 and ISO 9004-1 (formally, ISO 9000 and ISO 9004) are guideline documents and are to be used as reference. *They are not enforceable standards nor should they be consulted or interpreted as enforceable standards* (see chapter 8). I emphasize this point because too many individuals have made the unfortunate mistake of believing that the ISO 9004-1 document is an enforceable standard. Misguided by misinformed consultants and/or inaccurate promotions that do not know any better, potential customers of the ISO 9000 series have paid hundreds of dollars for videotapes about the series that are replete with misinformation. I would hope that similar mistakes are not repeated within the service industry.

Regarding the ISO 9000-1 document, its main objective is to help readers decide which of the three standards (ISO 9001, ISO 9002, or ISO 9003) best suits their needs (chapter 8 provides an overview of some of the author's concerns regarding ISO 9000-1). Both documents are significantly longer and more informative than the 1987 version.

As seen in Figure 2.1, the core of the ISO 9000 series consists of the three *hierarchically nested* standards 9001, 9002, and 9003. Hierarchically

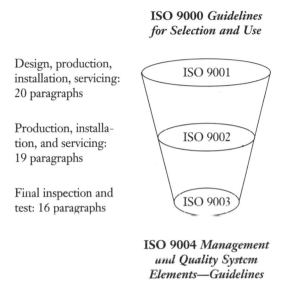

ISO 9000 *Guidelines for Selection and Use*

Design, production, installation, servicing: 20 paragraphs

ISO 9001

Production, installation, and servicing: 19 paragraphs

ISO 9002

Final inspection and test: 16 paragraphs

ISO 9003

ISO 9004 *Management and Quality System Elements—Guidelines*

Figure 2.1. Structure of the ISO 9000 series (1993).

nested means that as one progresses from ISO 9003 to ISO 9002 and ISO 9001, the scope of the quality assurance system is expanded by adding more paragraphs or subparagraphs.[10]

Differences Between ISO 9001, ISO 9002, and ISO 9003

Since servicing has been added to the ISO 9002 standard, the only difference between ISO 9001 and ISO 9002 is paragraph 4.4, Design Control, which does not apply to ISO 9002. As for the ISO 9003 standard, which used to be significantly shorter than the other two standards, its content has been aligned with the requirements of the other two standards. It is important to note that paragraphs on contract review, control of customer-supplied product, preventive actions, and internal audit have been added. Also, since the content of all (ISO 9003) paragraphs is nearly identical to ISO 9001, the ISO 9003 standard is considerably longer than the 1987 version. The only significant differences between ISO 9003 and the other standards follow.

4.1.2.1 Responsibility and Authority

This paragraph is significantly shorter. One only needs to define the responsibility and authority of persons who (all quotes from ANSI/ASQC Q9003, 1994):

- Conduct final inspection and tests; and

- Ensure that finished product that does not conform to specified requirements is prevented from being used or delivered.

4.2.3 Quality Planning

Since ISO 9003 does not include design control, there are only seven (instead of eight in ISO 9001 and ISO 9002) subclauses. The subclauses are slightly rephrased to reflect ISO 9003 emphasis on final inspection. For example, in ISO 9001, paragraph 4.2.3a reads: "the preparation of quality plans"; the same paragraph in 9003 reads: "the preparation of quality plans for final inspection and tests."

4.4 Design Control

Not applicable.

4.6 Purchasing

Not applicable.

4.8 Product Identification and Traceability

The paragraph is simplified to reflect the fact that ISO 9003 organizations do not produce, deliver, or install products.

4.9 Process Control

Not applicable.

4.10 Inspection and Testing

This paragraph consists of only two subparagraphs (General and Final Inspection and Testing), instead of the five found in ISO 9001 and ISO 9002. The final inspection and testing is further condensed to reflect the limitations of ISO 9003.

4.13 Control of Nonconforming Product

The paragraph is a combination of 4.13.1 and 4.13.2 found in ISO 9001 and ISO 9002. It reads as follows:

> The supplier shall establish and maintain control of product that does not conform to specified requirements to ensure that unintended use or delivery is avoided.
>
> Control shall provide for identification, documentation, evaluation, segregation (when practical), disposition of nonconforming product and for notification to the functions concerned.
>
> The description of repairs, and of any nonconformity that has been accepted under authorized concession, shall be recorded to denote the actual condition. (See 4.16.)
>
> Repaired and/or reworked product shall be reinspected in accordance with the quality plan and/or documented procedure requirements.

4.14 Corrective Action

As with paragraph 4.13, this paragraph also is substantially reduced. The requirements are that

> The supplier shall:
>
> a) investigate nonconformities that have been identified from the analysis of final inspection and test reports and customer complaints of product;
>
> b) determine and implement appropriate corrective action on the nonconformities;
>
> c) ensure that relevant information on the actions taken is submitted for management review (see 4.1.3).

4.16 Control of Quality Records
Minor rephrasing from 9001. The requirement to identify, collect, index, access, file, store, and dispose of records is deleted, thus reducing the length of the text. Requirements for subcontractor quality records also are left out.

4.19 Servicing
Not applicable.

4.20 Statistical Techniques
The Procedures paragraph is left out. The clause simply states: "The supplier shall identify the need for statistical techniques required for the acceptability of product characteristic," and implement and control their application.

All other paragraphs are essentially identical.

Which Standard to Select?
The criteria for selecting the appropriate ISO 9000 model can be found in paragraph 8.2, Selection of Model, of the ISO 9000-1 guidelines:

a) ISO 9001: for use when conformance to specified requirements is to be assured by the supplier during design/development, production, installation and servicing.

b) ISO 9002: for use when conformance to specified requirements is to be assured by the supplier during production, installation and servicing.

c) ISO 9003: for use when conformance to specified requirements is to be assured by the supplier at final inspection and test.[11]

An earlier version of the ISO 9001 document allowed for more flexibility by stating: "during several stages *which may include*, design/development . . ." (second sentence of paragraph a). Indeed, installation and servicing may not apply in all cases and, consequently, should be optional.

Finally, one should note, "In third-party certification/registration, the supplier and the certification body should agree on which standard will be used as the basis for certification/registration. The selected model should be adequate and not misleading from the point of view of the supplier's customers."[12]

In North America, the ISO 9003 standard appears to be popular in Canada, but not in the United States. In some European countries, specifically France, it appears that the 9003 model is viewed as a suitable model for small to medium-size companies (that seems to be the position of the French Association for Quality Assurance [AFAQ].[13] In fact, the use of the ISO 9003 model has nothing to do with the size of a company, but with the type of activity provided. There are some (probably limited) applications for this standard within the service sector. For example, warehouses, dealerships, or distribution centers could benefit from the ISO 9003 (1994 edition) standard. Yet, in most cases, ISO 9002 may be a better, more rigorous model to adopt.

I do not know why the ISO 9003 standard is such an unpopular standard except that the standard, which has fewer clauses than ISO 9001 or ISO 9002, may be unjustly perceived as being inferior to ISO 9001 or ISO 9002, or its emphasis on inspection and test is so narrow, that most organizations, consultants (including yours truly), and registrars simply recommend ISO 9002 as the appropriate model.

Therefore, with the possible exception of laboratories that may have to comply to the European Norm 45001 *General Criteria for the Operation of Testing Laboratories,* or to Guide 25, the decision as to which standard to adopt should be straightforward: ISO 9001 if design functions are performed; otherwise, select ISO 9002 or ISO 9003.[14] Design function for the service industry? What could that possibly mean?

Whenever a consulting firm or training agency develops training courses for a client, design activities are triggered. Parameters such as subject matter, time needed to develop the course, course duration, intended audience, method of delivery (lecture, video, workshop, combination), class size, maximum number of consecutive hours (in other words, three four-hour sessions, two six-hour sessions, or six two-hour sessions), place of delivery, and other issues must be agreed upon with the customer (in other words, purchaser of the course material).

Unfortunately, all too often many of these parameters are not carefully addressed or ignored by both the customer and/or the supplier. Certainly, a similar scenario could be envisioned (not in the near future) for certain types of courses developed within a university environment. The situation within a university environment is more complicated and delicate simply because the customer/student does not have the knowledge to decide what she or he needs to learn.[15] Therefore, contract negotiation and design review would be more delicate, if at all possible.

This should not discourage the faculty from surveying students to find out how to improve course(s). In fact, the process of developing and improving a course often parallels the manufacturing world. One starts with a new course, teaches it once, listens for comments from the students, modifies or improves the course, offers it a second time, and repeats the cycle ad infinitum, all the time following the basic tenets of continuous improvement without being aware of doing so.

For some architectural/engineering firms, the design process is the very nature of their service. This might consist of designing architectural structures, golf courses, or a landscape. The end product generally consists of a series of blueprints, computerized models, drawings, or process and instruments diagrams (P&ID) for an entire chemical plant. In each of these cases, the following activities are likely to take place with various emphasis, depending on the design activity.

- Design and development planning
- Activity assignment
- Organizational and technical interfaces
- Design input
- Design output
- Design verification
- Design changes

How these activities need to be interpreted within the service sector will be explored in chapter 5.

Interpreting the Standards

People who read a standard for the first time often are surprised by the brevity of the standards, which vary in length from two pages for ISO 9003 (1987) to seven pages for ISO 9001 (1987).[16] Soon after they read the standard (whichever applies to their need), a perplexed feeling ensues. "What does it mean?" or "How do I interpret this paragraph?" are often-asked questions.

When reading the standards, one must realize that there are two types of clauses, or paragraphs, within the standards: the *shall* clauses and the *where appropriate* or similarly phrased sentences. For example, paragraphs 4.1.1 and 4.8 of the ANSI/ASQC Standard Q9001 (1994) read as follows:

> 4.1.1 Quality Policy
> The supplier's management with executive responsibility shall define and document its policy for quality including objectives for quality and its commitment to quality. The quality policy shall be relevant to the supplier's organizational goals and the expectations and needs of its customers. The supplier shall ensure that this policy is understood, implemented and maintained at all levels of the organization.[17]

> 4.8 Product Identification and Traceability
> Where appropriate, the supplier shall establish and maintain documented procedures for identifying the product by suitable means from receipt and during all stages of production, delivery and installation.[18]

With respect to the *shall* sentences, the issue is clear-cut: you must address the requirements, however, the standard does not specifically tell you how you shall address the clause. Herein lies one of the major difficulties faced by most customers of the ISO 9000 series. Your mission is to ensure that the shall paragraphs are addressed. It is the registrar's mission, or more accurately, the auditor or assessor's role to determine whether or not you have adequately addressed the said requirements. Naturally, some subjectivity does come into play, but if the assessor has been properly trained, and if you have addressed the requirement to the best of your ability and needs, there should be no problem.[19]

Regarding the *where appropriate/suitable* or similarly phrased paragraphs, it is up to you or, more likely, your customers or regulatory agencies to dictate or determine if it is appropriate to apply the clause. For example, contrary to what is sometimes believed (and unfortunately wrongly advertised), paragraph 4.20 of ISO 9001 does not state that you must implement statistical process control (SPC) throughout your processes. Such programs usually are implemented at the request of one or more customers. The 1994 version of the statistical techniques paragraph states that "the supplier shall *identify* the need for statistical techniques required for establishing, controlling and verifying process capability and product characteristics." After you have identified the need, the standard requires you to establish and maintain documented procedures "to implement and control the application of the statistical techniques identified in 4.20.1."

In other words, the writers of the standard appear to be saying, now that you have identified some statistical techniques, make sure you maintain the process to ensure that the techniques are correctly implemented. I doubt that documented procedures will solve the problem, but remember that as users you are only required to identify the need for statistical techniques. You might arrive at the conclusion that there is no need for statistical techniques (see sample quality manual in Appendix A).

As a statistician, I urge you to seriously consider the value of statistically monitoring your processes. Having witnessed numerous misapplications of statistics, however, I also recognize that in many cases, statistical monitoring is impractical, unsuitable, or of dubious value. Naturally, if you have correctly implemented SPC or other techniques (for example, Pareto diagrams, histograms, run charts), you might as well say so in your quality assurance system.

One last example should clarify the interpretation of *shall* vs. *where appropriate* sentences. The second paragraph found under Product Identification and Traceability reads

> Where and to the extent that, traceability is a specified
> requirement, the supplier shall establish and maintain

documented procedures for unique identification of individual product or batches. This identification shall be recorded (see 4.16).[20]

Referring back to the *E. coli* case study of chapter 1, one can better appreciate how this extract would be interpreted from various points of view. As customers buying a hamburger or a chicken sandwich, most people would not demand to know from which beef or chicken farm the beef or chicken came. Traceability is not likely to be part of our contractual agreement with the fast-food restaurant (however, it may be required by the Food and Drug Administration). The situation is vastly different for the fast-food restaurant, particularly if a customer should become violently sick. Tracing where the chicken or beef originated is not always an easy task.

The Standards As Systems of Quality Assurance

Often the notion of systems, or quality systems, is not well understood by those in charge of implementing an ISO 9000–type quality assurance system. A system simply means that the whole (in other words, quality assurance) consists of many interacting, and thus interdependent, parts (see Figure 2.2). All too often the assumption is made that, since the ISO 9000 series of standards are models from quality assurance, the quality people should take care of it. Of course, the quality department (if such department exists) could, and generally does, try to implement or adapt/match the company's quality assurance system to one of the ISO 9000 models. There is nothing wrong with this approach as long as management and everyone else understands that the implementation of an ISO 9000–type quality assurance system involves everyone. Consequently, although the quality assurance department could lead the effort, others must join in order to ensure successful implementation.[21]

Some Major Changes from the 1987 Version

Comparing the 1987 versions with the 1994 updates, one immediately notices that the 1994 versions are longer. The ISO 9001 standard, which used to be only seven (two-column) pages is now 10 pages.[22] The shortest document (ISO 9003), which formerly consisted of only two pages,

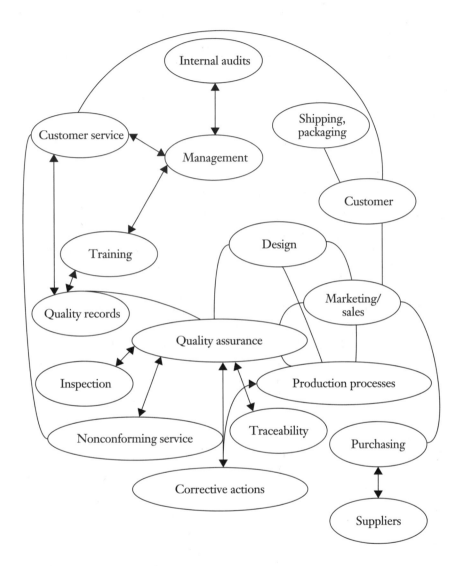

Figure 2.2. A generic quality assurance system.

is now 8 pages. Part of the reason for the increase in wordiness is that some paragraphs have been added while others have been rephrased. Perusal of Table 2.1 reveals that the only distinction between ISO 9001 and ISO 9002 is the Design Control paragraph. Servicing has been

Table 2.1. List of quality system elements (1994).

Title	Corresponding Paragraph (or Subsection) Nos. in		
	ISO 9001	ISO 9002	ISO 9003
Management responsibility	4.1	4.1	4.1a
Quality system	4.2	4.2	4.2a
Contract review	4.3	4.3	4.3
Design control	4.4	–	–
Document and data control	4.5	4.5	4.5a
Purchasing	4.6	4.6	–
Control of customer-supplied product	4.7	4.7	–
Product identification and traceability	4.8	4.8	4.8a
Process control	4.9	4.9	–
Inspection and testing	4.10	4.10	4.10a
Inspection, measuring, and test equipment	4.11	4.11	4.11a
Inspection and test status	4.12	4.12	4.12a
Control of nonconforming product	4.13	4.13	4.13a
Corrective action and preventive action	4.14	4.14	4.14
Handling, storage, packaging, and delivery	4.15	4.15	4.15a
Control of quality records	4.16	4.16	4.16a
Internal audits	4.17	4.17	4.17
Training	4.18	4.18	4.18a
Servicing	4.19	4.19	–
Statistical techniques	4.20	4.20	4.20a

All paragraphs ending with "a" are less stringent than ISO 9001. Element not present.

added to ISO 9002. The ISO 9003 standard resembles ISO 9002 without Design Control, Purchasing, Process Control, and Servicing, which have been removed from ISO 9003 (see also discussion on page 31). One improvement is the uniform numbering of paragraphs across all three standards. Some general observations are in order before reviewing the major additions to the 1994 standards.

There appears to be a conscious effort on the part of the contributors to insert the words "establish and maintain documented procedures" in almost every paragraph. The benefits of such editorial changes are dubious. I propose that some of the intended improvements could be perceived as regressions. Generally speaking, the standards are becoming more prescriptive. The tone and style appears more authoritative than the 1987 edition. I do not know if this is for the better. This tendency might be because contributors to the standards have attempted to improve the wording to avoid confusion or misinterpretation. For example, the standards' introduction devotes a few lines explaining that the standards "are generic, independent of any specific industry or economic sector. The design and implementation of a quality system will be influenced by the various needs of an organization, its particular objectives, the product and services supplied, and the processes and specific practices employed."[23] Given the broad range of companies applying for registration, these comments are a welcome improvement to the 1987 version.

One of the quickest ways to review the intent of the 1994 updates may be to reproduce the paragraph headings and subheadings and compare them with the 1987 version (see Table 2.2).

Although the 1994 version has more subparagraphs, this does not mean that more requirements have been added. In many cases (such as Design Control), the contents of the 1987 edition have been reorganized into a different format that consists of a redistribution of information, rephrasing, or clarification of certain themes into additional paragraphs or subparagraphs. In cases such as Amendment to Contract (4.3.3), subparagraph g of Process Control (4.9) (which adds "suitable maintenance of equipment to ensure continuing process capability"), and Preventive Action (4.14.3), the subparagraphs are additional requirements that shall be analyzed in Part II.

There are other subtle, yet significant, additions. For example, the Quality Systems paragraph now states, "The outline structure of the documentation covering the quality system requirements of this International Standard shall be defined in a quality manual. The quality manual shall include or reference the documented procedures that form part of the quality system."

This is a significant addition to the 1987 version, which did not even require a quality manual. The required manual also must reference documented procedures. No doubt, this requirement will facilitate the third-party audit process. Could it be that the amendment was recommended by a registrar?

Table 2.2. 1994 and 1987 ISO 9001 cross-reference.

1994		1987	
0	*Introduction*	0	*Introduction*
1	*Scope*	1.0	*Scope and Field of Application*
2	*Normative References*	2.0	*References*
3	*Definitions*	3.0	*Definitions*
4	*Quality Systems Requirements*	4.0	*Quality System Requirements*
4.1	*Management Responsibility*	4.1	*Management Responsibility*
4.1.1	*Quality Policy*	4.1.1	*Quality Policy*
4.1.2	*Organization*	4.1.2	*Organization*
4.1.2.1	*Responsibility and Authority*	4.1.2.1	*Responsibility and Authority*
4.1.2.2	*Resources*	4.1.2.2	*Verification Resources and Personnel*
4.1.2.3	*Management Representative*	4.1.2.3	*Management Representative*
4.1.3	*Management Review*	4.1.3	*Management Review*
4.2	*Quality Systems*	4.2	*Quality System*
4.2.1	*General*		
4.2.2	*Quality System Procedures*		
4.2.3	*Quality Planning*		
4.3	*Contract Review*	4.3	*Contract Review*
4.3.1	*General*		
4.3.2	*Review*		
4.3.3	*Amendment to a Contract*		
4.3.4	*Records*		
4.4	*Design Control*	4.4	*Design Control*
4.4.1	*General*	4.4.1	*General*
4.4.2	*Design and Development Planning*	4.4.2	*Design and Development Planning*
		4.4.2.1	*Activity Assignment*
4.4.3	*Organizational and Technical Interfaces*	4.4.2.2	*Organizational and Technical Interfaces*
4.4.4	*Design Input*	4.4.3	*Design Input*
4.4.5	*Design Review*		

Table 2.2. *(continued)*

1994		1987	
4.4.6	*Design Output*	4.4.4	*Design Output*
4.4.7	*Design Verification*	4.4.5	*Design Verification*
4.4.8	*Design Validation*		
4.4.9	*Design Changes*	4.4.6	*Design Changes*
4.5	*Document and Data Control*	4.5	*Document Control*
4.5.1	*General*		
4.5.2	*Document Approval and Issue*	4.5.1	*Document Approval and Issue*
4.5.3	*Document Changes*	4.5.2	*Document Changes/ Modifications*
4.6	*Purchasing*	4.6	*Purchasing*
4.6.1	*General*	4.6.1	*General*
4.6.2	*Evaluation of Sub-contractors*	4.6.2	*Assessment of Sub-contractors*
4.6.3	*Purchasing Data*	4.6.3	*Purchasing Data*
4.6.4	*Verification of Purchased Product*	4.6.4	*Verification of Purchased Product*
4.6.4.1	*Supplier Verification at Sub-contractors*		
4.6.4.2	*Customer Verification of Sub-contracted Product*		
4.7	*Control of Customer Supplied Product*	4.7	*Purchaser Supplied Product*
4.8	*Product Identification and Traceability*	4.8	*Product Identification and Traceability*
4.9	*Process Control*	4.9	*Process Control*
		4.9	*General*
		4.9.2	*Special Processes*
4.10	*Inspection and Testing*	4.10	*Inspection and Testing*
4.10.1	*General*		
4.10.2	*Receiving Inspection and Testing*	4.10.1	*Receiving Inspection and Testing*
4.10.3	*In-Process Inspection and Testing*	4.10.2	*In-Process Inspection and Testing*
4.10.4	*Final Inspection and Testing*	4.10.3	*Final Inspection and Testing*
4.10.5	*Inspection and Test Records*	4.10.4	*Inspection and Test Records*

Table 2.2. *(continued)*

	1994		1987
4.11	*Control of Inspection, Measuring and Test Equipment*	4.11	*Inspection, Measuring and Test Equipment*
4.11.1	*General*		
4.11.2	*Control Procedures*		
4.12	*Inspection and Test Status*	4.12	*Inspection and Test Status*
4.13	*Control of Nonconforming Product*	4.13	*Control of Nonconforming Product*
4.13.1	*General*		
4.13.2	*Nonconforming Product Review and Disposition*	4.13.1	*Nonconformity Review and Disposition*
4.14	*Corrective and Preventive Action*	4.14	*Corrective Action*
4.14.1	*General*		
4.14.2	*Corrective Action*		
4.14.3	*Preventive Action*		
4.15	*Handling, Storage, Packaging, Preservation and Delivery*	4.15	*Handling, Storage, Packaging, and Delivery*
4.15.1	*General*	4.15.1	*General*
4.15.2	*Handling*	4.15.2	*Handling*
4.15.3	*Storage*	4.15.3	*Storage*
4.15.4	*Packaging*	4.15.4	*Packaging*
4.15.5	*Preservation*		
4.15.6	*Delivery*	4.15.5	*Delivery*
4.16	*Control of Quality Records*	4.16	*Quality Records*
4.17	*Internal Quality Audits*	4.17	*Internal Quality Audits*
4.18	*Training*	4.18	*Training*
4.19	*Servicing*	4.19	*Servicing*
4.20	*Statistical Techniques*	4.20	*Statistical Techniques*
4.20.1	*Identification of Need*		
4.20.2	*Procedures*		

Finally, the note that used to be appended to paragraph 4.2 is now a separate clause (4.2.3, Quality Planning). Many of the requirements stated in this new paragraph are redundant and probably should have been kept as a suggestive note. Also worth noting is the complete rephrasing and retitling of paragraph 4.1.2.2, which used to confuse some people with its verification requirements. The paragraph is now simply retitled Resources.[24] Other observations could be made, but since most readers may not be familiar with the 1987 version, there is no need to pursue a detailed comparative analysis.[25]

Can the ISO 9000 Series Standards Be Applied to the Service Sector?

The adaptation of the ISO 9000 series to other industries, including the service industry, can follow two paths: one can either force the industry to fit one of the three ISO 9000 models (ISO 9001, ISO 9002, or ISO 9003), or one can adapt the ISO 9000 models to the industry. I believe the first approach is flawed simply because it usually leads to ludicrous propositions. Indeed, by wanting to force a particular clause or subclause to an industry or a sector within an industry, the auditor, consultant, or other so-called experts, fail to realize that diseconomies of scale might ensue. The impracticality of implementing a particular clause might be due to a variety of reasons: it does not make sense, it is not practiced within the industry (usually because it is not required by the customer), it would be too expensive, it is of little value, or it would be idiotic to do it as required by the standard.

One must remember that the standards' origins, and thus biases, have been strongly influenced by three military standards known as MIL-Q-9858A (*Quality Program Requirements*, 1963, but first published in 1959), MIL-STD-45662A (*Calibration System Requirements*) and MIL-I-45208A (*Inspection System Requirements*, 1963).[26] The influence of standards developed for the nuclear industry also is evident. Although these industries do provide a quality assurance model designed to suit their particular requirements, not all industries have the government or government regulatory agencies for customers. Moreover, the environmental and societal risks associated with certain nonconformances in a nuclear plant have little in common with contingency plans associated with low-risk industries. That is a crucial point often forgotten by certain ISO 9000 gurus and/or registrars (the distinction has become blurry). Certainly, an organization that has the Department of Defense as one of its customers is likely to pay attention to the government's requirements or guidelines, no matter how ludicrous some of these requirements might (appear to) be, simply because a successful bid may mean a steady stream of orders for several years. Also, since the government has enormous financial clout, it can be as demanding as it pleases. Naturally, we all know how costly these demands can be costly (for example, a $750 screwdriver).

I realize that these comments might arouse the ire of some readers. Some might say that the importance of a customer should not be measured in terms of dollars. Others might pontificate that there should be only one quality assurance model, irrespective of the type of customers. The fact remains that when a customer has a direct impact on the microeconomies of several regions, that customer can set his or her own rules; a luxury many of us, as customers, simply do not have. It is therefore the author's contention that different implicit and explicit rules apply depending as to whether the supplier of a product/service interacts with an omnipresent monopolistic (government agency); oligopolistic (Ford, GM, Chrysler) customer(s); or hundreds, thousands, or millions of customers. Moreover, since the implementation of international standards is intimately related to microeconomics (economics of the firm) and global economics, one must exercise wisdom when trying to implement standards whose origins and contents were/are greatly influenced by military standards. Thus, irrespective of the real or imaginary advantages that might befall an ISO 9000–registered company, one must recognize that a wrong or whimsical decision, designed to force or coerce a small supplier to adopt one of the ISO 9000 series standards may be detrimental to the supplier's economic and financial status.

These observations may lead one to question whether it is wise to simply adopt what are essentially standards derived from military applications and transplant them to any and all civilian industries. Indeed, despite recent changes in attitude vis-à-vis quality (in other words, adoption of total quality management [TQM] principles), most military standards still show the influence of an era where quality control inspection applied to the production of mass-produced standardized items. Consequently, despite the generic nature and robustness of the standards, I would suggest that, just as has been the case for the manufacturing, processing, and assembly world, one cannot simply transplant the ISO 9000 series to the service industry without carefully adapting the standards to the industry's idiosyncrasies. Moreover, the development of guidelines such as the ISO 9004-2 document are not likely to alleviate the problem.

The ISO 9004-2 Guidelines for Services

I do not know the origins of the ISO 9004-2 document, nor do I know who wrote it (although the spelling of *organisation* with an *s* would indicate that the document might have originated in the United Kingdom). No doubt, the document, entitled *Quality Management and Quality Systems Elements—Part 2: Guidelines for Services*, was drafted in an attempt to assist the service industry adapt a set of standards better suited for the manufacturing, processing, or assembly plants. The purpose of the standard is stated in the Scope where one can read the following:[27]

> This International Standard gives guidance for establishing and implementing a quality system within an organization. It is based on the generic principles of ISO 9004 and provides a comprehensive overview of a quality system specifically for services.
>
> This International Standard can be applied in the context of developing a quality system for a newly offered or modified service. It can also be applied directly when developing and implementing a quality system for supplying an existing service. The quality system embraces all the processes needed to provide an effective service from marketing to delivery and the analysis of service provided to customers.

With all due respect to its contributors, I am sorry to report that the document (although well written) falls short of its intended goals. One of the problems is that the standard (ISO 9004-2) is based on the generic principles of the ISO 9004 document, itself a guideline. Had the document delivered what its title promised, there probably would have been no need for this book. As it is, the guidelines are not really guidelines but an unsuccessful attempt to rephrase the standards with an apparent coat of servicing. The following paragraph helps illustrate my point.

> 5.2 Design Process
>
> 5.2.1 General: The process of designing a service involves converting the service brief (see 5.1.3) into specifications for both the service and its delivery, while reflecting the service organization options (i.e., aims, policies and costs).
>
> The service specification defines the service to be provided whereas the service delivery specification defines the means and methods used to deliver the service.
>
> Design of the service specification and the service delivery specification are interdependent and interact throughout the design process.[28]

This may mean more to you than it does to me. On the other hand, you might be asking yourself the same questions I asked when I first read these paragraphs: "What does it mean?" and "How does it relate to my industry?" In fairness to the guidelines, I should state that the Design Process section continues on for another page and a half attempting to detail what is meant by the opening general statement.

Nonetheless, similar comments can be made about many of the paragraphs found in ISO 9004-2. For example, under Statistical Methods (5.4.3), one can read that "Modern statistical methods can assist in most aspects of data collection and application, whether it be to gain a better understanding of customer needs, in process control, capability study, forecasting, or measurement of quality to assist in making decisions."

Fine prose indeed, but how can it be applied? Similarly, paragraph 5.2.4.6, Handling, Storage, Packaging, Delivery and Protection of Customers' Possessions, states: "The service organization should establish effective controls for the handling, storage, packaging, delivery and protection of customers' possessions which the service organization is responsible for, or comes into contact with, during the delivery of the service." What if you are in the business of delivering information via telephone lines? How would this clause apply?

I do not mean to suggest that the ISO 9004-2 document does not attempt to provide its readers with some guidance, but the prose often is so vague as to be of limited value. In other instances, the standard appears to overstep its boundaries. For example, paragraph 5.2.4.6 cited herein, is specific as to the nature and extent of the requirements for "protection of customers' possessions," yet one would think that the nature and extent of such requirements should be negotiated by the customer and the supplier, not suggested by a standard.

The basic problem with the ISO 9004-2 document is that it does not differentiate between service industries. As far as the contributors are concerned, a service is a service and that is all. Therein lies one of the fundamental mistakes. As will be shown in chapter 3, services (as manufacturing/assembly industries) obey particular laws of economic geography, which translates into the fundamental law that services are organized within a dual geographic and economic hierarchical structure. This hierarchical structure dictates the type, nature, and overall sophistication of the quality assurance system they must adopt.

It also should be emphasized that the ISO 9004-2 document is a guideline (hence the use of *should* rather than *shall* throughout). Finally, all over the world, the service sector is being audited to the ISO 9001, ISO 9002, and ISO 9003 models. For example, Swissair achieved ISO 9001 registration in December 1992. The Dutch meat and livestock industry (mentioned in chapter 1) has adopted the ISO 9002 model. Hospitals and other service industries in the United Kingdom also have adopted ISO 9002. In the United States, the service sector (including consulting firms) generally is registered under the ISO 9001 or ISO 9002 model. Therefore, based on these observations and in view of the fact that the ISO 9004-2 document is not particularly helpful, I see no need to refer to it. However, do not take my word for it. If you find this style helpful, I encourage you to purchase the document.

Why Achieve ISO 9000 Registration?

In the world of manufacturing and assembly, companies have been motivated to achieve ISO 9000 registration for a variety or combination of reasons.

• There is a perceived fear (occasionally well-justified, see item 5), occasionally fueled by some consultants or consulting firms that dictates that unless registration is achieved market share will (or might) be lost.

• Foreign or American companies that have successfully achieved ISO 9001, ISO 9002, or ISO 9003 registration are quick to advertise their ISO certification and promote it as a marketing advantage. Companies that are not yet registered to one of ISO 9000 standards usually feel pressured to respond by also achieving certification.

• As companies (American and foreign) achieve registration, they begin requesting their suppliers to also achieve ISO 9000 registration. Suppliers in turn request their suppliers also comply, and so on down the line. This cascading effect is a significant factor in the substantial increase in the United States of ISO registration ever since 1990 to 1991.

• The CEO (or vice president of quality) has decided that since ISO 9000 registration is supposed to eventually lead to some cost savings, it would be a good idea to achieve ISO 9000 registration. The claim that ISO 9000 registration can lead to savings is popular. How much savings really can be expected? A recent survey published by Deloitte & Touche reveals that, on average, ISO 9000–registered companies can expect to save $179,000 per year. That may appear substantial, but upon closer examination one learns that for companies with total annual sales of $11 million or less, the average annual savings averages $25,000—a very tiny percentage of annual sales. For companies with annual sales of $1 billion or more, average annual savings increases to $532,000, slightly higher percentagewise, but still tiny (which could indicate that larger organizations are more wasteful, on average).

These savings are even less encouraging when one learns that the total internal plus external costs associated with registration averaged $245,000 (one would really like to know the magnitude of the standard deviation, or better yet, the coefficient of variation). Consequently, simple arithmetic would seem to indicate that ISO 9000–registered firms have experienced (at least during their first year of registration) an average loss in revenues of approximately $66,000![29] I would therefore propose that immediate cost savings is not likely to be one of your primary motivations for achieving ISO 9000 registration.[30]

- The company recently has lost (or is about to lose) a significant European or overseas contract because it was not ISO 9000 registered.

- A combination of one or more of items 1 through 5.

Although the ISO 9000 phenomenon has not yet permeated the service industry, it is increasingly evident that the few service industries that have already achieved ISO 9002 (that appears to be the most common model chosen by the service sector) have been motivated to do so for similar reasons. Indeed, when I asked the director of quality of one of the major courier services what motivated management to achieve ISO 9002 registration he replied

> Our customers are major accounts. Some of them have businesses overseas. Many of them are well informed about TQM and ISO 9000. During their (second party) audits they would frequently ask us when we were going to achieve ISO 9000 certification. They looked at the delivery paragraph (of ISO) and said "we subcontract to xxx, so let's have them achieve registration." This was market/customer driven.

Such market-driven motivation apparently is shared by most organizations. Indeed, the July 1993 Deloitte & Touche survey revealed that 96 percent of the firms interviewed planned to use ISO 9000 registration status for public relation purposes.[31]

Conclusion
There is little doubt that the quality systems models of the ISO 9000 series can be adapted to the service industry. One of the themes of this chapter has been to warn readers and practitioners alike that some thoughtful adaptation (in other words, tailoring) and interpretation is

required if implementation is to be successful. The ISO 9004-2 guidelines, whose intent might have been to alleviate the implementation effort, provides the reader with very little interpretive assistance. Part of the difficulty is that the guidelines do not distinguish between the type of service industries. It is trite to suggest that not all service industries are alike. One only needs to look at the local corner store and try to compare it to the regional medical center to understand that the customer/service interface is not the same. Certainly, as with the manufacturing and assembly world, several basic principles do apply across the various customer/supplier interfaces, but one must also recognize that there are basic differences that must be analyzed in order to intelligently apply the standards. Attention will now focus on what these differences might be.

Notes

1. Quoted from *Completing the Internal Market. A New Community Standards Policy* 4. Commission of the European Communities (January 1992): 4–5, emphasis added.

2. Ibid., iii.

3. The International Organization for Standardization traces its origins to the International Federation of the National Standardization Association (1926–1939). From 1943 to 1946, the United Nations Standards Coordinating Committee (UNSCC) acted as an interim organization. In October 1946 in London, the name International Organization for Standardization was finally agreed upon. The organization, known as ISO, held its first meeting in June 1947 in Zurich. See Howard Coonley, "The International Standards Movement," in *National Standards in a Modern Economy*, edited by Dickson Reck (New York: Harper & Brothers, 1954).

4. *The Wall Street Journal, Business Week*, and most professional trade journals have carried at least one ISO 9000–related story.

5. Quality assurance is defined in ISO 8402 as: "All those planned and systematic actions necessary to provide adequate confidence that a product or service will satisfy given requirements for quality."

6. ANSI/ASQC Q9001, Introduction. It is the author's belief that the 1987 phrasing was both more elegant and concise.

7. ANSI/ASQC Q9001, Q9002, and Q9003, 1994, Scope, emphasis added.

8. ANSI/ASQC Q9001, Scope. The ISO 9002 standard essentially has the same text except it is for production and installation. The ISO 9003 standard states: "This International Standard is applicable in situations when the nonconformance of product to specified requirements can be shown with adequate confidence providing that certain suppliers' capabilities for inspection and test conducted on finished product can be satisfactorily demonstrated.

9. ANSI/ASQC Q9001, 1994, paragraph 3.1, notes 2–4.

10. As of 1994, ISO 9002 includes servicing.

11. ISO 9000-1, paragraph 8.2.1.

12. General Guidance, ANSI/ASQC Q9000-1, 1994, paragraph 8.1.

13. "Honours for ISO 9003 and Small/Medium Firms" in *ISO 9000 News* 2, no. 5 (September/October 1993): 7–10.

14. I am not suggesting that all laboratories will have to obtain EN 45001 certification. Only laboratories that wish to have their services recognized by the international, and particularly the European community, would need to seek EN 45001 certification.

15. In the manufacturing world, many suppliers would argue that their customers often do not have a clue as to what they want. Similar comments would apply within the software industry where specifications change numerous times during the course of a project.

16. The standards are getting longer. The 1994 versions will have a few more pages, mostly for clarification purposes.

17. ANSI/ASQC Q9001, 1994, paragraph 4.1.1. The 1987 version reads as follows: "The supplier's management shall define and document its policy and objectives for, and commitment to, quality. The supplier shall ensure that this policy is understood, implemented, and maintained at all levels in the organization." ANSI/ASQC Standard Q91-1987, p. 1.

18. ANSI/ASQC Q9001, 1994, paragraph 4.8.

19. These issues have been discussed at some length in my *ISO Preparing for Registration* and *Implementing the ISO 9000 Series.*

20. The 1987 version reads as follows: "Where, and to the extent that, traceability is a specified requirement, individual product or batches shall have a unique identification." Certainly that version is more concise. Notice the emphasis (1994) on documented procedures. ANSI/ASQC Q9001, paragraph 4.8.

21. For further information see chapter 4 of my *Implementing the ISO 9000 Series* (New York: Marcel Dekker, 1993).

22. One wonders what the pagination will be for the next updates.

23. ANSI/ASQC Q9001, 1994, Introduction. Let us hope registrars/ auditors remember to read these lines.

24. "The supplier shall identify resource requirements, provide adequate resources and assign trained personnel (see 4.18) for management, performance of work and verification activities including internal quality audits." ISO/DIS 9001 (1993), paragraph 4.1.2.2.

25. For a slightly different point of view the reader may want to read I. G. Durand, D. W. Marquardt, R. W. Peach, and J. C. Pyle, "Updating the ISO 9000 Quality Standards: Responding to Marketplace Needs," *Quality Progress* 26, no. 7 (July 1993): 23–28. I am curious as to which marketplace needs the authors are referring to: the ubiquitous customer who represents billions of individuals, the microscopic community of ISO voting members, some enforcers of the standard, or the unlikely combination of all three?

26. It is often believed that the ISO 9000 series of standards first originated in the United Kingdom with the British Standards 5750 series (parts 1–3). The BS 5750 series merely adapted the military standards, in the 1970s, for nonmilitary applications. Subsequently, the British Standards Institution played an important role in convincing the International Organization for Standardization to adopt and rename the series as ISO 9000–ISO 9004. Several additional standards have since been added to the 9000 series.

27. ISO/DIS 9004-2, Scope.

28. Ibid., 18.

29. Mark Morrow, "Companies Find Savings with ISO 9000," *Quality Digest* (November 1993): 20. One should note that external third-party costs associated with registration rarely exceed 5 to 20 percent of total cost.

30. A survey conducted by the Singapore Institute of Standards and Industrial Research (SISIR) revealed that "Only a limited number of companies have reported tangible benefits. . . . Other companies have not been able to correlate sales with the effect of certification as they were unable to isolate the effect of the business cycle and other seasonal factors." The survey revealed that first-time reject rate decreased by as much as 50 percent. "Singapore Survey Cites Market Forces," *ISO 9000 News* 2, no. 6 (November/December 1993): 12.

31. Mark Morrow, "Companies Find Savings with ISO 9000," *Quality Digest* (November 1993): 20.

3 The Service Sector

Generally, people in the service sector or in the marketing and customer service divisions tend to think that
quality control belongs to manufacturers and to people
who work in the manufacturing divisions. This is a mis-
taken assumption. As long as a person is selling a piece
of merchandise or a service, he must be responsible for
its quality. (Kaoru Ishikawa, *What Is Total Quality
Control?*)

This chapter explores several themes that need to be considered when
applying an ISO 9000–type quality assurance system to the service
sector. The focus will be on identifying unique characteristics of the
various service sectors including public institutions. Special attention
will be devoted to the spatioeconomic aspects of the industry in general
(characteristics that also apply to the manufacturing world). The chapter concludes with a brief review of some of the difficulties and challenges of applying TQM to the service sector and asks whether or not
similar challenges await ISO 9000 implementers.

Introduction

Although almost everyone would agree with Zimmerman and Enell's definition of a service as "work performed for someone else," experts do not seem to agree as to how similar the service industry is to the manufacturing/assembly industry.[1] Karl Albrecht and Ron Zemke concur with Theodore Levitt of the Harvard Business School, who states that "the service and nonservice distinction becomes less and less meaningful as our understanding of service increases. There are only industries whose service components are greater or less than other industries."[2] Carol A. King probably would disagree since the author identifies as many as 11 differences between service quality and product quality.[3] Reviewing King's argument, one probably could contend that many of the so-called differences are not differences in kind or nature, but in emphasis. As Zimmerman and Enell suggest, "from a quality viewpoint, the nonservice industries have much in common with manufacturing, as they engage in processing of materials and (often) produce finished goods."[4]

One must nevertheless acknowledge that irrespective of how similar service companies are to manufacturing companies, service companies share certain characteristics that are not always typical of the manufacturing world.

Characteristics of the Service Sector: Does It Matter?

Reviewing the works of Jacques Horovitz, Carol A. King, Karl Albrecht, and Charles Zimmerman, one observes that in their attempt to differentiate the service sector from the manufacturing sector, each author tends to favor his or her own set of attributes. For example, Horovitz differentiates between short and long contact point, high and low interaction.[5] King, as explained, presents 11 points ranging from a customer evaluating a service based on his or her expectations, to the (arguable) suggestion that services do not generate scraps or rejects. Albrecht and Zemke speak of "help me," "fix it," "value added," "unskilled," "skilled," "industrial," "mass consumer," and "high-technology" services.[6] Finally, Zimmerman and Enell provide the most inclusive and generic set of characteristics when they suggest that service companies generally share the following characteristics.

- An emphasis on direct sales to the customer.
- More direct contact with the customer.
- Service delivered on demand rather than weeks or months later.
- Shorter completion time.
- Output created as it is delivered.
- The product is not always a physical product.
- The output cannot always be stored or transported.

Although Zimmerman and Enell recognize that many manufacturing companies may share these characteristics, the thrust of their argument is that service companies are more affected by the characteristics.[7]

John McKnight provides some interesting observations regarding the service sector in general. The first of McKnight's observations is that "[S]ervice production has none of the limits imposed by goods production limits such as natural resources, capital and land. Therefore, the social service business has endless possibilities for expansion as there seems to be no end to the needs for which services can be manufactured."[8] Secondly, McKnight astutely points out that, "[I]n business terms, the client is less the consumer than the raw material for the servicing system. In management terms, the client becomes both the output and the input."[9] Finally, McKnight notes that, in some cases, the client can "consume" the product. McKnight is not referring to the consumption of food but consumption of answers provided by the professionalized servicers (for example, consulting firms, experts, MDs).[10]

One must consider at least two more types of service sectors: the public sector and the nonprofit sector (sometimes referred to as the third sector).[11] David Osborne and Ted Gaebler recognize that the public sector is somewhat unique from the private sector in that[12]

> *Most public agencies don't get their funds from their customers.* Businesses do. Public agencies get most of their funding from legislatures, city councils, and elected

boards. And most of their "customers" are captive: short of moving, they have few alternatives to the services their governments provide. So managers in the public sector learn to ignore them. The customers public managers aim to please are the executive and the legislature—because that's where they get their funding.

Interesting as they are, these characteristics do not necessarily determine whether or not a service company should or should not apply for ISO 9000 registration. Indeed, the standards are generic enough to apply to all industries. However, the characteristics in question do play a significant role when the time comes to interpret and adapt the standards' contents to the myriad of services. Moreover, there are other important characteristics that have not yet been considered by experts that must be taken into consideration when one looks at the feasibility of implementing the ISO 9000 series in a particular service industry.

Types of Services

As is the case with any other industry, the service industry is not monolithic. One must distinguish between monopolies, oligopolies, and competitive services. Such distinctions are important because they help determine the relevance of the standards, as well as provide some suggestions as to how the system should be implemented.

I recently had a difference of opinion with my local cable company, a monopolistic service par excellence. My original objection concerned the fact that the cable company (as most, if not all, cable companies) wanted to charge me a monthly fee for each television outlet. I will not elaborate on all the arguments and counterarguments, but one of the key propositions presented by the cable company was that their service was not imposed (which service is?). Therefore, they argued, if I didn't like their policy, I didn't have to subscribe. Is that premise true? Since regular antenna reception is rather poor (strangely enough, more so than it used to be years ago) I, and thousands of others, really do not have any choice. Although I could tolerate poor antenna reception, or opt for the (expensive) satellite option, I simply cannot shop around for another cable service, much as I would like to. Moreover, the city, which grants these cable monopolies, can provide no assistance whatsoever. What about the quality of service? Predictably, it is less than average. Certainly, everyone is courteous, as long as you want to subscribe, play along, and don't ask annoying questions. But if you begin to politely ask questions and inquire as to which law or regulation applies, courtesy tends to evaporate. Thus, as with manufacturing companies, the true test of quality of service is not so much with the routine processes, but with the employees' ability to handle exceptions to the rule (in other words, process deviations).

Public utility companies and government organizations offer the same set of difficulties. Since it is impossible to negotiate rates or tax brackets, contract review becomes essentially a moot point. I am not suggesting that the application of ISO 9000 is impossible within a monopolistic (regulated or nonregulated) industry, I am merely pointing out that in such cases, much wisdom, self-control, and well-designed customer opinion surveys are required on the part of the service agency to ensure that the customers' needs are served. If we are to focus on the competitive sector of the service industry, there are other important factors to consider.

The Hierarchy of Service

The observation that services, and industry in general, are not randomly distributed within the spatioeconomic landscape, but are distributed in a hierarchical network, had been noted by economic geographers as early as the 1930s.[13] This observation, generally ignored by most authors, is significant because it helps set implementation efforts in their proper perspective. To understand the hierarchical nature of the spatial economy, one must first define three basic concepts known as: *threshold*, *range*, and *order* of a product or good.

Threshold is the minimum amount of sales needed per time period to bring a firm into existence and keep it in business. Similarly, one defines the threshold for a firm selling a product/good or service as the minimum market needed to bring it into existence and to keep it going.

The *range* of a product/good is the average maximum distance people will go to purchase it. Thus, the range for a loaf of bread is shorter than that for a gold bracelet.[14]

The *order* of a product/good is a direct function of its threshold. Consequently, low threshold products/goods have low order and high threshold products/goods have high order. Generally speaking, expensive, infrequently purchased goods such as jewelry, cars, or open-heart surgery have high thresholds and are considered high-order goods. Goods purchased at your local convenience store or at the local gas station tend to be low threshold and low order.[15]

To complete the explanation, the agglomeration of high- and low-order places are clustered into hierarchies of *central places*. These central places usually are referred to as hamlets (low-order central places), villages, towns, and cities (highest order central place). One of the characteristics of central place theory is that high-order places offer all of the goods and services offered by the lower order places. For example, when shopping at a regional shopping center, one is likely to also find most of the activities, goods, and services found at your local shopping center, plus all of the activities not available at your local center, but readily available at the regional shopping center. Enough of economic geography, let us return to the ISO 9000 series and its significance to the service industry.

If services are nested in a hierarchical network of central places that differentiates between the local gas station and the regional hospital, then the customer-supplier relationships at each of these service centers also must be based on some form of hierarchical interrelationships designed to suit a particular need.

Significance of Central Places to the ISO 9000 Series

The reader will remember from chapter 2 that the ISO 9001, ISO 9002, and ISO 9003 standards are organized in a hierarchical fashion (see Figure 2.1). Since the service industry also follows a hierarchical structure, a mapping between these two hierarchies must exist. On the one hand one has the nearly infinite categories of services ordered according to the range and threshold of the goods and services they provide; conversely, one has the three (or perhaps only two) ISO 9000 standards. The mapping (as depicted in Figure 3.1) maps many services onto three standards (ISO 9001, ISO 9002, or ISO 9003). Naturally, this *many to three* mapping also is present in the manufacturing world and may be the source of much initial confusion.

As people began to struggle with the standards, those left with the responsibility of auditing to the standards were faced with the unenviable task of interpreting the paragraphs and reaching a verdict. As customers began wrestling with the standards, they wanted clear and precise answers. The perception was, and continues to be, that there must be one and only one correct way to satisfy or interpret a particular clause. Surely, the registrars, as third-party auditors, would have the answers. Unfortunately, the registrars do not always have the answer; they too learn as they go. Just because they have been in business for several years does not mean they often reach the correct verdict. Sometimes the decisions or interpretations that they render are wise and sometimes they are idiotic. The hit-and-miss approach of their recommendations is understandable because the

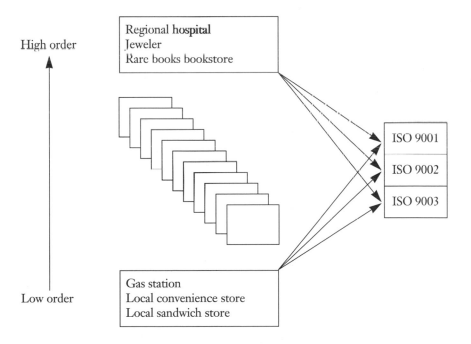

Figure 3.1. Service to ISO standards mapping.

standards are routinely applied to all sorts of industries for which they were not designed. Unfortunately, rather than confess ignorance, the registrars/auditors have felt compelled, as experts, to answer all questions.

In an attempt to alleviate the problem, a host of guidelines is now being written. Unfortunately, these guidelines often are perceived as standards, and thus, rather than alleviate the problem, they amplify it by limiting or narrowing the range of options available to a supplier. A partial solution to the difficulty has emerged over the last couple of years as registrars include an industry expert within their team of auditors.[16] I emphasize *partial* because the use of industry experts can lead to yet another difficulty as these individuals begin to arbitrarily decide what is or is not a correct adaptation or interpretation of a specific clause. The subject, interesting as it is, is too complex and beyond the scope of this book to be addressed presently.

What Is Meant by Quality of Service

The hierarchical nature of services has been emphasized because it will impact the way a service organization interprets and implements the ISO 9000 series. Quality professionals might question this statement by countering that there is but one service quality, independent of the type of service. As one author remarked, "I know quality when I see it." This explanation is too facile for it avoids many important issues. To say that quality of service applies equally to everyone is saying everything and therefore nothing.

Most people have seen how the word *quality* is used in almost every context. Thumbing through the business listings of my local phone book, I found an impressive listing of quality organizations (Table 3.1.)

One can reasonably assume that the services in Table 3.1. provide a quality service; after all, that is what is claimed by their very name. However, if each of the listed service organizations were to implement one of the three ISO 9000 models for quality assurance, they would experience their own set of difficulties simply because they provide a different order of goods. This implies that their customer-supplier relationships will be different, and their processes and inspection control mechanism will range in complexity, as well as a host of other criteria.

Table 3.1. Examples of some services with the word *Quality* in their company name (suggested ISO standard in parentheses).

Quality Air (questionable, but likely to be ISO 9002)
Quality Business Forms and Printing (ISO 9001/ISO 9002)
Quality Business Systems, Inc. (ISO 9002)
Quality Carpet Cleaners (ISO 9002)
Quality Concrete Products, Inc. (ISO 9002)
Quality Consumer Referrals (ISO 9002)
Quality Control Printing & Graphics (ISO 9002)
Quality Control Software, Inc. (ISO 9001)
Quality Express Plumbing (ISO 9002)
Quality Financial Plans, Inc. (ISO 9001/ISO 9002)
Quality Finishing, Inc. (ISO 9002)
Quality 1st Frame Company (ISO 9002)
Quality Foreign Auto (ISO 9002)
Quality Home Painting (ISO 9002/ISO 9003)
Quality I&R Services (ISO 9002?)
Quality In-House Video (ISO 9002/ISO 9003)
Quality Interiors (ISO 9001/ISO 9002)
Quality Landscape Services (ISO 9001)
Quality Landscapes (ISO 9001)
Quality Linen Service (ISO 9002)
Quality Machine Staining, Inc (ISO 9002).
Quality Marble Care (ISO 9002/ISO 9003)
Quality Micro Repair & Equipment (ISO 9002)
Quality Nutrition Center (ISO 9001/ISO 9002)
Quality Pacific Inc. (questionable, ISO 9002)
Quality Quilting (ISO 9003)
Quality Rentals (ISO 9002)
Quality Sewing & Vacuum (ISO 9002)
Quality Sewing & Vacuum Center (ISO 9002)
Quality Systems, Inc. (consultant? ISO 9001)
Quality Tax Service (ISO 9001/ISO 9002)
Quality Tire (ISO 9002)
Quality Tool & Supply, Inc. (ISO 9002/ISO 9003)
Quality Transmission, Inc. (ISO 9002)

Perusal of the list reemphasizes some of the points made by Horovitz and others regarding contact time, intensity of interaction, and nature of service (customized vs. standardized). Indeed, the contact time and intensity of interaction will be different between Quality Tax Service and Quality In-House Video. Both services are of a different order. The tax service is of a higher order than the video store. Although one could argue about which one offers the customized product/service and which one offers a standardized service, the tax service is more likely to customize its service to its clients' needs than the video store, which basically offers videos for rent. The contact time and intensity (customer-supplier) are obviously very different (intense vs. ephemeral).

Naturally, the quality assurance system of the tax consultant will be different than the video rental store. That does not mean that they will not address the same issues—they will, but with a different emphasis. This is an important point. I am not suggesting that one organization is free to ignore more ISO 9000 paragraphs than the other. On the contrary, both organizations will have to address most paragraphs (some will have no relevance whatsoever), but they will satisfy these paragraphs differently. These are the very issues that will need to be explored in Part II, when the ISO 9001 is applied to a few service industries.

Are All Firms Equal?

The hierarchical distinction between firms brought about by economic geographers partly demonstrates that the undifferentiated and universal application of the ISO 9000 series to all industries is ill-advised. Similarly, research by some economists indicates that one must differentiate between firms. In the late 1960s, Robert T. Averitt concluded in his *The Dual Economy: The Dynamics of American Industry Structure* that a distinction must be made between *center* and *periphery firms*.[17] Although some of the themes presented by Averitt have become slightly outdated, I believe his observations regarding center and periphery firms still apply. "The center firm," he observed, "is large in economic size as measured by number of employees, total assets, and yearly sales. It tends toward vertical integration (through ownership or informal control), geographic dispersion (national and international), product diversification, and managerial decentralization. Center firms excel in managerial and technical talent; their financial resources are abundant."

As for the periphery firm, Averitt observes that it "is relatively small. It is not integrated vertically, and it may be an economic satellite of a center firm or cluster of center firms. Periphery firms are less geographically dispersed, both nationally and internationally. Typically, they produce only a small line of related products. Their management is centralized, often revolving around a single individual. . . . Periphery management below the top executive is, on the whole, less able than its center counterparts. Financial limitations pose a major problem to periphery firms."[18]

Similar observations would apply to the service industry. Some sectors sell a few items in large volume (hamburger stand) while other sell hundreds or thousands of items in small volume (department store). Within the service sector, the hamburger stand could be a satellite from a major center firm, or it could be a small, family-owned periphery firm. Which one is more likely to have documented procedures?

What is especially relevant in Averitt's study is the implication that different styles of management are found in each type of firm. In fact, Averitt goes as far as suggesting that various modes of productions (hence, various processes) have a direct correlation with managerial styles.[19] Although Averitt's analysis is somewhat weak on empirical data, his observations concur with the work of others (including my own data accumulated over the last five years of interviews). In essence, Averitt proposes that as an industry shifts from mass production to process (continuous) production, there is a shift from a *formal* management system to an *informal* one.[20]

What is interesting about Averitt's crude process differentiation is the distinction he makes between the two styles of management: formal (in other words, rigid) vs. informal (in other words, loose). I have observed this dichotomy countless times in managerial styles. Center firm managers, especially those who have had experience with one or more of the many military (quality assurance) standards, are more apt to readily accept the need for documented procedures. These firms are more likely to have long-run processes where thousands of pieces/items are produced in a relatively short period of time (hours) or short runs (tens or less to hundreds of items) built over a relatively long period of time (six to 12 months or more).

Acceptance does not necessarily mean compliance. Indeed, it has been my experience that although formal managers often readily agree with the need for documented procedures and would claim that their system is fully documented and compliant, audits of the quality assurance system reveal many discrepancies.

Managers favoring the informal system generally have greater difficulty understanding the need for a formal (procedure-driven) quality assurance system. Although these managers (who tend to work in periphery rather than center firms) would concede that some generic procedures should be implemented to improve overall performance, they invariably will resist and question the need for documented procedures as prescribed by the majority of the ISO 9000 clauses.

For the most part, their objections are centered around one common comment: "We do not build mass-produced items. Our products are highly customized." Managers within some sectors of the service industry could certainly raise similar objections.

Even though these observations are undeniably true, one should not focus on the unique characteristics of any and all processes; rather, the objective is to concentrate on the overall business purpose or raison d'être (in other words, the reason for being in business). Consequently, behind every customized service (manufactured or otherwise), there must be a basic supporting structure that identifies the basic tenets, principles, and beliefs of any organization. The ISO 9000 models attempt to focus on these fundamental principles (see chapter 7).

TQM and the Service Sector: What Can We Learn?

Over the past decade, the principles of TQM have been applied to various sectors of the service industry with mixed results. Some of the most outstanding applications of TQM to the private and public sectors have included educational institutions (from high schools to universities), hospitals, city governments, law firms, and various agencies of the federal government.[21]

Despite some very positive results presented by Osborne and Gaebler, the application of TQM to academia and other institutions has met with some resistance and skepticism. For example, David H. Entin explains that "[T]he pronounced reluctance of academic divisions (except business schools) to adopt TQM is alarming and may represent a serious disjunction between market forces and the academic enterprise and indicate that faculty are not currently interested in satisfying their students and other customers."[22] Entin concedes that although "a few minor systems have been analyzed and have definitely improved," major problems have not yet been solved. Entin concludes by observing that, "one interpretation might be that TQM is off to a successful start. . . . Another interpretation would be that the results so far do not match up to the hype, hopes, and initial investment in time and money."[23]

Although the special issue of *Change* (May/June 1993) contains several examples of successful applications of TQM within academia, other authors do share Entin's concerns. For example, Peter Ewell states that, "[A] final trap is the 'pleasing the Customer Syndrome,' . . . The result is a narrowly reactive approach where the recognized bottom line is immediate student satisfaction, or, as one horrified faculty member recently put it, 'where the inmates are running the asylum.'"[24] Steven E. Brigham and, to some extent, Osborne and Graeber, echo Ewell's concerns when he states that, "[U]niversity TQM advocates may need to rethink the place of quality management on campus, lest TQM wind up being about parking stickers and billing complaints."[25] Similar concerns also are raised by Howland Blackiston who notes, "I see a lot of law firms doing what I call 'dustball' projects—measuring how long it takes to answer a phone but not tackling anything significant."[26]

The fundamental difficulty of implementing TQM within service industries such as law firms, hospitals, or academia is that, in most cases, professionals within these services either provide good services or perceive themselves as performing good service. On a score from 1 to 10 (10 being best quality of service), most law firms rated themselves an 8.5. Moreover, the perception seems justified when one learns that only 1 percent of the population of customers surveyed cited quality as a concern, but 60 percent thought that law firms charge too much.[27]

Brigham proposes that similar to MDs, faculty think they "know their job and are *already* providing quality."[28]

One should also note that one of the implementation flaws of TQM may be that practitioners often refer to "the voice of the customer." Naturally, I am not questioning the value of listening to customers. Rather, I would suggest that the constant referral to the voice of the customer is much too simplistic because no two customers are alike. Therefore, to avoid the trivialization of TQM, already cited, one should refer to the voices of the customers. Indeed, since "people don't want standardized services any more," the task of moving away from one-size-fits-all services could be made easier if advocates of TQM would modify their anthem to: "Always listen to the voices of the customers, and learn to discriminate."

Will the difficulties and challenges of implementing TQM delineated herein be experienced by anyone wishing to adopt the ISO 9000 series? Perhaps but probably not with the same emphasis. Certainly, the issues raised by the aforementioned authors or writers transcend TQM and would naturally apply to the ISO 9000 series. Nonetheless the implementation hurdles are likely to be different in nature precisely because the ISO 9000 series in many respects, is more specific because it provides its users with well-defined models of quality assurance.

As will be illustrated throughout the following chapters, the models do not always neatly fit the application. The fact that models are provided simplifies the task somewhat. At a minimum, the ISO 9000 series of standards, with its many paragraphs and subparagraphs, does identify for the user the specific tasks that will have to be addressed. In this respect, the ISO 9000 series is both easier and occasionally more difficult to implement (see chapter 6). It is easier because one knows that in order to achieve ISO 9000 registration, a quality policy will have to be written, internal audits will have to be conducted, procedures will have to be written, documents will have to be controlled, and so on.

It is more difficult, because in some cases, the application or justification for application of a particular clause or subclause will be either tenuous, tedious, or dubious. Hence the dilemma and challenge to intelligently apply the standards. Finally, many people would probably acknowledge that one of the appealing advantages of achieving ISO 9000 registration is that it is an internationally recognized standard. Achieving true TQM (for example, à la Baldrige) may be more meaningful and rewarding (if not more costly), but (as of now) the only recognized international standard for quality assurance is the ISO 9000 series.

Which Standard for the Service Sector?

As was explained in chapter 2, the selection of a standard is the responsibility of the user. Nonetheless, the following examples (listed in Table 3.1) are provided in an attempt to assist readers who may still be undecided. Referring to the table, one observes that the majority of services would apply for ISO 9002. A few would apply for ISO 9001 and fewer still may apply for ISO 9003. The selection of ISO 9002 over ISO 9003 as the most popular standard for the service industry is rather easy to justify since most service organizations have processes that should/could be controlled.

The occasional hesitation between ISO 9002 and ISO 9003 (home painting, in-house video, marble care, quilting, and tool and supply) is caused principally by the fact that one would have to visit the facilities to determine which standard best applies. In the case of the video store, one easily could argue that the store is basically a warehouse of videos that are rented to customers. One of the primary functions of the video store is to ensure that the customer returns the videos in good condition (preferably rewound). Basically, this is a rent and inspection function. The service is very basic, although perhaps not as basic as a gas station, which could limit its service to selling gasoline and oil (I am not suggesting that the gas station should consider ISO 9003 registration). For the remaining companies, it depends whether they are essentially warehouses/distributors where customers come to buy their products, or they perform additional services such as installation; thus the hesitation.

The choice of ISO 9001 for the software, landscape, nutrition center, and the consultant(s) is obvious, but not necessarily clear cut (few things are with the ISO 9000 series). The software company is likely to design software for a company. The landscape company or the landscape architect certainly needs to design landscapes for customers. One would think that the nutrition center also designs a nutritional program best suited to satisfy the needs of each customer. Finally, one would hope that the consultant does not always offer the same canned advice, therefore some design activities should take place; particularly if training and course development is required.

Conclusion

The generic nature of the ISO 9000 series of standards is a valuable asset for it indicates that the basic principles of quality assurance can be applied to a broad range of industries. This does not mean that the quality assurance system of a hospital should resemble that of a bank. Nor does it mean that each (ISO 9000) paragraph should be interpreted from the same point of view. These remarks might appear trite to some readers, but they need to be stated simply because some auditors do view every industry through the same tinted glasses. Thus, the need to write this chapter and hopefully raise the awareness of not only the implementer, but also the auditors. Having hopefully convinced the reader that not all firms are created equal, we now need to explore in Part II, how the standards can be applied and transferred to the service industry.

Notes

1. Charles D. Zimmerman and John W. Enell in J. M. Juran's, *Juran's Quality Control Handbook* (New York: McGraw-Hill, 1988): section 33, 33.2.

2. Karl Albrecht and Ron Zemke, *Service America*, (New York: Warner Books, 1985), 4. For a similar view see Raghu N. Kacker, "Quality Planning for Service Industries," *Quality Progress* (August 1988): 39–42.

3. Carol A. King, "A Framework for a Service Quality Assurance System," *Quality Progress* (September 1987): 27–32.

4. Zimmerman and Enell in J. M. Juran's, *Juran's Quality Control Handbook*, 33.3

5. Jacques Horovitz, *La Qualite de Service: A la Conquete du Client.* (Paris: Intereditions, 1987).

6. Albrecht and King, op. cit.

7. Zimmerman and Enell, in J. M. Juran's, *Juran's Quality Control Handbook*, 33.5, 33.6.

8. John McKnight, "Professionalized Service and Disabling Help," in *Disabling Profession*, ed. Ivan Illich (New York: Marion Boyars, 1987): 70.

9. Ibid., 74.

10. "I, the professional, am the answer. The central assumption is that service is a unilateral process. I, the professional, produce. You the client, consume." Ibid., 83.

11. David Osborne and Ted Gaebler, *Reinventing Government* (New York: Penguin Books, Plume Book, 1993), 43–47.

12. Ibid., 167. Oddly enough, Osborne and Gaebler do not mention that the legislature or city councils do collect taxes from citizens (their customers). Nevertheless, their argument is still valid.

13. These theories, which postulate that the spatioeconomic landscape consist of hexagonal market areas upon which a hierarchical structure of towns and cities is superimposed, were developed by the German geographer Walter Christaller (1933) and the German economist August Losch (1950s). Many others (such as W. Isard, W. Alonso) have also contributed throughout the decades.

14. From Ronald Abler, John Adams, and Peter Gould, *Spatial Organization* (Englewood Cliffs, N.J.: Prentice-Hall), 364–365.

15. Anthony R. de Souza and J. Brady Foust, *World Space-Economy* (Columbus, Ohio: Charles E. Merrill Publishing Company), 243.

16. An industry expert always is required whenever the third-party audit is conducted for a regulated product. To my knowledge, such requirements do not (yet) apply to the service industries.

17. Robert T. Averitt, *The Dual Economy* (New York, W. W. Norton & Company, 1968). See pages 35–37 for Averitt's discussion on the hierarchy of american industry structure.

18. Ibid., 1–2. I am not sure one could still argue that the management of periphery firms is less able than its center counterpart.

19. Averitt distinguishes between "unit and small batch," "large batch and mass production," and "process (continuous) production."

20. Ibid., 34.

21. For a recent survey of TQM in education see, the May/June 1993 issue of *Change* (The Magazine of Higher Learning). For applications within the legal profession, see Stephanie B. Goldberg, "The Quest for TQM," *The ABA Journal* (The American Bar Association Journal) (November 1993): 52–58. For many examples within the public sector, see Osborne and Gaebler, op. cit. See also, David Charters, "U.S. Postal Service Delivers Total Quality," *Quality Digest* (June 1993): 25–31; T. S. Pevic, "Government in Action: A Look Inside the Federal Quality Institute," *Quality Digest* (June 1993): 34–37; Brad Stratton, "How the Federal Government Is Reinventing Itself," and Karen Bemowski, "Trailblazers in Reinventing Government," *Quality Progress* (December 1993): 21–34, 37–42.

22. David H. Entin, "From Boston: Less than Meets the Eye," *Change* (May/June 1993): 31.

23. Ibid.

24. Peter T. Ewell, "Total Quality and Academic Practice: The Idea We've Been Waiting For?" *Change* (May/June 1993): 55.

25. Steven E. Brigham, "TQM: Lessons We Can Learn from Industry," *Change* (May/June 1993): 48. David Osborne and Ted Graeber concede that "[E]ven public schools, for instance, will act like businesses when forced to compete for their students and dollars; they will manipulate test score." Osborne and Graeber, op. cit., 186. John McKnight argues that "[U]nlike most servicing systems, the school is transparent in its institutional definition of the client's role. The school client is evaluated in terms of his ability to satisfy the teacher. The explicit outcome of the system is professional approval of behavior and performance." McKnight, op. cit., 88.

26. Quoted in Stephanie B. Goldberg, "The Quest for TQM," *The ABA Journal* (November 1993): 53.

27. Survey reproduced in Goldberg, op. cit.

28. Steven E. Brigham, op. cit., 48.

Part II

ISO 9000 Series Standards in the Service Industry: How Well Do They Apply?

The division between services
and manufacturing is becoming
steadily less useful.

—*Quality Digest*
June 1993

4 ISO 9001, ISO 9002, and the Restaurant Industry: A Fictitious Example

The restaurant sector has not been selected as the first case study because restaurants are likely to rush toward ISO 9000 registration, but because everyone is familiar with it. Expanding on concepts developed in chapter 3, one must first recognize that there are many orders of restaurants each having a different *threshold* and *range*. There are cafeterias, low-scale coffee shops, upscale coffee shops, fast-food restaurants, diners, specialty or trendy restaurants, ethnic restaurants, and expensive restaurants. Within the restaurant sector, most of the ISO 9002 paragraphs apply equally well to all (from the cafeteria to the expensive restaurant). In other words, although the type of foods, nature of service, and ambience will vary drastically from the All You Can Eat cafeteria to Chez Maxime, both restaurants will have to address the same ISO 9002 paragraphs. Certainly, there will be some differences in emphasis as to how certain paragraphs are handled, but all paragraphs would have to be addressed.

ISO 9001 or ISO 9002?
The decision as to which standard to apply should be rather simple, but as will be shown, subtle issues need to be considered. First of all, similar to their counterparts in the manufacturing/assembly world, not all

restaurants prepare meals. Fast-food restaurants usually reprocess frozen or refrigerated food delivered by many suppliers or subcontractors. When I order a Bordeau burger at a local restaurant, I know that most of the ingredients making up the burger were delivered frozen to the restaurant, which in turn heats it up, adds a few french fries (also delivered frozen), and serves it. A totally different process takes place when I order my favorite Moroccan couscous at another of my favorite restaurants. There, I can actually see the chef prepare my meal using raw ingredients. Even there, however, the chef must use some preprocessed food.

Therefore, if we are to focus only on the preparation of food, the single most important activity of most restaurants, a distinction must be made between the two restaurants; a distinction usually reflected in the price of the final product. Is there any design involved? One could suggest that since some restaurants (or rather chefs) design their own recipes, 9001 could be the required standard. Is that a correct assumption? It all depends on what is meant by designing recipes. Indeed, there are at least two major scenarios to consider: the case of the restaurant that belongs to a chain and the case of the specialized, generally high-priced, restaurant. Let us first consider case two, the specialized restaurant.

Usually, when a customer orders a meal from a menu she or he is not involved with the design process of the recipes. Certainly, the customer may request her or his steak to be well done and ask for some substitutions (not tolerated by most chefs), but these requests really are deviations from the standard process; they do not call for a major reformulation of the recipes (a similar argument could be made for many assembler/manufacturers who must customize their standard products to satisfy the broad range of customer requirements). The next issue to consider is whether or not a recipe is a precise formula (a process) that can be quantified and proceduralized. Some would say "yes," others, who have tried to obtain recipes from chefs (as opposed to cooks), would likely say "no." Recipes often are considered to be secret procedures that are jealously kept by their originator(s) and are passed on only to a select group of individuals. So much for design control in such cases.[1]

The first scenario (restaurant belonging to a chain) would perhaps allow for design control of recipes. In such cases, chefs often are requested to develop menus for an entire chain of restaurants. In order to ensure that the same menu (standardized portions, standardized preparation, and so on) is served throughout the various restaurants, the menu must be designed and controlled to avoid deviations from the original menu. However, even in such cases, I am not aware of any customer participation within the design loop.[2]

Menus are designed, priced, and launched. To the best of my knowledge, customer specifications are not set a priori. Rather, they are specified (fine-tuned) a posteriori during the contract review phase (much as is done in various sectors of the manufacturing world). The chef designs his or her menu in the hope of satisfying as many customers as possible. This is partly achieved by offering as wide a variety of meals as is economically feasible. If certain items are not popular, they are eventually removed from the menu. In the process of designing a menu a chef will identify specifications such as size of the portion, ingredients to be used, preparation, and presentation. These internal specifications will have to be respected.

The obvious difficulty is that in a restaurant, much as in the manufacturing world, there are at least two types of design activities. The first type consists of the fine-tuning already described. During this phase the customer may specify certain deviations from the standard menu. In such cases, although much of the design control activities of paragraph 4.4, Design Control, are performed by the kitchen staff, I do not foresee any restaurant wanting to implement documented (re)design control procedures.

The second type of design control (in other words, new recipes) is identical to the new product design phase experienced by manufacturers. In this case, the marketing/sales force suggests that a new product be launched. The customer may or may not be involved during these early phases when engineering is asked to design a product in anticipation of customer needs (see Design Function in chapter 6, for additional explanations).

Both models (ISO 9001 and ISO 9002) may be applied to the restaurant industry. However, since it is unlikely that restaurants will opt for the ISO 9001 model, this text will focus on the ISO 9002 model. If one is to assume that the ISO 9002 model is better suited to the restaurant industry, let us review how the quality assurance system of a restaurant would address each paragraph.

Management Responsibility (4.1)

This opening paragraph consists of the following subclauses.

- Quality Policy (4.1.1)
- Organization (4.1.2)
    –Responsibility and Authority (4.1.2.1)
    –Resources (4.1.2.2)
    –Management Representative (4.1.2.3)
- Management Review (4.1.3)

The first difficulty encountered by individuals faced with the task of implementing a quality assurance system is the formulation of a quality policy. Often, the words *quality policy* are interpreted to mean mission statement. The confusion is understandable since a clear definition of the terms quality policy and mission statement has yet to be written. The ISO 8402 definition standard does provide some assistance by defining *quality policy* as "the overall quality intentions and direction of an organization with regard to quality, as formally expressed by top management." The associated notes provide some additional clarification by specifying that "The quality policy forms one element of the corporate policy and is authorized by top management."[3] Thus, it would appear that the quality policy is a subset of the corporate policy, often phrased in the form of a mission statement.

To satisfy the quality policy requirements, the restaurant's upper management—which could consist of the owner(s) and other executives—will have to *define* and *document* its objectives for and commitment to quality. Once these objectives and commitments are stated, upper management must then find means to ensure that the policy is understood and maintained throughout the organization. Satisfying the first part of this requirement (objectives and commitments) should not be difficult. Ensuring that these stated objectives and commitments to quality are understood and implemented throughout the restaurant or chain of restaurants is more difficult for it requires some sort of management review (see also chapter 7, How Much to Write?, particularly point 4, for additional comments).

The purpose of these management reviews, which must be scheduled at prescribed intervals (defined by the restaurant owner[s]), is not only to ensure that the restaurant's quality system conforms to all of the requirements of the standard, but also to continually review that the system is suitable and effective. In other words, there is no need to overdesign a quality assurance system that cannot be maintained in the long run. The first step should be to make certain that the minimum requirements set by the standard are satisfied. Improvements can occur later.

For example, in order to satisfy the opening paragraph (management responsibility), the restaurant owners still have to address three more subparagraphs. The responsibility, authority, and interrelationship of personnel who manage, perform, and verify work affecting quality must first be defined and documented. Specifically, third-party auditors would like to know who has authority to

- Initiate action to prevent the occurrence (and by implication recurrence, see later paragraphs) of any process, product, or quality system nonconformities.

- Identify and record any product, process, and quality system problems.

- Initiate, recommend, or provide solutions through designated channels.

- Verify that the solutions have been implemented.

- Control processing, delivery, or installation of nonconforming product until corrective action(s) have been successfully implemented.[4]

In addition, management must ensure that adequate resources of trained personnel are assigned to conduct verification activities that include internal audits (Resources). Finally, an upper management representative must be appointed, irrespective of other responsibilities, to ensure that the ISO quality requirements are established and maintained. In addition, the representative must report to management as to the performance of the quality system. So much for the opening subparagraphs, only 18 more to go. What does it mean to a restaurateur?

If a restaurant wishes to apply for ISO 9002 certification, it will have to adapt its quality assurance system to the requirements stated herein. The quality policy and objectives should not be too difficult. Each restaurateur will have to come up with its own policy statement and objectives. One of the typical methods is to brainstorm with a few colleagues (two to six) what the policy should be. Avoid unachievable or difficult to measure criteria such as "the best food in the world at unbeatable prices" or the "fastest service in town." It is difficult to determine what is the best food. It is even more difficult to truly assess if one's prices are unbeatable; besides that might not be that important to your customers. So, prior to starting on your quality policy mission and objectives, why not interview a few customers (20 to 30 should do). Interview face-to-face rather than rely on a questionnaire. If you rely on a questionnaire, you might still miss what is really important to your customers and only measure what you think is important.

Having captured your customers' quality objectives and defined your policy that will help you satisfy these requirements, you must write it all down and ensure that the information is not only transferred to every member of your staff, but also practiced by each and every one of them. This is not as difficult as you might think but it does require training, time, and persistence. Since training is a requirement of the standard, you might as well inform your staff of your new policy (and desire to achieve ISO 9002 certification) via some official media. Some restaurants train every member of their part-time staff in an eight- to 10-hour series of workshops coupled with on-the-job training, which includes a two-hour explanation of the restaurant's quality policies.

How do you ensure that your policies are understood and practiced? Simple. Conduct internal audits (yet another requirement of the standard). These audits will have to be conducted at regular intervals (to be determined by you) by trained personnel. In other words, it is not enough to say that you will conduct audits, you must also ensure that the personnel assigned to conduct audits know how to perform them.

Moreover, these audits are not only designed to verify that your policies are practiced, but that all aspects of the standards are followed. In other words, the remaining 18 paragraphs (to be described) must be adhered to. We will return to internal audits later.

The responsibility and authority section probably will include (depending on the type/order of restaurant) the chef(s) and assistant chefs—if several shifts are in effect—the host(ess), the bartender, the waiters/waitresses, and busboys. Each have a specified set of responsibilities that include tracking and correcting nonconformances.[5] For example, the following list of responsibilities could be specified for the chef.

- Purchase all main ingredients.

- Set criteria of acceptance for all fruits, meat, and vegetables (and perhaps more).

- Ensure that all ingredients are of acceptable quality.

- Verify that all menus are prepared correctly or according to specific recipes.

- Ensure that all meals are cooked within a reasonable amount of time. (*Note:* You may want to be more specific as some restaurants do, however, that may be considered rather tacky in an expensive French restaurant where customers might be served when the chef is ready.)

- Answer any special request.

- Modify recipes as per customer requirements.

(*Note:* For restaurants of a different order [as defined in chapter 3], this set of responsibilities is much too involved. For other restaurants, one would have to include the pastry chef, sauce chef, and so on.)

Responsibilities for other key positions also will have to be defined, including the busperson whose important job is to

- Clean tables within his/her station.

- Ensure that all seats are clean.

- Set table.

- Provide a glass of water for each guest.

The management representative responsible for ensuring that the quality systems are established, implemented, maintained, and reported to management may be the restaurant's manager who would report to the owners or district manager, depending on the arrangement. It is important to understand that upper management must be part of the verification loop. That is, management (more specifically, upper management) must be kept informed via management review—for which records (for example, minutes) must be kept—of the system's effectiveness and suitability. If internal audits reveal that any part of the quality assurance system is found to be deficient or inadequate vis-à-vis the restaurant's own quality system or the ISO 9002 standard, nonconformances must be addressed and corrective actions implemented to prevent recurrence. This is what is meant by effectiveness and suitability.

For example, if kitchen sanitation is found to be in violation of some sanitation code, or if a particular procedure (for example, final inspection by a waiter) is not in line with written documents/procedures or policy, the nonconformance must be reported to management and a corrective action must be initiated and enforced. The corrective action may require a change in procedure, which in turn will have to be approved, documented, and applied. This may require additional training or retraining.

The reader may now understand what is meant by a quality assurance system. Remember that so far only the first four paragraphs of Management Responsibility have been presented and already three additional paragraphs were invoked: Training, Procedures (or process control), and Internal Audits.

Quality System (4.2)

The 1987 version of this paragraph was simple to satisfy for it stated that the restaurant in question had to have a documented quality assurance system that would address all of the paragraphs of the ISO 9002 standard. The 1987 version had an extensive note that was purely advisory. The note is now included in the 1994 version as clause 4.2.3, Quality Planning. Fortunately, the clause states that "The supplier shall give consideration to the following activities, as appropriate, in meeting the specified requirements for products, projects or contracts.

a) the preparation of quality plans;

b) the identification and acquisition of any controls, processes, equipment (including inspection and test equipment), fixtures, resources and skills that may be needed to achieve the required quality;

c) ensuring the compatibility of the design, the production process, installation, servicing, inspection and test procedures and the applicable documentation;

d) the updating, as necessary, of quality control, inspection and testing techniques, including the development of new instrumentation;

e) the identification of any measurement requirement involving capability that exceeds the known state of the art, in sufficient time for the needed capability to be developed;

f) the identification of suitable verification at appropriate stages in the realization of the product;

g) the clarification of standards of acceptability for all features and requirements, including those which contain a subjective element;

h) the identification and preparation of quality records (see 4.16)."[6]

Assuming the service sector can find applications for most of these requirements, the system will consist of documented procedures that have to be effectively implemented. Consequently, be careful not to develop endless procedures that you know will never be enforced and/or maintained. Finally, the restaurateur will have to specify how he or she intends on satisfying his or her own quality requirements, namely, how the quality system will be enforced.

One of the standard methods often recommended during implementation of a quality assurance system, is to adopt the quality of pyramid structure. The conceptual pyramid divides any quality assurance system into four tiers.

- Tier one, the highest level document, consists of the quality manual (now required by ISO 9001, ISO 9002, and ISO 9003) where each of the ISO 9000 paragraphs are addressed. The quality manual is a control document that must satisfy all of the document control requirements set within the ISO 9000 series standards. Some of the aforementioned examples for responsibility and authority should be included in a quality manual.

- Tier two is an optional (but recommended) tier that consists of all standard operating procedures. These could be global or high-level departmental procedures that address the pertinent ISO 9000 paragraphs. Internal customer/supplier interrelationships could be identified within the second tier.

- Tier three documents are more specific and consist of work instructions or assembly instructions.

- Tier four is the actual quality records that indicate that an inspection or analysis has been performed.

(*Note:* Each tier should refer to the tier below.)

For a restaurant, the quality manual would have to address every one of the ISO 9002 paragraphs. The manual generally does not exceed 25 to 40 pages, depending on the style of the writer(s) and nature of the business. Although no specific format is required, it is recommended that the quality manual mimics the structure and format found in the standards. The only advantage for doing so is that it facilitates the task of the auditor. If you already have a quality manual and do not wish to rewrite it because you feel it adequately addresses all of the clauses, you may simply add in an appendix, a matrix that would cross-reference, or map your paragraphs or pagination to the standard.

Tier two would likely consist of area-specific standard operating procedures. For example, the kitchen would have its own set of kitchen procedures, a set of generic procedures on how to wait on a customer, how to bus, hosting, and so on, which would make up the second tier. These procedures would not have to be elaborate, but they will likely include several other subprocedures. For example, one of the subprocedures to be included within the how to wait on a customer procedure would include the contract review procedure, which will be reviewed shortly.

Tier three procedures may include specific how-to work instructions. Examples of tier three procedures could include: recipes, how to operate and maintain certain equipment (for example, French fries machine), and hosting procedures (what to say, what information to ask for, and so on). One should not assume that a whole set of written procedures will be required for every piece of equipment or job description. Indeed, the amount of documentation is (in some ways) directly correlated to the amount of training or experience of the individual. In today's age of multimedia and increasing computerization, one must remember that several media are available; procedures do not have to be written. Many jobs are best explained by simply demonstrating the task during a brief training session. For example, I doubt that a restaurateur would want to write a detailed tier three procedure on how to bus a table. However, the restaurateur may want to prepare a brief video on how to properly bus a table or how to wait on a customer. Since these videos contain documented instructions used for training, they will have to be controlled as any other document (see Document Control section).

Tier four consists of all records relating to the operation and maintenance of the quality system. These records consist of purchasing orders; customer order entry forms (in other words, receipts); records of instrument calibration; personnel training records; records of internal audits; minutes from meetings in which corrective action and preventive methods are discussed, formalized, and implemented; records required for health inspection officials, vendor assessments, or ratings; inspection records (other than visual); and so on.

Contract Review (4.3)

The contract review clause is written to address issues pertaining to the restaurant's ability to satisfy its customers' requirements. The procedure that will have to be written must ensure that the following points are satisfied.

- Written or verbal requirements are adequately described and documented.

- Deviations and/or amendments from the tender are transferred to functions concerned and resolved.

- The supplier has the capability to meet contract or accepted order requirements.

In a restaurant (or similar establishments, such as catering services) all of these conditions for contract review should be practiced daily. Customers read a menu (the equivalent to the manufacturer's catalog), ask the waiter/waitress for clarification, and occasionally request deviations from the standard menu. When in doubt, the waiter/waitress verifies with the kitchen to ensure that the deviation can be satisfied and amends the order on his or her recordkeeping pad.[7] All that would be required from the restaurateur is to describe the above steps (and additional ones, if required) in the restaurant's quality manual or include the procedure within a second tier document.

Design Control (4.4)

This paragraph is not likely to apply in the restaurant industry and will therefore be reviewed in chapter 6.

Document and Data Control (4.5)

The document and data control paragraph requires that a procedure be written explaining how control of document and data that relate to the requirements of the ISO 9000 series standards is achieved. The document and data control clause consists of two major subclauses entitled: Document Approval and Issue and Document Changes. The essence of these paragraphs is to

- Ensure that documents and data are reviewed and approved for adequacy by authorized personnel prior to issue.

- Ensure that pertinent documents are available at locations where they are needed for the effective operation of the quality system.

- Ensure that obsolete documents are removed from point of use. Obsolete documents preserved for legal and/or knowledge purposes will have to be properly identified.

- Ensure that changes are performed by the same organization/ function that performed the original approval and issue.

- Establish a master list or equivalent document which would identify the current revision status of documents so as to preclude the
use of invalid and/or obsolete documents.

Although the requirements for document and data control are
equally pertinent for the restaurant industry, the emphasis probably will
be different than that in the manufacturing world. The quality manual is
a controlled document since it describes the quality assurance system.
One would like to know who wrote it and when, which revision is in
effect, what changes have been made and by whom, what paragraphs
were affected by the changes, who approved the changes, how many
controlled copies were printed, and the location of these copies.

The same document and data control procedure would apply for
tier two and tier three documents. For example, kitchen procedures
would probably be written by the chef or his/her delegate. These procedures (or videos) would have to have an effective implementation date.
Revisions or amendments also would have to be identified, signed, and
dated by whomever is responsible (in other words, has the authority) to
enforce the procedure. The same would apply for other operational or
administrative procedures. As for data control, I do not believe such procedures would be required for a restaurant. Although restaurant managers handle a considerable amount of data pertaining to profitability/
efficiency, restaurants are not primarily in the business of handling the
amount of data required by the ISO 9000 series. Surely, one could maintain equipment calibration records and conduct customer surveys.
However, I do not believe a restaurant would have to control and maintain elaborate procedures for such data. Within the restaurant industry,
the bulk of the document control procedures would address the quality
manual as well as second and/or third tier procedures.

Purchasing (4.6)
The purchasing clause includes three major subclauses—Evaluation of
Subcontractors, Purchasing Data, and Verification of Purchased
Product—broken down into further subparagraphs. With the exception of cleaning or maintenance services (which could apply for ISO
9002 registration), restaurants do not have many subcontractors, rather
they have vendors that provide them with various food and beverage

supplies. Since all restaurants purchase raw materials in various stages of value added and transform them into finished goods by cooking, freezing, or mixing them (providing additional value added), the purchasing paragraph is significant.

The purchasing paragraph takes on a different meaning depending on whether it is an expensive restaurant providing gourmet dishes or a fast-food restaurant. This is not to say that certain requirements need not be satisfied by either restaurant, but that both restaurants would have to adapt the paragraph to their needs. Both restaurants would have to address the following issues.

- Describe how vendors and subcontractors are evaluated on the basis of their ability to meet quality assurance requirements.

- Define the type and extent of control exercised by the restaurant on their vendors.

- Maintain records of acceptable subcontractors and vendors.

In addition, the restaurants will have to

- Have well-defined requirements specifying the type, class, grade of product.

- Verify that purchasing documents are adequate prior to release.[8]

  (*Note:* Some restaurants may verify the purchased goods at the subcontractor/vendor premises. If that is the case, a description of how goods are released/approved should be written.)

A brief tier two procedure would easily address the requirements specified within the purchasing clause. The restaurateur would have to demonstrate that the purchasing process accounts for all of these requests. A list of approved vendors would have to be prepared, and the vendors would have to be assessed. Since the standard does recognize a subcontractor's previously demonstrated capability and performance, vendor audits are not absolutely necessary. However, some records of vendor performance would have to be maintained to back up claims. These records would keep track of whatever would be considered appropriate measures of effectiveness by the restaurateur.

Control of Customer-Supplied Product (4.7)

This paragraph is not applicable to the restaurant industry. The paragraph is intended for cases when a customer provides a supplier with components that are incorporated into the finished product. Since customers are not likely to provide restaurants with their own food or wines, the paragraph is not applicable. The paragraph is applicable to other service industries. For example, a consultant or training agency that has been subcontracted by a client to train its employees may be requested to include some specific material (videos, articles, and so on) provided by the customer and to be inserted within the consultant/agency's course material. In such cases, the ISO 9000 clause could apply.

Product Identification and Traceability (4.8)

This paragraph is pertinent to the restaurant industry, but difficult to implement. Since the theme has already been presented in chapter 1, I will only add that the restaurateur has to carefully analyze (perhaps with the help of his lawyer) how this one clause will be implemented.

There is one difficulty that needs to be studied. Paragraph 4.8 states that "the supplier shall establish and maintain documented procedures for identifying the product by suitable means from receipt and during all stages of production, delivery and installation." Although installation does not apply to the restaurant, can a restaurant really economically identify each fish, T-bone steak, ice cream cone, and so on, during all stages of production (in other words, frying, grilling, scooping) and delivery to the customer? I don't think so. Fortunately, the clause is a *where appropriate* clause, so one could argue that since food circulates rather quickly, one does not need to identify and trace food and beverages beyond some delivery expiration date. The question remains as to how the vendor identifies the batches.

Process Control (4.9)

A restaurant has many processes that would include the following: hosting, order placing, kitchen (many subprocesses), dishwashing, table busing, and other specialized processes. Within the restaurant industry all of these processes directly affect the quality of service. Therefore, it is important for the restaurant owner to ensure that these processes are carried under controlled conditions. As far as the ISO 9000 standard is concerned, controlled conditions mean

• *Documented procedures are in place.* The purpose of these procedures would be to ensure, among other things, that a certain repeatability of service standard is maintained.

• *Use of suitable production, installation, and servicing equipment operating within a suitable working environment.* In a restaurant, the most important instrument would be cooking or refrigerating devices. In most cases these instruments would have to operate under various health and safety regulations. The word *suitable* seems to have replaced the 1987 use of the word *appropriate.* Either way, the state or county agencies are likely to determine what is suitable or appropriate since subclause c refers to "compliance with reference standards/codes, quality plans, and/or documented procedures."

• *Monitoring and control of suitable process parameters and product characteristics.* An example of a control parameter is likely to include temperature. However, I cannot envision a chef or cook carefully monitoring the temperature of a skillet as he or she prepares a Saumon a la Norvegienne. Other process parameters might include time needed to prepare or deliver an order (not likely to be monitored in a haute cuisine restaurant, but likely to be monitored at the All You Can Eat restaurant). Customer surveys also could be used as a form of monitoring the overall satisfaction process.

• *The approval of processes and equipment, as appropriate.* Since this is an *as appropriate* clause, each restaurant would have to decide if and how it would want to implement this clause.

• *Criteria for workmanship, which should be stipulated in the clearest practical manner.* The most favored method that applies to kitchen procedures is to include pictures (often reproduced in the menu). Videos explaining how to perform various activities could be used.

• *Suitable maintenance of equipment to ensure continuing process capability.* This is a new subclause. The purpose is to ensure that preventive maintenance is practiced whenever necessary. The clause, in some respect, duplicates the requirements specified in clause 4.11. One easy and cost-effective way to satisfy this clause is to subcontract maintenance agreements for stoves, refrigerators, freezers, or similar devices, as required.

The clause concludes with a reference to special processes, that is, processes, "the result of which cannot be fully verified by subsequent inspection and testing of the product and where, for example, processing deficiencies may become apparent only after the product is in use." These processes must be identified, qualified, and operated by qualified personnel. The application to the restaurant industry is perhaps limited to the kitchen where meals (special processes) are to be prepared by qualified operators (that is, certified chefs or cooks). One could also classify processes relating to sanitation as special processes. If special qualifications and/or training are required to operate within a particular area, records of said qualification shall be specified and filed somewhere. For certain restaurants, these special processes may include the sauce chef, the main course chef, the dessert chef, and others. For most restaurants, special processes (if such processes are identified) would probably be limited to the preparation of meals).

The process control clause concludes with a reference to clause 4.16, Control of Quality Records. Besides training and/or qualification records required for particular jobs (in other words, bartender), I do not foresee restaurants keeping records of qualified processes or equipment.

Inspection and Testing (4.10)

This paragraph consists of five major subparagraphs (4.10.1 through 4.10.5). The basic requirement is that the supplier (restaurant) shall maintain documented procedures for inspection and testing activities to "verify that the specified requirements for product are met." The inspection activities are broken down into three major activities: receiving, in-process, and final inspection and testing. Naturally, records of all inspections must be kept.

Before examining these clauses it is important to remember that the standards emphasize verification activities based on specified requirements. If these requirements are nonexistent or ill-defined, the verification activities also will be nonexistent or poorly defined. In the restaurant industry, specified requirements are likely to be loosely defined. One could order from suppliers grade AA lean beef, premium ice cream, and fresh vegetables, however, I am not aware of any particular standards that would allow a restaurant owner or the chefs to specify these requirements and inspect them. This is not to say that various forms of incoming inspections (in other words, visual, tactual, olfactory, or taste) are not performed on a daily basis—they are. Within the restaurant industry, however, I am not aware of any inspection and testing procedures besides those that rely on taste, smell, and appearance (experts within the food inspection industry may say otherwise). Nevertheless, since incoming, in-process, and final inspections are performed, the quality assurance system will need to explain how they are performed and by whom.

In a restaurant, incoming (receiving) inspection is likely to be the most important activity because the quality of the final (assembled) product is dependent on the quality of each and every one of the sub-components supplied by a variety of suppliers or subcontracted to others (for example, desserts). Therefore, as an assembler and processor of foods, the restaurant is likely to pay particular attention to the quality of its incoming ingredients.

In-process and final inspections are ongoing activities, however, they are not likely to consist of detailed testing procedures. Moreover, the implementation of some of the clauses is not practical. Under in-process inspection, the standard requires that product is held "until the required inspection and tests have been completed or necessary reports have been received and verified except when product is released under positive recall procedures." The required inspection can only be visual. As for positive recall, the application is of limited value within the restaurant industry since the meal can be returned instantly by the customer.

Similar comments would apply for final inspection. In most cases, the waiter verifies that the prepared meal conforms to the written order. If anything is missing, an immediate corrective action is taken and the meal is delivered to the customer who has the final say. If something is not to the customer's satisfaction, immediate corrective actions are activated. Thus, although the inspection clause applies to the restaurant, simplified procedures are likely to apply.

Similarly, the maintenance of test records would have to be adopted to the restaurant and related industries. A simple procedure could be implemented where the chef or cook simply initials the order as it is delivered to the waiter. I have seen this procedure applied in some restaurants.

Control of Inspection, Measuring and Test Equipment (4.11)

This is one of the longest paragraphs. It should be easy to implement within most sectors of the service industry. This assertion is based on the fact that for most service (tangible and certainly intangible) industries, the reliance on instrumentation to deliver said service is either not crucial to the business or not required. This is partially because in many cases requests for measurements are not very precise. Most customer requests are measured either on a nominal (yes-no, hot vs. cold) scale or an ordinal scale (such as, rare, medium, well-done; hot, warm, cold). By their definition, these scales do not allow for sophisticated measures of accuracy and precision.

The paragraph requires that the supplier "maintains documented procedures to control, calibrate and maintain inspection, measuring and test equipment (including test software) used by the supplier to demonstrate the *conformance of product to the specified requirements*" (author's emphasis). The clause identifies several subclauses (a–i) designed to ensure that the supplier performs a host of tasks which include: determining the accuracy and precision required, determining the calibration frequency, maintaining calibration records, and a few other requirements that may not be needed for most service industries. I have emphasized "conformance of product to specified requirements" to illustrate the need to demonstrate conformance may not be a specified customer or regulatory agency requirement.

Since customers are not likely to order their steaks to be cooked at 375°F or want their ice cream to be served at 38°F, the paragraph does not have the same significance as it has for the manufacturing world. Even if an odd customer (perhaps a retired auditor with too many years of experience) were to request specific cooking temperatures, one wonders how the customer would verify his or her request. (*Note:* One must recognize that one customer [state agencies], may have specific requirements for cooking time and minimum temperature.)

There are some applications. In a restaurant, some equipment or measuring instruments might need to be under control of inspection. It would be a good idea to have thermometers calibrated at least once a year to ensure that meat is cooked/heated at the correct temperature for a set period of time. Similarly, refrigerated food must be kept at a certain temperature. The requirement for instrument precision and traceability to national standards is not applicable in this particular case study. Nevertheless, if calibration services are subcontracted, traceability to national standards usually are provided.

Inspection and Test Status (4.12)

This paragraph has some relevance to the restaurant or food processing industry although it would have to be adapted to the various needs. The paragraph requires that "the inspection and test status of product shall be identified by suitable means, which indicate the conformance or non-conformance of product with regard to inspection and test performed." The clause is meant to apply throughout all stages of production, installation, and servicing and is designed to ensure that only product that has passed the required inspection or test is released. There could be some applications for the clause during incoming inspection, where product could be tagged to indicate delivery date (see Storage requirements on page 101). However, product that is nonconforming (visually or otherwise) is likely to be returned immediately.

The clause is not likely to be applied during production because the time lag between production and installation (in other words, consumption) is short: a few minutes at the most. Moreover, the tagging of food as it is being prepared is not likely to be practical or of interest to the customer. Therefore, for the most part, only a small portion of this paragraph could apply to the restaurant industry.

Control of Nonconforming Product Review and Disposition (4.13)

These two clauses (4.13.1 and 4.13.2) translate well to the service sector. However, once again some thoughtful adjustments will be required. The paragraph requires that documented procedures be maintained to "ensure that product that does not conform to specified requirements is prevented from unintended use or installation." Nonconforming product must be identified, segregated (if practical), and disposed by someone who has the authority to decide whether the product should be

- Reworked to meet specific requirements
- Accepted with or without repair by concession
- Regraded for alternative applications
- Rejected or scrapped

When required by contract, concessions must be approved by the customer. Finally, records of corrective action shall be maintained including reinspection in accordance with the quality plan and/or documented procedures. How could these requirements be applied to the restaurant industry?

Nonconforming products are part of the food processing industry. In fact most of the activities just listed are practiced every day in countless restaurants throughout the nation. (A meal is not cooked to the right specifications, the wrong vegetables have been substituted, the bacon is not extra crisp, and so on.) In all cases, the nonconformity is resolved on the spot and the corrective action is implemented within minutes. The responsibility for reviewing the nonconformity with the customer and the authority to implement the proper disposition usually is placed with the server.

In some cases, the nonconformity might be more serious and the meal might have to be rejected and scrapped. Perhaps the meal is so salty that you cannot eat it, or the salsa is so hot that your ulcer will not let you have another bite, or your taste buds are simply offended by your (unfortunate) selection (for example, escargots served in warm yogurt). Even in these cases, management usually is understanding and will allow you to order another meal or simply cancel your order.

The implementation of paragraphs 4.13.1 and 4.13.2 (Control of Nonconforming Product Review and Disposition) should not be too difficult. The quality system should describe in a brief statement (a documented procedure) how the examples of nonconformity are addressed. Naturally, there is no need to outline each and every type of nonconformity. It would be much more practical to identify two or three categories of nonconformity and define who has authority to resolve said nonconformity.

Corrective and Preventive Action (4.14)

These two paragraphs are a logical extension of paragraph 4.13 (Control of Nonconforming Product). The intent of the paragraphs is to encourage the supplier to implement corrective actions procedures that would prevent recurrence of nonconformities. This means that whenever nonconformities occur, they should be investigated to determine what was/were the root cause(s) and corrective actions should not only be implemented, but also tested for their effectiveness. These corrective actions may require changes in processes that may necessitate developing new or modified training procedures. As in most cases, records of all investigations and changes must be maintained.

The corrective and preventive action paragraphs should find a ready application within the service sector. In the case of a restaurant, the corrective actions are likely to be unique and specific to each particular order. In most cases, corrective actions probably are generated when a customer orders a specific set of deviations from the menu. In most cases, the deviations are duly recorded on the contract/order form by the server (who might even rephrase the order to ensure accuracy). Therefore, if there are nonconformities, they are likely to originate from the kitchen which might not have been able to decipher the server's handwriting and simply assumed that the order was standard. Irrespective of the cause or nature of the nonconformity, a procedure should be initiated to formulate how nonconformities should be analyzed and resolved to prevent recurrence.

One way to quantify nonconformities would be to come up with a set of half a dozen typical nonconformities and prioritize them at the end of each week (or any frequency of your choice) in the form of a Pareto diagram. The purpose of Pareto diagrams would be to focus on the first two or three most important nonconformities (where importance is measured in terms of customer inconvenience) and formulate a strategy on how to remove or reduce these nonconformities. Brief brainstorming sessions with members of the kitchen staff probably will be required to achieve the best solution.

The documented procedure required to satisfy the intent of the *Corrective and Preventive Action* paragraphs need not go into the details of how corrective and preventive actions are handled. That is, the procedure need not explain how the Pareto diagram is prepared and analyzed. However, it could state that Pareto diagrams are prepared and analyzed via brainstorming sessions.

Handling, Storage, Packaging, Preservation and Delivery (4.15)

The opening sentence sets the tone: "The supplier shall establish and maintain documented procedures for handling, storage, packaging, preservation and delivery of product." For the restaurant industry, the very nature of most of its processes is to handle food and meals. Having observed how various foods are handled in restaurants, I am not aware of special procedures except for those relating to hygiene. Some fast-food restaurants that specialize in serving delicatessen sandwiches require that their sandwich makers wear plastic gloves. Such practices would look rather peculiar for some restaurants.

Storage requirements designed to prevent damage or deterioration of product (pending use or delivery) are appropriate to the restaurant and other service industries. Of particular significance to a restaurant owner is the following sentence, which requires that "In order to detect deterioration, the condition of product in stock shall be assessed at appropriate intervals." Restaurants and their customers could benefit from this clause. Most of us have had the unfortunate experience of ordering a meal which, once delivered, tasted past its expiration date. The clause also specifies that "appropriate methods for authorizing receipt to and dispatch from such areas shall be stipulated."

The packaging clause is not likely to be of major significance to restaurants except for restaurants such as pizzerias whose specialty is to deliver food. Indeed, the clause specifies that "The supplier shall control packaging and marking processes (including materials used) to the extent necessary to ensure conformance to specified requirements." In the case of the pizzeria, the specified requirements would have to be set by the pizzeria and would have to set some heat retention parameters to guarantee delivery of a hot pizza. In such cases, the specifications are not explicitly set by the customer but are implicit and must be met by the pizzeria in order to satisfy customers.

The preservation clause suggests that the supplier implements "appropriate methods for preservation and segregation of product. . . ." Each restaurant would have to decide how the clause needs to be implemented. In the case of a delivered product (in other words, meal), most restaurants deliver the product within minutes of its preparation. Restaurants ensure that the meal is served hot by either temporarily placing the food under hot lights or by having the first available waiter serve the food (or a combination of both).

The clause does not only apply to finished product but also could be applied to ingredients that eventually find their way in a meal (for example, mustard, mayonnaise, creams, sauces). These ingredients would also have to be appropriately preserved.

The last subclause, entitled Delivery, probably would only apply to restaurants such as pizzerias that specialize in home delivery. These "restaurants" would have to "arrange for the protection of the quality of product after final inspection and test." Since destructive tests (in other words, sample consumption) are not likely to apply, one is left with a final, probably visual inspection and verification of the order. For the restaurant industry, satisfying the Packaging clause will simultaneously satisfy the delivery clause. Naturally, for all other restaurants where the food is consumed (tested) on site, the delivery clause is a minor issue since it is delivered just in time for consumption.

Control of Quality Records (4.16)

The need to keep quality records is invoked by most clauses. The purpose of the quality record paragraph is twofold: to demonstrate conformance (product and service) to specified requirements and document the effective operation of the quality system. Once records are kept, they must be legible, kept for a predetermined period of time (to be decided by the supplier), and stored in such a fashion as to minimize deterioration.

The application of paragraph 4.16 (Control of Quality Records) to the restaurant should not be too complicated since few requirements are specified. Customer requirements are entered by the waiter on either a pad (order book) or, in some high-tech restaurants, on a computer terminal. (I have even seen the use of portable, hand-held terminals, which allow for the order to be placed instantaneously with the kitchen.) Restaurants relying on personal computers for their record entries usually make use of software that manages all record keeping and inventory tasks. Restaurants that depend on the old-fashioned notepad perform similar tasks either by hand or they rely on cash register records. Other records would consist of purchasing records, supplier evaluation records/surveys, and receiving inspection records (such records are retained). Retention time is up to the restaurant owner: one day, one week, one month, or longer.

Internal Quality Audits (4.17)

After the quality assurance system is implemented, it must be monitored for suitability and effectiveness. One of the best procedures to adopt is to conduct periodic internal audits. These audits must be planned and conducted by trained persons. Moreover, they must be carried out by personnel independent of those having direct responsibility for the activity being audited. Finally, results of the audits shall be recorded and corrective actions shall be brought to the attention of the appropriate management authority to ensure proper implementation. It is important to remember that the internal audit activities cover all aspects of the quality assurance system as defined by the standard. For example, in the case of a restaurant, the audit will not only limit itself to the kitchen area, but also to all other functions/processes: hosting, busing, cleaning, order taking, inspection, purchasing, and training.

Training (4.18)

The training needs of all persons whose jobs affect quality (in other words, not only quality of the food but also of the overall operation of the restaurant) must be identified within a documented procedure. The standard does not specify what is meant by "the training of all personnel performing activities affecting quality." In the case of a restaurant, quality is likely to mean more than just quality of the food, it would also include quality of all other processes already mentioned.

The training paragraph does recognize a variety of training qualifications: appropriate education (perhaps for managers), training and/or experience (waiters, kitchen help, and so on). Naturally, the requirements would vary from restaurant to restaurant. Some restaurants apparently consider it quite acceptable to have their staff refer to their customers as "you guys," or "Honey or hon." Others would find such an etiquette unacceptable.

The clause concludes by stating that "appropriate records of training shall be maintained." I have never understood the reference to appropriate records. I do not know what an inappropriate record is. At any rate, some form of records should be maintained to identify who has received what type of training. In an industry where part-time help comes and goes with high frequency, management might question the necessity of training the staff only to have them leave within a few months. Nevertheless, as was explained earlier, training, no matter how brief, is likely to be a worthwhile investment that should guarantee satisfied, loyal customers.

Servicing (4.19)

This can be a confusing clause particularly when interpreted within the context of the service industry. The clause is limited to those cases when servicing of a product is called for as part of a contractual agreement. I cannot think of any applications within the restaurant industry where servicing would come into play. (See chapter 6 for examples of where the clause could apply.) Certainly, many industries within the service sector are in the business of servicing a variety of activities (servicing your lawn, your car, your appliances, and so on). However, in such cases, the service industry in question has an entire set of procedures that would require certification to ISO 9002 or perhaps ISO 9003.

Statistical Techniques (4.20)

The 1987 version of this paragraph was less prescriptive because it allowed the supplier, or its customers, to determine whether or not the use of adequate statistical techniques was appropriate. The updated version now requires the supplier, to "identify the need for statistical techniques required for establishing, controlling and verifying process capability and product characteristics." Once the need has been established, the supplier shall then "establish and maintain documented procedures to implement and control the application of the statistical techniques identified."

It is well known that most restaurants rely on a multitude of basic statistics to measure various efficiencies. For example, the serving of liquor is often closely monitored to determine if correct portions are used. Some restaurants/bars can even identify which bartender tends to have a generous hand. Still, the use of such descriptive statistics are not imposed by the customer and are therefore not part of a contract review between the restaurant owner and customers. Nevertheless, the use of statistical techniques can be of value to a restaurant manager. The application of statistical process control to determine process capability could be beneficial to restaurants that have implemented various forms of the "lunch served within 15 minutes, or it's on us" program. However, in such cases, the service characteristic (namely, quick lunches) is not necessarily imposed by the customer (although it is certainly appreciated if the meal is not literally thrown together, as is sometimes the case).

This is not to say that paragraph 4.20 is of little value to the service industry. Indeed, various sectors of the service industry (particularly marketing and related agencies) long ago discovered the virtues of statistical techniques such as analysis of variance, factor analysis, and regression analysis. Each industry will have to identify its needs. If process capability (in the statistical sense) is of little concern to you, or if your customers are satisfied with your current capability (in other words, serving meals within 15 to 20 minutes), you probably should not be too concerned with paragraph 4.20.

Conclusion

The purpose of this chapter has been to expose the reader to the requirements of the ISO 9001 standard. This was achieved by illustrating how the ISO 9002 model could be applied to a restaurant. As was demonstrated, the ISO 9002 model is well-suited for direct application to restaurants as most of the paragraphs find an easy and logical application. The point also was made that in some cases a few of the paragraphs needed to be interpreted slightly differently or treated as nonapplicable, depending on the order (high vs. low) of the service being provided. Thus, although it is true that every restaurant wishing to achieve ISO 9002 registration will have to have a quality policy, a receiving procedure, conduct internal audits, and so on, not all restaurants will develop the same policies and procedures. By extension, although the standard can easily be applied to the restaurant industry, it remains to be seen if the standard transfers equally well to other service industries. Chapters 5 and 6 will analyze that issue.

Notes

1. A close parallel can be found in the manufacturing world. In the highly competitive world of high technology, managed by thousands of entrepreneurs in charge of their small enterprises, the fear of design control is very real. Some of these industrialists prefer to avoid having to register their plant to ISO 9001 simply because they want their processes to remain secret. In fact, that is the reason why they keep documentation to a minimum; just in case a employee should transfer to a competitor.

2. Because of the great variety of palates, it would be difficult to take into account the multitude of customer specifications. The chef must design a meal with broad enough specifications.

3. ISO 8402, *Quality Management and Quality Assurance—Vocabulary* (Geneva, Switzerland: ISO, 1994), 14.

4. Paraphrase of ANSI/ASQC Q9001, 1994, paragraph 4.1.2.1.

5. A common practice is to include in the quality manual a high-level organization chart that defines global responsibilities. Such organization charts generally are not sufficient because they do not always address the specific requirements already mentioned and set forth in clause 4.1.2.1, Responsibility and Authority.

6. ANSI/ASQC Q9001, 1994, paragraph 4.2.3.

7. Many restaurants have automated the order process to the point of having the waiter/waitress actually enter the customer's order by using a hand-held terminal (about the size of a large pocket calculator). The order is automatically forwarded to the kitchen where a software package takes over the inventory process.

8. The purchasing paragraph contains Supplier Verification at Subcontractors and Customer Verification of Subcontracted Product subclauses. These clauses are not likely to apply in the restaurant and most service industries. The clauses, influenced by their military origins, address the case when a supplier or his or her customer would wish to inspect the supplier's subcontractor's premises. It is highly unlikely that a customer would want to inspect the restaurant's vendors facilities prior to ordering a meal or a drink. The customer simply assumes that all is in order. A restaurant may wish to conduct inspections of the subcontractors; however, most restaurants rely on federal or state agencies.

5 ISO 9000 in Hospitals, Banks, and Other Services

The first question that comes to mind when considering ISO 9000 registration for hospitals, banks, or similar institutions is "Why?" Is registration absolutely necessary, and, if so, what would be the benefits. To say that achieving ISO 9000 registration might be good for a hospital or a bank is not convincing enough because one still has to prove the assertion. That is difficult to do without first having the hospital or bank go through the registration process.

I cannot think of any compelling argument in favor of ISO 9000 registration for those service industries except to propose that (1) it might well be easier than anticipated because (2) the current quality assurance system might already approximate one of the ISO 9000 models, and (3) as explained in the Preface and previous chapters, the models (ISO 9001, ISO 9002) are slowly but surely being adopted by hospitals and other service institutions in Europe, the United States, and other parts of the world.[1] If these arguments are still not convincing, the reader might want to wait until a major customer requests ISO 9000 certification (which is precisely what happened to one service firm that never thought it would have to deal with the ISO 9000 series).

Although it is unlikely that patients will ask hospitals to achieve ISO 9000 registration, their insurance companies may think otherwise.

Indeed, as more companies achieve ISO 9000 registration, insurance companies may learn of the benefits in requesting hospitals to look into the ISO 9000 registration process.

ISO 9002 and Hospitals

The standard can find a niche within hospitals; whether it would be accepted is another question.[2] As an increasing number of hospitals continue to adopt various forms of TQM, they will find that most of the requirements imposed by the standard should already be practiced.[3] In France, registrars have decided that it would be wise not to attempt registering the medical functions of a hospital. Rather, the focus has been on all administrative and convalescence aspects of a hospital. The decision to leave the medical profession out of the scope of registration probably is based on the difficulty of having individuals outside the medical profession propose to the medical staff a quality assurance system derived from manufacturing application. Similar resistance has been experienced in the United States by TQM practitioners. The usual argument proposed by doctors is that they already practice the highest level of quality assurance when dealing with a patient's life. Therefore, what could they possibly improve on? (See chapter 3.)

Many of the quality assurance issues raised by the ISO 9000 series certainly are not new to the medical profession. For example, the practice of quality surveillance in the health care delivery systems has been applied for several decades. The extensive use of medical records and medical audits, including audit of nurses, also dates back to at least the 1960s.[4]

To find out how hospitals implement their quality assurance system, I interviewed the quality manager of one of the major hospitals in Seattle. I realize that a sampling of one hospital is statistically inadequate, but since the hospital in question is recognized by many as a model of good practices, I feel reassured by the validity of the statements made. The questions were designed to find out how a hospital would address ISO 9002 requirements. In essence, the interview was conducted much as a preassessment audit, except that verification was not undertaken.

Although one could consider the 9001 model for research institutions—usually hospital attached to universities—I do not have the competence to comment on the application of the standards to such institutions. Unlike third-party audits, none of the facts stated during the interview were verified. The interview was granted by a hospital administrator in charge of quality and was conducted in her office. As you read the administrator's answers, try to determine which ISO 9002 paragraph would apply to the answer.

Lamprecht: "What could you tell me about your quality policy?"

Administrator: "We don't really have a quality policy, but rather a plan which is written in our quality manual. Our quality assurance system is audited and accredited by the Joint Commission on Accreditation of Healthcare Organization (JCAHO). This is a voluntary system. Accreditation is good for three years. The laboratory is also accredited by the College of American Pathologists."

Lamprecht: "How are laboratories accredited?"

Administrator: "This too is a voluntary system. Audit teams consist of volunteers from within the region. The process starts with a self-audit. An inspection team follows. Lab equipment is audited on paper trails as well as procedures. All equipment is checked, even centrifuges. Some equipment is covered by manufacturer maintenance contracts, others are done internally. The certificate is good for two years." (*Note:* My interlocutor often mentioned the Biomed laboratory without ever mentioning radiology, MRI, chromatography, and so on. I would suspect, but cannot confirm at this stage, that these departments are also accredited and certified.)

"JCAHO does mostly a paper work inspection." (*Note:* ISO audits are more than paper trail audits.) They can also inspect instruments, but they mostly check records. We also are subject to Medicare yearly audits. Although we do have hazardous chemicals, we are rarely audited by OSHA or the EPA. In recent years, the focus of JCAHO has been toward *preventive action* and customer contract. We are in fact mandated, by JCAHO, to have a *quality improvement* system.

Lamprecht: "What is the average length of stay of patients?"

Administrator: "The average length of stay is 4.2 days. For open heart patient it's 6–7 days. This (reduction in hospital stay) is being pushed by the insurance companies. We also have lots of expensive equipment (millions of dollars). Young doctors are more likely to want to use the latest technology because that is what they have been trained to do. Older doctors are less likely to use the fancy (expensive) equipment."

Lamprecht: "What service does the hospital provide?"

Administrator: "The hospital essentially provides a nursing function. It also provides care, food, equipment, and doctor expertise. Doctors, who must be approved by our board, bring the patients. Nurses keep the doctors in check if they try to perform functions for which they are not qualified."

Lamprecht: "How do you address contract review?"

Administrator: "We have three clients: physicians, patients, and the insurance companies. Insurance companies are not the immediate patient but they are the most demanding. They, in fact, impose requirements without always understanding (or seeing) the big picture. The body is a holistic organism and insurances tend to look at it as being made up of separate entities."

Lamprecht: "What about risk management?"

Administrator: "This is certainly important for us."

Lamprecht: "How do you control your documents?"

Administrator: "Document control is decentralized by department. Obsolete documents are promptly removed from the point of issue." *(An auditor would certainly check that statement.)*

Lamprecht: "What about storage requirements?"

Administrator: "We have professional standards for the shelf life of many products, including instruments."

Lamprecht: "And what about quality records?"

Administrator: "Patient records are kept indefinitely (archived). Lab records are kept for two years and some records are microfiched for longer."

Lamprecht: "How do you evaluate your suppliers?"

Administrator: "It depends on the product. We do have specs for product and require certificate of analyses from some of our suppliers. Some products are tested by our lab. Other (cotton balls) are accepted as is. Pharmacy also has many standards. We also subcontract some of our instrument work and require proof of certification. Various media are certified and/or inspected by Biomed."

Lamprecht: "What about in-process and final inspection?"

Administrator: "We have many procedures such as standards of performance and core competency. We seem to have procedures for everything. We, in fact, have many internal customers/suppliers teams who interact with each other as the patient moves from being an in-patient to an outpatient. The teams consist of specialized individuals. There are crossfunctional groups of specialists" *(For example, lab tech, dietician, radiologist, health keeping, engineer, transporter, social worker, physician, nurses).*

Lamprecht: "How do you ensure that your staff has adequate training?"

Administrator: "We do keep records on all staff personnel for all training sessions. We also have an in-house education department responsible for most of our technical training needs."[5]

Lamprecht: "How do you address nonconformity and corrective actions?"

Administrator: "We conduct periodic meetings during which we address all corrective actions. Minutes of these meetings are kept for our records."

Lamprecht: "Do you conduct internal audits?"

Administrator: "Each department conducts its own internal audits." *(It appeared as though little, if any, corrective actions were implemented. Internal audits were not conducted in the spirit of ISO requirements.)*

J. L.: "Do you use statistical techniques?"

Administrator: "Yes, we do a lot of SPC. Biomed, radiology, and respiratory care, all use a variety of statistical techniques. Recently we have begun to look at measuring administrative functions (nursing functions), customer surveys, and so on. We also do trend analysis. We trend complaints and send result of surveys to managers and the nursing congress." *(This is very good, however, I could not determine how corrective actions were implemented.)*

Lamprecht: "In what areas do you need to improve?"

Administrator: "We need to dialog with the customer. This is difficult because in most cases, our direct customers don't pay the bills, insurances do."

These comments reveal several interesting facts that would indicate that with some adjustments, the hospital eventually could pass an ISO 9002 audit. Such a statement probably would surprise the hospital administrator who seemed to believe that passing an ISO 9002 audit would be a mere formality. Such an attitude is not uncommon among individuals who know little about the ISO 9000 series and the audit process. The self-assurance of some individuals, commendable as it is, is sometimes based on false assumptions or premises. This casual or over-confident attitude is partly due to the fact that the ISO 9002 audit process is mistakenly viewed as a mere routine paper trail audit. Also, the assumption is that since the organization already is accredited, ISO 9002 registration can only reconfirm what already has been established.

Unfortunately, that is not always the case. Third-party audits go beyond a desk audit in that their main purpose is to (1) verify that all aspects/requirements of the standard have been addressed, and (2) the system is *applied* and practiced on a daily basis, not just during the announced audit. In other words, the quality assurance system must be understood by all and implemented at all levels within the organization.

Reviewing the administrator's answers one can establish (but would need to verify) that the hospital has

- A quality assurance system that is audited and accredited for a period of three years (similar to ISO 9000 registration)
- A quality manual
- Laboratory equipment that is audited (desk audit)
- Several types of customers, thus several contracts
- A preventive action and quality improvement program
- A decentralized document control process
- Professional standards regarding storage requirements and shelf life of products and instruments
- A supplier evaluation program
- Documented procedures (core competency and standards of performance)
- Training programs

- Corrective action meetings

- Internal audits by department

- Statistical process control for various processes

Although these points cover many of the ISO 9002 paragraphs, the interview did reveal that some corrective actions would have to be undertaken by the hospital if it wanted to achieve ISO 9002 registration. Some areas of apparent concern would include[6]

- In-process inspection: Procedures may well exist but need to be verified for compliance, particularly for special processes, which are very relevant within the medical field.

- Instrument control: Appears to be adequate but an auditor would like to verify the system's effectiveness.

- Internal audit procedures appear to be informal and not documented.

- A clear definition of responsibility and authority needs to be stated.

- Contract review (not addressed at all).

- Document control (low concern since it seems to be performed, but this would have to be verified).

- Purchasing procedures (not really explored during the interview).

- Corrective and preventive actions. These actions seem to be in place, however, their effectiveness would have to be tested. Documented procedures for corrective actions seem to be missing.

- Medication traceability: Hopefully under control but would need to be verified.

These are only a small sample of questions and issues that will have to be investigated by the auditors. Now let us turn our attention to a different sector of the service industry—banking.

ISO 9002 in Banking

Banks could benefit from ISO 9002 registration. In order to find out how well the standard could apply within the banking industry, I interviewed the vice president in charge of quality at one of Seattle's leading banks. The fact that this bank had a vice president of quality already was impressive. As the reader must have surmised from earlier comments in chapter 1, my bank does not have a vice president of quality. It has, however, many posters advertising a host of commitments to quality.

The interview format was similar to the hospital interview. My purpose was to determine whether or not a bank could implement an ISO 9002 quality assurance model (ISO 9001 is unlikely and ISO 9003 is not likely to satisfy all of the activities performed by a bank).

Lamprecht: "When did you first implement your TQM program and how did you go about it?"

V. P.: "Our bank has had a quality program since 1989. Most of our implementation was done in-house and without the help of external consultants. We used the services of our marketing department to assess and implement changes. We first defined our external customers and began surveying them. We found out that our lobby hours needed to be extended to accommodate our customers. Our customers also told us that the amount of time spent at a teller line was too long. Based on this information, we began implementing our '5 minutes or $5' policy. If customers feel they have waited more than five minutes we pay them five dollars (we have clocks at each station). Although automated service is also available (for transfer of funds, payments, balance, and so on, we also offer a 24-hour service with a live person. This is rather expensive, but it is much appreciated by our customers."

Lamprecht: "What training program do you have in place for your staff?"

V. P.: "We have a college where our staff can, on a voluntary basis, obtain training. The college provides a curriculum of two days of training plus eight days on-the-job training for our staff that is mostly part-timers. The training emphasizes face-to-face interaction, phone etiquette with our external and internal customers."

Lamprecht: "How do you control/monitor your processes?"

V. P.: "We have set up some standards known as service level contracts. These contracts identify what each department, as an internal supplier, promises to its internal customer. For example, the statement department has a contract with the retail department. We have 50 of those contracts. We also collect and analyze statistics. The results are reported during our weekly meeting and in our newsletter.

"We also monitor some of our key processes. For example, we have leading service indicators which monitor

1. Cash machine up time

2. Turnaround time on cash card (specifications are set for a one week turnaround)

3. Check order turnaround time

4. Standardized method of measuring time in line; some departments were measuring it differently, so we had to standardize the methods

"Many of our service indicators are driven by our *customer focus groups*. I believe very much in these groups which are led by an outside facilitator."

Lamprecht: "How do you improve your services?"

V. P.: "Besides our regular surveys we also listen to our customers when they object to some of our policies. For example, we have learned to deal with voice mail. Voice mail cannot be used during business hours. We believe the sound of a live voice is important to our customers. We also adhere to our motto which states that: 'We make banking easy for you.' In order to honor that motto we offer banking at various department stores and we also have cash card machines at the checkout counter of these stores."

Lamprecht: "How do you ensure that your system is effective, efficient, and practiced?"

V. P.: "I frequently go out on visits to the various branches to collect data and talk with the staff. On one such visit we discovered that one of our screen menus was too difficult to interpret for some of our customers. So we had our MIS staff redesign the menu. We also have begun forming interdepartmental work teams—which is difficult when you have part-timers—these teams use the basic problem-solving tools to solve their problems."

Lamprecht: "How do you assess your subcontractors?"

V. P.: "We do have detailed contracts with outside vendors. We also verify samples of our checks and test the microcoding during incoming inspection. We have significantly reduced our supplier base."

Lamprecht: "Do you perform any servicing activities?"

V. P.: "Yes, we service our cash machine (in-house)."[7]

Lamprecht: "What about document control? How do you ensure that the latest version of your procedures and manuals are available at various points of issue?"

V. P.: "For document control we have our *Management Staff Guide.* For special or rarely used procedures we rely on our hot line to handle these unique, once-in-a-while questions. The task of the hot line staff is to know who is best suited to answer specific questions."

Lamprecht: "Do you conduct internal audits?"

V. P.: "We do not conduct audits besides my periodic branch visits. We are, however, audited once a year by the feds and by the state for lending policy, compliance with various federal requirements, serving minorities, management issues, real estate portfolio, regulation E for ATMs, and so on. The Office of the Comptroller also audits us."

It appears that this bank would have little difficulty implementing an ISO 9002 quality assurance program. As was the case with the hospital, many of the requirements postulated by the standard are already in place, or nearly so. Reviewing the answers, it is evident that the bank monitors certain key processes (4.9), controls documents (4.4), services its ATMs (4.19), trains its staff (4.18), conducts corrective actions (4.14), performs receiving inspection (for checks) (4.10.1), and evaluates it suppliers (4.6.2). Naturally, many more questions relating to other parts of the standard would have to be asked and, as always, the effectiveness of the system would have to be tested. Nevertheless, I was so favorably impressed that I even considered switching banks.

ISO 9001 in Engineering Design

The ISO 9001 model is increasingly being considered and, in some cases, adopted by some engineering consulting firms. These firms either design or redesign complex industrial plants such as chemical plants, foundries, or paper mills, to name but a few (see also Design in the Service Industry in chapter 6). The end product consists of a multitude of piping and instrumentation drawings (P&IDs), prepared on CAD workstations (which naturally does not guarantee accuracy). These P&IDs are then delivered to the primary contractor for implementation. In an increasing number of cases, known as turnkey operation, the contractor and the engineering consulting firm work as one team.

When the ISO 9001 model is applied to the engineering consulting firm, few paragraphs do not apply. One could argue that the receiving inspection paragraph does not apply simply because "we don't inspect everyday office items," however, there are instances where the paragraph could apply. For example, it is not unusual for firms to subcontract small jobs to other consultants. In these cases, one can find a direct application for the evaluation of subcontractor and the receiving inspection paragraphs.

Software is another important area that will need to be considered. Consulting firms rely heavily on purchased software as well as software developed in-house. Since the software is likely to be used in activities that directly affect the quality of the final product, one would like to know if and how the software is tested for functionality and other characteristics. The standard does not require the purchaser of software to perform a lengthy and costly evaluation and reliability analysis of all purchased packages. The standard (paragraph 4.11) only refers to test software "used as suitable forms of inspection." This could include software used for various computations or modeling. The standard practice is to assume, until proven otherwise, that the software is delivered with no catastrophic bugs.[8] Nonetheless, for software developed in-house, one would still like to know if and how the program was tested for functionality and reliability. In other words, what are the procedures for testing and verifying software.

Servicing is another paragraph that might be considered not applicable, yet most engineering firms do provide technical assistance after they release a design. The contractor who inherits the design may have a host of questions for the engineering firm. He or she may need some clarification on one section of the design. He or she want to know if a different valve or slightly smaller pipes can be substituted. In all of these cases, and countless others, the engineering firm essentially is asked to service its design.

With the possible exception of Supplier Verification at Subcontractor (4.6.4.1), Customer Verification of Subcontractor Product (4.6.4.2) and Statistical Techniques (4.20), most of the remaining ISO 9001 paragraphs would apply to the engineering consulting firm.[9]

ISO 9002 and Distributors

The following example, adapted from a distributor of software products, could apply to any other distributor.

A software distributor has one objective: to deliver software to customers. This task appears simple were it not for the following additional constraints.

- The software must be competitively priced.

- The software must be delivered within 24 to 48 hours.

- Accuracy in delivery (in other words, type and quantity) must be 100 percent.

- A broad variety of software must be made available (flexibility).

- The distributor must be able to satisfy major accounts as well as individual orders.

In order to satisfy these requirements, distributors usually operate from one or more distribution centers that operate on two or three shifts. Customer orders are taken by a sales force located at remote sites. Prior to approving the order, the salesperson must first verify whether or not the item is available. If available, a sales order entry is initiated and the order is transmitted to the nearest distribution center and processed within a few hours. The processing of an order might take two forms, depending on the size of the order. In most cases, an order picker is assigned to the order and processes the order by picking the necessary items from various bins. For large orders, a team of pickers may be assigned to sections of the order. As each phase of the order is completed, it is sent down the line for the next team. Eventually the order arrives at quality control, which verifies every order for accuracy and initiates corrective actions, as required. After the order has passed quality assurance, it is sent to packaging and shipping where the order is checked for any special delivery instructions.

An important process for most distributors is the return process. Returns are not necessarily limited to bad or defective products. Customers may return product simply because they don't like it or it is not what they supposedly wanted. Whatever the cause, returns are inspected, the cause of the nonconformance noted, and if the product is not damaged, it is restocked for future use.

These processes follow all the paragraphs of ISO 9002. Indeed, although not specified in the description, traceability of an order is an important requirement. Training, and some times a picker certification program, is in place. Servicing also is provided since some software distributors provide technical assistance on a variety of software for their customers.[10] Incoming inspection from the hundreds of suppliers, as well as for returns, is very important. The nature of the incoming inspection usually consists of a quantity count and condition of the container or package. It should be mentioned that such incoming inspections are not always performed by all distributors. For example, distributors of valve, pipes, or related hardware do not usually inspect goods delivered to them by their suppliers. This can occasionally lead to a difficult situation when a distributor ships to customers products that were inadvertently packaged (at the source) in error. A simple receiving inspection program might alleviate the problem.

The only paragraph that does not seem to apply to the software distributor (but could apply to others) would be Control of Inspection, Measuring, and Test Equipment. However, in the case where a warehouse relies on a computerized bar code system to control the access and removal of product, it might be a good idea to verify the software during the early stages of testing. The reader should review each of the ISO 9002 paragraphs and verify that the application is logical.

ISO 9002 and Packaging

The application of the ISO 9002 standard to the packaging industry should provide few difficulties. It is not unusual to have suppliers rely on subcontractors to handle, store, package, preserve, and deliver a product to their customers. A courier service or shipper would be subcontracted by the software distributor firm to deliver packages. In some cases, the courier also is asked to store and preserve the product to be delivered at a later date. One subcontractor I worked with basically handles one product that is delivered to several customers. The subcontractor is responsible for all of the activities of paragraph 4.15. In addition he must ensure that the right amount is delivered to the client. In this particular case, storage is a major activity since the subcontractor has essentially become a (hidden) warehouse for the supplier who claims that he does not produce nonconforming products, but regraded products.

In both of these cases, even though the handling, storage, packaging, preservation, and delivery activities are the very essence of the subcontractor activities, a host of other (ISO 9002-related) processes are in place to ensure that all activities are performed correctly.

Other examples include the software industry, which relies on many peripheral services to duplicate and package millions of diskettes that are eventually shipped to warehouses throughout the nation (see Appendix B). In recent months, the disk duplication industry within the Seattle area has adopted the ISO 9002 series as the most practical model.

ISO 9000 and the Hotel Industry

This last application of the ISO 9000 series to the service industry is logical. Having spent too many days in hotels throughout the country, I have had ample opportunity to test whether or not hotels could benefit from ISO 9000 registration. There are a wide range of hotels and, as any professional traveler knows, the quality of service and comfort is not always directly related to the price. As a customer, I have found that many hotels seem to be designed by architects who apparently have either never had to sleep in the hotels they design or are very sound sleepers. Indeed, my main complaint about hotels is that often they are not designed for maximum quiet. Certainly, design engineers have done an excellent job blocking out external noise, partly by relying on the white noise generated by the air conditioning unit. But what about internal noises? What about the neighbor who comes in at 2:00 A.M. and slams the door, or the noisy conversations down the hall at 1:30 A.M? Could a better door closing design or insulation be installed? Probably, but at what cost? Since these personal objections would have to be addressed by the architectural firm, I see no need to belabor the point.

Before applying the standard, one would first need to define the scope of the audit. This is likely to be influenced by the type of hotel. Since a four-star hotel is likely to provide more services than a one-star hotel, the quality assurance system of each will be different. Also, as with any organization, a hotel consists of numerous interrelated operating systems. Some of these systems may require their own quality assurance system. For example, one could separate the restaurant functions from the rest of the hotel and request two registrations (I would not necessarily recommend this approach). For most hotels (and many inns or motels), there are at least half a dozen major quality assurance subsystems (in other words, services within a service): Check-in/out, room service (food), housekeeping, maintenance (for example, plumbing, electrical), bellperson, restaurant, conferences, general information, as well as a host of ancillary services. The implementation of a quality assurance system that would conform to each and every one of the paragraphs will require some coordinating efforts to avoid duplication. In some cases, a paragraph may apply to several of the subsystems (for example, training) while in other cases, a paragraph will only apply to one or two subsystems (maintenance or instrument calibration).

Benefits of the ISO 9000 Series

When I first decided to interview the quality director of a national courier, I had no leads (I actually had to look up the phone number in the white pages). When I called headquarters, I simply introduced myself and asked the operator to transfer my call to the quality director. Within seconds I had the director on the line who proceeded to inform me that his company had recently achieved ISO 9002 registration. Encouraged by my success, I thought it would be interesting to interview another courier firm. What transpired is interesting and worth recounting.

Lamprecht: "May I speak to someone in charge of quality control or quality assurance?"

Operator: "Sir, I don't know what you mean. What is your specific problem? Did you lose a package?"

Lamprecht: "No, I haven't lost any packages. I simply would like to ask a few questions to one of your managers. Don't you have someone in charge of operations?"

Operator: "What is your number? I'll have someone call you back."

Two days later someone did call back and the following conversation ensued.

Lamprecht: "Do you have anyone in charge of quality assurance? I would like to know if you are considering implementing an ISO 9000 quality assurance system."

Man: "That would probably be handled by headquarters."

Lamprecht: "Could I talk to someone at headquarters?"

Man: "No, but if you give me your name and address we will have someone write to you." *(Note that I had not stated any problem. Therefore, what was there to write about?)*

Lamprecht: (Trying to once again explain my purpose) "I think it would be easier if I were to talk to someone at headquarters."

Man: "I am sorry, sir, that is impossible. Besides, I am sure that if there is a need to look into this ISO 9000 system, they are already well aware of it."

Lamprecht: "Alright let me give you my address."

I somehow managed to obtain the address of the man I had been talking to. I mailed him some information. No news ever since.

Notice the drastic difference in corporate culture between the two companies. One is very open, the other secretive and certainly not communicative. When I tell the story to seminar participants, I ask them to guess the name of the company. To my surprise, many guess who it is before I even finish my question (perhaps you too have guessed who it is). People usually are very eager to tell me some of their horror stories relating to lost packages or packages delivered late. It would seem that the company in question could certainly benefit from ISO 9002 registration, however, management is so convinced it is doing a good job that it is not likely to consider it for a long time.

Conclusion

The generic nature of the standards demonstrate that in many cases they can be successfully applied within environments as diverse as a hospital, bank, distributor of software, hotel, or architectural/engineering consulting firm. The application of an ISO 9000–type quality assurance system need not be very involved. Under proper guidance and training, a firm can establish a working system within six months, or less for smaller firms. Still, despite the flexibility of the standards, one should not conclude that the standards (or guidelines) can be, or need be, applied to all industries. Some difficult questions still remain to be answered. Chapter 6 explores how certain clauses may (when applied within certain industries) lead to some annoying difficulties.

Notes

1. The standard already has been applied in the United Kingdom to the National Health Service. See E. M. Rooney, "A Proposed Quality System Specification for the National Health Service," *Journal of the Institute of Quality Assurance* 14, no. 2 (June 1988): 45–49. The article fails to address many important issues of the 9001–9002 models.

2. Leonard S. Rosenfeld demonstrates that the issues of what constitute quality of care can be traced in the United States to at least 1914. See, L. S. Rosenfeld, "Standards for Assessing Quality of Care," in *Quality Assurance of Medical Care*, Regional Medical Programs Service, U.S. Department of Health, Education, and Welfare (January 1973): 9–34. Some of the issues relating to the difficulty of monitoring the medical profession are covered by Selig Greenberg, "The Defenseless Consumer," Chapt. 7 in *The Quality of Mercy* (New York: Atheneum, 1971).

3. Robert Burney, "TQM in a Surgery Center," *Quality Progress* (January 1994): 100.

4. See, for example, Donald C. Harrington, "The Relationship of Quality Surveillance to Various Health Care Delivery Systems;" H. Kenneth Walker, "The Problem-Oriented Medical Record in Medical Audit"; Maria C. Phaneuf, "Quality Assurance—A Nursing View," all in *Quality Assurance of Medical Care*, Conference of February 1973, U.S. Department of Health, Education, and Welfare.

5. The Healthcare Quality Certification Board (HQCB) promotes excellence and professionalism in health care quality management. For more information call 800-346-4722.

6. I must emphasize *apparent* because objective evidence was not collected.

7. The author is aware of at least two suppliers of automated teller machines that are currently either implementing or about to implement an ISO 9001 quality assurance system.

8. These are not necessarily the worst bugs. A formula that is incorrectly programmed can have a much more serious impact, particularly if the error is only noticeable within certain ranges of the independent variable(s). See Henry Petroski, *To Engineer Is Human*, "From Slide Rule to Computer: Forgetting How It Used to Be Done" for many good examples.

9. Since consulting firms work on unique projects, the application of statistical techniques is not likely. This is not to say that some applications could not be found but they should be practical and of value to the user.

10. Technical assistance to ensure that the customer uses the product correctly is a good example of what John Goodman, Arlene Malech, and Colin Adamson wrote about in "Don't Fix the Product, Fix the Customer," *The Quality Review* (Fall 1988): 8–11. Of course, a better design or better documentation might alleviate the problem.

6 Some Potentially Difficult Paragraphs to Interpret for the Service Sector

The purpose of this chapter is different from chapters 4 and 5, which explained how clauses of the ISO 9002 standard applied to the restaurant, hospital, banking, and other industries. I have selected eight of what I perceive to be the most difficult or challenging paragraphs of the ISO 9001/ISO 9002 standards and offer suggestions and comments on how each paragraph could be interpreted or applied across various service industries.

Difficult to Interpret Paragraphs

The list of what I have identified as difficult to interpret paragraphs is one man's opinion and could be challenged by some readers. Certainly, I recognize that the difficulty of a paragraph depends on the interpreter and on the type of industry she or he represents. Naturally, a difficult paragraph for someone operating in one industry might be an easy or nonapplicable paragraph for someone else. Nonetheless, after some reflection, I have found the following paragraphs are likely to cause some difficulties for certain service industries: Contract Review (4.3), Design Control (4.4), Receiving and Inspection and Testing (4.10.2 and 4.10.3), Control of Inspection, Measuring and Test Equipment (4.11), Inspection and Test Status (4.12), Preventive Action (4.14.3), Handling, Storage, Packaging, Preservation and Delivery (4.15) and Servicing (4.19).

Difficulties in interpretation should not imply nonapplicability. In most cases, some logical application or translation/adaptation can readily be devised. In other cases, the application seems to either be missing or artificially conceived. Faced with a particularly difficult clause, an individual often feels compelled to find an acceptable or elaborate scenario rather than recognize that the clause may have no particular or limited relevance to the organization or customer requirements. Such exercises are futile but, unfortunately, this tendency to relentlessly want to fit the standards to any and every scenario, rather than tailor the clauses to the situation, seems to be prevalent among some circles. Hence this chapter.

In the following pages, I try to give as many examples as possible to illustrate how various situations could lead to potentially difficult interpretations of the standards for certain organizations. Whenever possible, I try to provide solutions or suggestions as to how the dilemma might be resolved. In certain cases, some of these organizations (for example, universities) are not likely to perceive themselves as an industry, let alone a service industry. Nonetheless, since the use of the models provided by the ISO 9000 model already has been suggested for application within the educational sector, the challenge cannot be ignored.

Contract Review

The contract review paragraph is a rather straightforward clause. It basically requires that

- A contract review procedure be written (although verbal contracts also are recognized).

- Contracts are reviewed by the supplier to ensure that requirements are adequately defined and documented.

- Disagreements are resolved. That assumes that differences in interpretation are caught during the contract review phase. I will illustrate one case where, despite the issuance of numerous detailed specifications, disagreements can occur after completion of the project.

- The supplier is capable of meeting the contract.

These requirements are reasonable. One would hope that a contractor is capable of meeting contractual obligations. Unfortunately, that is not always the case.[1] The difficulty with clause 4.3 (Contract Review) has little to do with its contents, but with the fact that in many cases contracts within the service industry are poorly defined or specified (this also can be true within the manufacturing sectors). This invariably leads to some lengthy subjective interpretations as to what was requested or intended. Also, the identification as to who is the customer can be murky. As shall be seen in the case of a book publisher, several customers are involved. Ultimately, there are only two parties negotiating the contract: the book publisher and the author. Nonetheless, the author also must satisfy other customers and their representatives.

A similar scenario occurs when hospitals were examined. Suppose a hospital decides to implement an ISO 9002 quality assurance program. How would a hospital (or university) handle clause 4.3? One of the first comments from a hospital administrator will be that hospitals have at least two customers: the patient and the patient's insurance company. Legally, there is one customer—the one who signs the admission papers. Even then, many thorny questions remain. Suppose you are to be admitted in the emergency ward. Are you in a position to negotiate your contract? Is there a contract? How do you verify the hospital's capability to deliver its service which itself is subcontracted to doctors?

Let us examine a less dramatic scenario. You are scheduled for a physical with your doctor. What will be the nature of your contract review? What are your requirements and how do you ensure that they are adequately defined? In the majority of cases the requirements or symptoms are poorly defined. Shortness of breath, frequent headaches, pain in the lower right side, and so on. From these ill-defined symptoms (input), the doctor must then formulate a set of hypotheses, which must be verified via a process of elimination by ordering a battery of tests, which may or may not solve the problem. To my knowledge, few patients would want to argue or negotiate a contract with a doctor (I have once, regarding some overcharges on a minor surgery). Moreover, even in the case of an operation, no formal written contract specifying deliverables is ever written. The closest a patient comes to examining a contract is when she or he is confronted, a posteriori, with an incredibly long, itemized bill. Then it is usually too late to argue. In most cases, you find yourself arguing with the hospital and your representative (in other words, the insurance company).

There is an implied or latent contract between a patient and his or her physician. The latent contract presupposes that the doctor will either alleviate or preferably eliminate the trauma or pain. The contract is left open until the problem is resolved by your doctor or another doctor (for example, a specialist), or until your insurance decides that enough is enough and stops payments.

Yet, despite the apparent vagueness of the contract review, a hospital could maintain documented procedure(s) outlining its contract review phases. Contract review is not referring to the various contracts between the hospital and its staff of nurses, laboratory technicians, and adjunct doctors. Instead, it refers to the contract review(s) between doctors and patients. Naturally, there are likely to be several types of contract reviews that would depend on the type of visit (emergency vs. scheduled).

Contract Review in Universities or Educational Institutions

Since most of the issues relating to this section are addressed in the following section (design), I will limit my comments to a few lines. One of the first difficulties faced when applying this paragraph to educational institutions is to decide which parties are involved. If one focuses on contract review between the faculty/staff and the university (as an employer), the paragraph is easily interpreted. However, if the customer comprises the community of paying students, the paragraph takes on a different meaning. Similarly, in some universities where government (U.S. or foreign) research is an important source of revenues, the customer is yet another entity who, in this case, usually knows quite a bit about contract review and usually would insist on clearly stated terms. Consequently, depending on the scope of the registration, applicants (paying customers) may be left out of the contract review process (see TQM discussion in chapter 3).

Design and the Service Industry

The design control clause (Paragraph 4.4) often causes so much consternation that many firms that have major design activities choose to forego ISO 9001 registration and apply for ISO 9002 registration as an interim solution. The decision to delay ISO 9001 registration often is influenced by registrars who recommend this procedure. Technically, such recommendations are correct, however, I have never understood why firms appear to have so little confidence in their design process, but not in their manufacturing process—which is impacted daily by the engineering/design functions.

If the design control functions create anxiety attacks for manufacturers of tangible products, one can imagine the frustration experienced by potential implementers within the service industry as they struggle with the concept of a designed service. Before proceeding any further, let us first review the intents of the Design Control paragraphs that consist of several subclauses.

The Design Function

What is design? There are as many definitions of design as there are authors. John R. Dixon, in *Design Engineering*, views design as part inventiveness, analysis, decision making, and, above all, problem solving.[2] Victor Papanek, in *Design for the Real World*, favors the intuitive aspect of design. He believes design should be viewed "as the conscious and intuitive effort to impose meaningful order."[3] D. J. Leech and B. T. Turner, in *Engineering Design for Profit*, provide no less than five definitions within two paragraphs. They see the full design process as much more than the production of drawings: "It embraces many tasks from customer liaison and specification writing, through drawing, prototype manufacture, development, proving, product support, and product support to modification."[4]

Design is a complex activity that is full of conflicting requirements. Quoting the designer David Pyle, Henri Petroski explains that, "The requirements for design conflict and cannot be reconciled. . . . It is quite impossible for any design to be 'the logical outcome of the requirements' simply because, the requirements being in conflict, their logical outcome is an impossibility."[5]

The basic premise of the design control paragraph is that the supplier "shall maintain documented procedures to control and verify the design of the product in order to ensure that the specified requirements are met." What are specified requirements and who specifies them? In the manufacturing world (as in the service world), many interested parties usually are involved in the specification of requirements—invariably the customer, who may or may not have very specific requirements; marketing, which may dream up some abstract or very real customer requirements; sales, which generally will agree to just about any customer requirements; engineering, which takes it all in, quantifies it as best it can, and occasionally cuts specifications or tolerances in half just to test manufacturing or operation's patience; and manufacturing, which can (if it is fortunate enough to participate during the early discussions), always rely on deviations to do the best it can. One should not ignore the forgotten field service staff that eventually discovers what the requirements and specifications should have been in the first place.

I hope the reader will recognize the levity of the last paragraph although many of you may be smiling for different reasons. I would like to remind the reader that not everyone believes that the design of new products should involve marketing or even the customer. Akio Morita, in *Made in Japan*, states: "Our plan is to lead the public with new products rather than ask them what kind of products they want. The public does not know what is possible, but we do. So instead of doing a lot of market research, we refine our thinking on a product and its use and try to create a market for it by educating and communicating with the public."[6] Morita's remark will be relevant when the design process is reviewed within certain sectors of the service industry.

Within ISO 9001 (1994 revision), the design process, which can cover either new designs or modifications/adaptation of old designs, is broken down into the following stages:

- Design and development planning
- Organizational and technical interfaces
- Design input
- Design output

- Design review
- Design verification
- Design validation
- Design changes

Let us see how these subclauses may apply to the following services: education, consulting, and landscaping. I have selected these professions for two reasons: (1) I have either some personal experience or know friends who work within these sectors, and (2) some important questions will have to be answered as to whether or not the service provided is recognized as a service (for example, a university) and, if so, who is the customer. Consequently, by focusing on these services, other ISO paragraphs also will have to be invoked.

Design Control in Education

The thought of comparing universities with factories has had a long history. As early as 1921, Arthur E. Morgan observed, "an educational institution has certain points of resemblance to a factory" and although, "the academic type of educator may object to this comparison . . . a study of the points of similarity might profitably be made by many colleges. The small college, like the small factory, must select an output that the larger institutions either have neglected or cannot deal with efficiently, and should fortify its position by selection of its materials in a manner which the wholesale methods of its large competitors have made impracticable."[7] A few years later, the same idea was recaptured by Alfred H. White when he proposed that, "[T]here is some analogy between the college and the manufacturing plant which receives partially fabricated metal, shapes it and refines it somewhat, and turns it over to some other agency for further fabrication. The college receives raw material. . . . It must turn out a product which is saleable. . . . The type of curriculum is in the last analysis not set by the college but by the employer of the college graduate."[8]

Today, many of the same arguments are hotly debated. Ralph Frammolino, in an article published in the *Los Angeles Times*, wrote that, "schools are under increasing pressure to prove they are getting results. . . . We have to show something has happened to [students] during their four years besides seat time and grades. The Western Association of Schools and Colleges has become so concerned about public accountability that it is considering a plan to measure how well students are educated and making public the results, as well as other findings of the accreditation process." Quoting Weisner, Frammolino concludes by observing that, "[T]here is a very significant body of opinion in higher education that says to the public, 'Trust us. And don't require us to produce any evidence [of results].' What we are saying is that those days are over. Institutions and faculty have got to demonstrate that good things are happening to students. We think they are . . . but we've got to talk about our strengths and weaknesses in public."[9]

Perhaps some of these debates could be partly resolved if academia were to consider third party accreditation. In fact, some universities already are considering this novel approach, however, as shall be shown, some adjustments will have to be made.

The application of ISO 9001 and ISO 9002 to education was thought of some time ago and, in the United States, a guideline (ANSI/ASQC Z1.11 *Quality Management and Quality Assurance Standards—Guidelines for the Application of ANSI/ASQC Q91 or Q92 to Education and Training Institutions)* is already published. As with most guidelines, the Z1.11 document also could be improved. The first difficulty we are faced with when trying to apply ISO 9001 to the education sector (private or public) is to ask whether or not institutions such as universities perceive themselves as providers of a service.

I am well aware of the fact that an increasing number of universities and other educational institutions are beginning to either implement or look into the implementation of TQM programs, but based on my experience with several institutions of higher learning, I would propose that despite the difficult economic situation faced by many universities, many still do not perceive themselves as providers of a service.[10]

Let us not forget that universities (for the most part) grant degrees. I say "for the most part" because one can always purchase degrees from certain nonaccredited universities. Consequently, as far as some universities are concerned (at least those in which I taught), their perception is that they do not have customers, but applicants. I believe the distinction is important because an applicant must first fill in an application.[11] If accepted, the applicant can spend her or his money on tuition, which does not guarantee graduation.[12]

Therefore, if indeed there were to be a contract and a contract review phase (the nature of which will have to be explored later), the applicant/customer is not guaranteed delivery of his or her diploma (final product) since the processes that would lead to graduation are principally the responsibility of the applicant and not of the supplier/ provider of the service (see Figure 6.1).

If accepted, the student is granted the privilege of attending classes for which she or he has no, or little, preliminary input. The class format and content was designed much as Morita designed his Walkman.® This

The question as to whether or not students should be perceived as customers leads to yet another fundamental question: Can a university really afford to treat students as clients?[13] The question came to mind when I learned from a friend that the university he graduated from some years ago had begun implementing a total quality program. Intrigued, I asked my friend to elaborate. I was not prepared and yet, somehow not very surprised, for what I was about to learn.

The story begins when the university, located in the United States, but serving thousands of Canadian students, lost its accreditation from the Canadian government. Within months, the flow of Canadian students and money was cut off. Facing a difficult financial crisis, the president decided to implement a total quality program. Students were to be treated as paying customers. This might appear to be a sensible thing to do, but how does one treat students as customers? Moreover, since the university and by extension, its faculty has now formally transformed itself as a supplier of diplomas, what must the faculty do to please their customers? Simple—the faculty, as instructed by the school president, can no longer fail students. Indeed, customers who have failed a course would no doubt become very irritated, and as every provider of a service knows, irritated customers are not a good way to guarantee return business. The story becomes even more interesting when one learns that these customers no longer bother to attend courses. Why should they? They apparently are guaranteed a passing grade by simply signing up for the course! Incredible, but true.

The phenomenon of grade inflation, partly motivated by such policies is not new to academia. What is more disturbing, however, is the ensuing devaluation of the university's degree and the enormous economic impact such an action has on society as a whole.

Figure 6.1. Should students be treated as customers?

is not to say that a design process did not take place. Indeed, in universities with which I am familiar, new courses must first be submitted to the department chair for approval. The process usually consists of writing a detailed course proposal designed to justify the course. These proposals can resemble marketing studies outlining potential needs and benefits to students. If accepted by the department chair and a peer review, the course proposal is then forwarded to the dean who may or may not approve the course based on the recommendations of the department chair. After the new course is approved, a more detailed design must take place. Most of the design activities specified in the *Design Control* paragraph take place.

The *design and development activities* consist of the course proposal, its outline, course duration, intended contents, course objectives, grading policy, and so on. If the course is to be jointly taught with a faculty from another department, *organizational interfaces* must be addressed (for example, who will teach what subject when). The *design input* would consist of the topics to be covered, sometimes detailed to weekly (or even hourly) presentations. The *design review* may consist of the department chair offering some suggestions. *Design output* usually is provided in the form of tests and student reports. *Design verification* would consist of student evaluation and can only be submitted after the course is delivered once. These evaluations can/should be used to improve the product. The *design validation* is manifested by the fact that students keep enrolling. If the class is not accepted by the student community, the course will not last more than a few quarters, or may only be offered once in a while, to keep testing the market. *Design changes* are a normal part of course improvement and revitalization. If a course is not periodically modified, it usually becomes stale. Besides, within a university environment, if a course is not periodically changed or upgraded, students will start selling course notes (or give them away).

Much the same activities take place when a course is developed by a consultant or a consulting firm for a client. I used to design/develop statistical process control and design of experiment courses for a major employer in Seattle and several consulting firms. Unfortunately, within the reality of the everyday business world, design control activities are not always as carefully planned as they should be; supposedly, because it would cost too much money. For instance, courses always had to be developed in about one fifth of the required time. If I required a month of development time, I would be lucky to be given five to seven course development days. Management's rationale for such drastic cuts in course development activities was somewhat predictable: Development of anything was perceived as a nonvalue-added activity. After all, we were paid to teach, why did we need development time?

Trying to find out some information about the intended audience (design input) was always a major effort (manufacturers will no doubt understand). What invariably happened was that the courses were first launched and then constantly modified via poorly controlled design changes after design changes (a process reminiscent of some practices within the software industry where software versions are released with known minor bugs to be fixed at a later time).[14]

These design changes led to some occasional confrontations simply because everyone (all four of us) had authority over change approval. The process was not as chaotic as one might think. Although anyone could recommend changes to any course, all changes were reviewed (usually on Fridays) by the staff, which consisted of four instructors. After the changes were approved, one of us would volunteer to insert the changes and distribute copies of the new version to the other members.[15] Naturally, the courses would evolve and improve as we obtained more instructor and student input.

Design and Consulting

Consulting means any activity for which advice and/or solution to problems are sought by a customer. The solution might consist of a design study complete with blueprints. Examples of such consulting activities would include a broad range of engineering studies such as environmental impact studies, engineering (architectural) designs, product design, plant design leading to a complete process and instrument diagram(s), and computer simulation model building. Other consulting activities would range from art consultants, interior decorating, diet, physical fitness, financial consulting, as well as a host of other activities, including consultation on how to design an effective ISO 9000 implementation plan.

Consulting activities could greatly benefit from the suggestions introduced within the Design Control paragraph of ISO 9001 (the clause is only found in the ISO 9001 standard). In the case of engineering design firms, most of the activities outlined within the subclauses of the design control paragraph are practiced, however, not all consulting firms practice good design control. There are many reasons why. In many cases, the nature of the service is either vaguely defined or poorly specified. This problem is not necessarily the sole property of the service industry. Manufacturers of product suffer the same fate, which is only one of the many reasons why so many design changes and deviations are constantly issued. For example, software developers often are faced with the difficulties of an ever-changing set of customer requirements that evolve and become more specific as the product (software) evolves.

As is often the case within the manufacturer/assembler world, the product characteristics or process objectives are not always clearly thought out and cannot be until the consultant analyzes the problem. A specific example relating to ISO 9000 consultation will help illustrate some of the difficulties.

When a customer contracts for an ISO implementation job, one of the elements of the contract review phase usually specifies that part of the contract would consist of an evaluation or preassessment phase. The purpose of this phase is to determine what needs to be done, by whom, and how it will be done. Thus, the contract and design for implementation can begin only after a preliminary assessment (or a precontract phase) is first completed.

As far as the supplier (in other words, consultant) is concerned, the objective is clear: Ensure that the customer achieves ISO 9000 registration. These are the specified requirements that must be met. Can the consultant guarantee ISO 9000 registration? No, simply because the consultant rarely has control of the whole implementation process, nor should he or she have such control. Invariably, the customer wishes to retain some control over the process, which may lead to implementation or prioritization conflicts. I would propose that the customer must always be responsible for the implementation. Unfortunately, some customers, who supposedly cannot or do not want to allocate the time or resources, would rather hire a consultant to take care of everything. Technically, such an approach could be cited as a nonconformance. (*Note:* Do you know which paragraph applies to this situation? *Hint:* Go back to chapter 4 and reread some of the early clauses.)

The early design phases of the implementation, which would consist of the development planning and organizational interfaces, are invariably performed with the customer. It has been my experience (perhaps not shared by others) that these phases usually are followed, however, they may not always be well documented. As for the formulation of design input and design output, usually it is left out of the process. Yet, the design input phase is crucial if it is to bring about a successful implementation. For example, design input would consist of defining the nature of the commitment, the type of resources, the preliminary implementation schedule, and a definition of responsibilities specifying the consultant's domain of responsibilities and differentiating these responsibilities from the client's. This input is most important and usually difficult to specify, particularly if the director or president of the company is not committed to the implementation program.

As for design review, verification, and validation, they are rarely, if ever, performed. This does not necessarily mean that ISO implementation efforts are doomed to fail. If they were, few companies would have achieved registration. This could mean that, with respect to ISO 9000 consulting activity, design control is not an important activity or that the design control activities are performed by the consultant during his or her many activities. Indeed, one could conclude that these design control activities become part of the hidden requirements of most consulting jobs.

Design in Landscaping

Unlike some consulting activities, landscaping requires some carefully planned design processes. Landscaping can begin with vague contract requirements. A client or owner requests a landscape concept to be formulated. The concept proposed by an owner/client in collaboration with a landscape architect consists of a theme (Oriental, Mediterranean, Hill and Dale, Alpine) to be developed within a certain budget ranging anywhere from $10,000 to several million dollar contracts. After the concept has been agreed upon, the team of landscape architects (there can be several architects on major jobs) begin the task of designing the landscape. Throughout the design phase, *planning* activities are coordinated with the client (owner), who provides *design input* throughout the development phases, and the structural engineer, who also provides design input and *design output* to ensure that the input parameters satisfy architectural features and various safety codes. The coordination of activities between the landscape architect(s) and the structural engineer cover all of the requirements specified in the Organizational and Technical Interfaces paragraph (4.4.2). As the design evolves, the landscape architect translates the customer/client's visions and the structural engineer requirements (in other words, two sets of input parameters) into a list of specifications (design input). The list, which for big jobs can consist of 30 to 50 pages of hardscape and landscape specifications, is simultaneously translated into output requirements. Output requirements would include various pipes, fittings, sprinkler systems, plants, trees, shrubs, grading requirements, type of pots, fences, filling material, and numerous other items.

Once completed, the design is subcontracted to a landscape contracting firm that will install the design. Prior to installation and during the construction process, the various blueprints and set of specs go through the usual set of *change orders*, which can be initiated by just about anyone. Change orders can consist of *addendums*, that is change/upgrades to the original contract, or *bulletins*, which are approved and (usually) signed changes to the blueprints. As is often the case in manufacturing, these bulletins can be red penciled by the landscape architect and later are officially released with blueprint updates. *Design verification, review, and validation* are also performed by all interested parties (landscape engineer, structural engineer, client, and subcontracted firm).

Upon completion of the job, an audit (known as a punch list) is performed. During these audits, the client, architect, general contractor, and the subcontractor walk the job to ensure that all specifications and contractual requirements have been met. Corrective actions resulting from these audits are the responsibility of the subcontractor. One might wonder why corrective actions are still needed after the job is completed.

After all, the aforementioned processes do indicate that much information constantly flows between all interested parties throughout the life cycle of the project. Nevertheless, the translation of a landscaping concept cannot always be completely captured by a set of blueprints and a mountain of details and specifications. Artful and artistic interpretive subjectivity still rules.

Perhaps the only flagrant nonconformance to the standard (with respect to Design Control) is that, although all of the design activities are performed, most firms would be hard pressed to furnish a documented set of procedures that would outline or otherwise describe the procedures. If, however, a firm wanted to apply for ISO 900 registration, it could describe its design process. Naturally, that would satisfy only one-twentieth of ISO 9001. The other 19 paragraphs also would have to be addressed!

Inspection and Testing

This paragraph (4.10) consists of five subparagraphs entitled: General, Receiving Inspection and Testing, In-process Inspection and Testing, Final Inspection and Testing, and Inspection and Test Records. Of the five paragraphs, I believe receiving and in-process inspection and testing are likely to be the two most difficult paragraphs to implement and may not even be applicable in some cases.

Of course, many service industries can apply all of the inspection paragraphs. For example, hospitals conduct some receiving inspection and testing for certain materials and chemicals. If one is to treat a patient as an incoming product (rather coldhearted, I will grant you), then medical records (blood pressure, temperature, laboratory analyses, physical tests, and so on) could be considered as a form of receiving inspection. During an operation, the monitoring of various vital signs would make up the in-process test and data bank.

Some banks sample their receiving materials (such as cash cards and checks) for nonconformities. Records of such inspections are maintained. I suppose one could say that a university samples its incoming applicants when it requests SAT or GRE scores. Similarly, the in-process inspection and testing would consist of the many tests students have to take in order to pass their courses and eventually graduate (the ultimate final inspection and testing). Records are kept for an apparent eternity. This would of course satisfy clause 4.16 (Control of Quality Records).

There are cases where the supplier of a service would be hard-pressed to implement a receiving and in-process inspection. For example, I do not know what type of receiving inspection the consultant could implement. Even if an application could be found, I am not sure it necessarily would be beneficial. Similar remarks would apply to the other subparagraphs. In some cases, such as a restaurant or related industry, performing an in-process inspection or testing is either not practical or not necessary.[16] Certainly, as was already stated, a properly trained or qualified cook continuously monitors his or her cooking, however, documented procedures are not required.

One should note that the standards do not require the supplier to have documented procedures for in-process inspection and testing. Subclause a of 4.10.3 states that, "The supplier shall: a) inspect and test product as required by the quality plan and/or documented procedures."

If the quality plan simply requires the chef to visually inspect the meals and allows the chef to rely on his or her experience and training to decide when the product is acceptable, then that should be good enough. If a third party auditor objects to the restaurant's documented procedures, my advice would be to find another registrar.

Control of Inspection, Measuring and Test Equipment

This is likely to be the most difficult paragraph for many industries. I have already identified sources of application for paragraph 4.11 in the restaurant industry and hospitals (laboratory).[17] Nevertheless, many service industries do not rely on instruments, at least not in the sense described in the ISO 9000 series of standards. As far as the standard is concerned, the paragraph is written for all equipment or software used to monitor quality. If one is to find other applications, one must expand the definition of an instrument.

Within the service industry, an instrument can be a questionnaire used for customer surveys or a test used to verify someone's knowledge of a topic. Psychological tests could be used (on a voluntary basis) by registrars to determine an auditor's psychological profile. The information might help determine why certain auditors grade the same audit differently. A marketing agency is likely to use several questionnaires (instruments) to measure/test public opinion. A training organization (internal or external to a firm) might rely of some in-house tests to verify competency for a host of technical expertise.

Unfortunately, the use of tests in industry is often ignored during training sessions. Yet they are a valuable tool for assessing, and therefore measuring, not only how much has been learned, but also the effectiveness of the training material. What often is ignored by trainers/instructors/teachers is that questionnaires used to assess knowledge of a subject, need to be tested for reliability and reproducibility.[18] Some questionnaires need to be upgraded periodically (calibrated) to account for various shifts in the socioeconomic profile of a population.[19]

The clause sometimes appears to be forced upon customer by ill-informed auditors. The following anecdote was recounted to the author during an interview with the quality assurance director of a major courier firm, which eventually did achieve ISO 9002 registration.

Lamprecht: "What were the difficult implementation issues?"

Q. A. Director: "We had difficulties adapting the instrumentation paragraph (4.11) to our needs. We think the auditor was wrong in interpreting this paragraph for our industry. He went to the vehicle maintenance department and asked the mechanic for some procedure regarding the inspection of a pin used to determine when the pin needed replacement. The mechanic told him that sometimes the inspection was visual and sometimes he took a measurement. The auditor did not like that. We had to write a procedure. But we still feel that the question had nothing to do with our product (delivery of packages). Besides, we allocate 10 percent of our fleet to cover in case of mechanical breakdown. So we had (the delivery issue) covered anyway. We really fought it, but they (third-party auditors) would not give-in. It actually upset management, particularly those who were not in favor of registration in the first place."

Lamprecht: "What about your scales?"

Q. A. Director: "Oh, we have them calibrated by an agency once a year. We also use a 50-pound weight to check that the scale is within percentage."

The director is correct, the requirement for the pin maintenance procedure had nothing to do with the scope of the audit. Certainly, the auditor would have been correct if the maintenance department had been part of the audit, but as it turned out the auditor visited the maintenance department (a remote facility) as an afterthought.

It is easy to understand the auditor's logic. The maintenance department maintains a fleet of trucks that are used to deliver packages, the very heart of the company's business. Therefore, since the maintenance of trucks is an integral part of the quality assurance system, maintenance procedures must be in place. Maintenance/scheduling procedures were in place, but not the one for pin inspection.

Well, if one is to interpret every paragraph with the same rigor, one will always find a missing procedure. The important question to ask (and it should be asked by the firm, not the auditor) is: "Was the pin procedure required to improve or ensure delivery of the package?" The answer, from the company's point of view was "no," because the risk and cost were not worth the investment. Besides, a contingency plan already was in place.

Inspection and Test Status

This is likely to be a paragraph with limited practical application for many service industries, especially the so-called intangible service industry where the service cannot really be tagged or labeled simply because it may consist of an idea or concept. Even in the restaurant or hotel industry, the paragraph would find limited application.[20] The paragraph requires, among other things, that the "inspection and test status of product shall be identified by suitable means which indicates the conformance or nonconformance of product with regard to inspection and test status performed."

Distributors or transportation firms could find applications for the paragraph (and many already do). Transportation firms often label the contents of trucks with a certificate of analysis guaranteeing the quality of the contents. Distributors that need to store items often identify items with various labels and tags. It has been suggested that the paragraph could perhaps be applied to any process that requires the processing of claims or applications (insurance claims, credit cards applications, and so on). One would think that in such cases, the activities already are carefully monitored.

Preventive Action

The preventive action clause may cause some frustration leading to migraine headaches. The clause is a significant expansion from the 1987 version of the standards which had only one sentence. The preventive action clause consists of four items.[21]

> Procedures for preventive action shall include:
>
> a) the use of appropriate sources of information such as processes and work operations which affect product quality, concessions, audit results, quality records, service reports and customer complaints to detect, analyze and *eliminate potential causes of nonconformities;*
>
> b) determination of the steps needed to deal with any problem requiring preventive action;
>
> c) initiation of preventive action and applying controls to ensure that it is effective;
>
> d) confirmation that relevant information on actions taken is submitted for management review.

I have some difficulty interpreting subparagraph a, which calls for the analysis and elimination of potential causes of nonconformities. When I ask other people to interpret the subparagraph, a variety of opinions are suggested. Some suggest that failure mode and effect analysis (FMEA) could be used, while others believe that the standard is referring to field reports. I suppose one could use FMEA, although I always thought the technique was most effective when used during the design phase, not after the product is in circulation. An analysis of field reports also is a good suggestion since field service often reports on potential problems.[22]

The difficulty I have with subclause a is that I interpret the words "potential causes of nonconformities" to mean that the causes are latent and have therefore not yet occurred and may not even ever occur. In these cases, I don't know how one can analyze latent causes, unless one possesses a crystal ball. The application to the service industry probably will be challenging.

The analysis of potential causes of nonconformities can be hard to predict as the following amusing story, extracted from the *Billings Gazette*, illustrates.[23]

> Council members have been asked to declare an emergency and suspend bidding requirements so the city can buy a new electrical switch for the water treatment plant. Westinghouse Corp., the supplier, has estimated it will cost about $30,000 to replace a switch that exploded last week.
>
> The unexpected expense resulted from the misadventures of a rabbit that got inside equipment at the treatment plant, according to Joe Steiner, treatment plant superintendent.
>
> Apparently attracted by the warmth of the switch gear, the rabbit pushed against a metal shield covering a 6-by-10 inch vent. Once inside the mechanism, the rabbit's feet and nose formed an electrical connection and triggered an explosion.
>
> "He took 12,000 volts. This is a fried bunny; he's a bunch of fuzz and not too much rabbit," said Steiner, who took pictures for insurance purposes.

No amount of analysis (FMEA or other techniques) could have anticipated that a rabbit would eventually cost the city of Billings, Montana, $30,000. Yet, one wonders if a corrective action was ever implemented. Certainly, I would think that at $30,000 a rabbit, some redesign of the metal shield might be worth the investment. No doubt, a cost benefit analysis is under way.

Handling, Storage, Packaging, Preservation and Delivery
These subclauses are not always readily applicable to the service industry except if the nature of the service is to deliver a product. For example, a dry cleaning service would have to properly handle, package, and

preserve (and perhaps deliver) the products it processes. A fast-food restaurant or pizzeria would find an application to all of the subclauses. Courier services must ensure that packages or letters are properly handled, stored, and delivered to the correct address. A dentist, however, has little need for the paragraph except for products that must be stored or autoclaved within the office in order to perform his or her job (chemicals, drugs, gloves, masks, and related items). Services of intangible (intellectual) products, however, would struggle with these paragraphs. A book publisher could apply the paragraphs, in most cases books are durable and can be boxed and delivered to various customers without many precautions. A wholesaler of pharmaceutical products would adapt the paragraphs differently than the publisher.

An office specializing in translation services also may have difficulties with this paragraph. It is not uncommon for organizations specializing in the translation of software to actually store the product on disks and then deliver it electronically via a wide area network. In such cases, various verification activities regarding the integrity of the proper storage and transmission of the translated text and programming code is routinely performed by standard packages. If an error occurs during transmission, the computer simply retransmits.

Servicing

The service industry usually does not service its products mostly because the product often is consumed on the spot, as it is being produced, or shortly thereafter.[24] At any rate, the requirement is not compulsory since it only applies "where servicing is a specified requirement," which is infrequent within the service industry. Hence, it may be difficult to apply the clause to the industry in general. However, one can again rely on the hotel industry for an example of a service industry where the service paragraph would apply. Hotel rooms must be serviced (that is, cleaned) every day. The servicing activity, although not an explicit part of the contract, is a very strong implicit requirement.[25] Cable companies and phone companies also provide services (for a fee). The phone company will service/maintain the very service they provide (the line inside your house and all outlets) for a nominal monthly fee.[26] The fee is a warranty that guarantees that if anything should go wrong with your line, the phone company will provide maintenance for a mere $14 to $15 subscription fee per year. Similar comments would apply for the cable company.

Engineering firms that design building structures (for example, paper mills, hotels, and so on) often have to service their designs to the contractor. Contractors often need clarification regarding a variety of characteristics (hardware or software) of a design. Sometimes, a subcontractor may want to know if a different valve or pipe may be substituted from the one called for in the specifications. Whenever questions emerge, the subcontractor must rely on the design engineer for clarification. Most engineering/consulting firms will routinely provide interpretive assistance of their product (in other words, design) to ensure correct interpretation and/or suggestions.

Conclusion

This chapter's purpose has been to review some potential limitations of the standards. The basic premise is that the standards do not necessarily universally apply to all scenarios, thus the need for careful reflection. Nevertheless, one can conclude that, even in the case of so-called difficult paragraphs, one usually can find sensible applications within most industries. With the possible exception of universities and other related organizations that deal with so-called intangible services, the applications need not be artificial. For example, I alluded earlier that tests could be designed; in fact, they must be designed. A good test/questionnaire must be calibrated and verified for its effectiveness. Before designing a test one must first decide the purpose of the test (in other words, what is it testing?). One must come up with test items (input). The validity of each item/question also must be verified; in other words, one must determine the good and bad questions by first trying out the test on a sample of students. (*Note:* a bad question is a question that tends to be correctly answered by students who score below average on the test as a whole, but wrongly answered by the above average students.) Questions may have to be rephrased or eliminated. These activities would satisfy the design output, verification, validation, and change activities of paragraph 4.4.

One must conclude that in many, but not all, cases, practical applications to most of the standard's paragraphs can be found without much difficulty. Generally speaking, many of the requirements called for by the standard already are practiced in some form or another by the industry. In some cases, the practice may not be recognized. In other cases, the practice is haphazard and, worse yet, no documentation can be found.

Trying to implement a quality assurance system modeled after ISO 9001, ISO 9002, or ISO 9003 should help achieve some degree of formalization and normalization of certain procedures. After the structure is in place, it can be updated and improved as required. Notice that I was careful to avoid the use of the word *standardization*. I do not believe that the entire purpose of achieving ISO 9000 registration should become an exercise in standardization. As with any other industry, the service industry must be flexible and respond quickly to customer demands or changes in attitude. These objectives cannot be achieved if a rigid structure is adopted, which would allow for little or no deviations. In my view, the ISO 9000 series of standards, and more specifically ISO 9000 semi-official de facto interpreters, known as third-party auditors, can only benefit the service industry and industry in general if the need to preserve adaptability and fast response is recognized by all. E. F. Schumacher, anticipating Alvin Toffler, Tom Peters, and others perhaps said it best when he stated[27]

> In any organization, large or small, there must be a certain clarity and orderliness; if things, fall into disorder, nothing can be accomplished. Yet, orderliness, as such, is static and lifeless; so there must also be plenty of elbowroom and scope for breaking through the established order, to do the thing never done before, never anticipated by the guardians of orderliness, the new, unpredicted and unpredictable outcome of a man's creative idea.
>
> Therefore any organization has to strive continuously for the orderliness of *order* and the disorderliness of creative *freedom*. And the specific danger inherent in large-scale organizations is that its natural bias and tendency favor order, at the expense of creative freedom.

Notes

1. I once contracted with a home improvement firm that promised me that they could finish a job within 20 days. Forty-five days later the job was finally finished.

2. John R. Dixon, *Design Engineering: Inventiveness, Analysis, and Decision Making* (New York: McGraw-Hill Book Company, 1966).

3. Victor Papanek, *Design for the Real World* (Chicago: Academy Chicago Publishers, 1992).

4. D. J. Leech and B. T. Turner, *Engineering Design for Profit* (New York, John Wiley & Sons, 1985).

5. Henry Petroski, *To Engineer Is Human* (New York, Vintage Books, 1992).

6. Akio Morita, *Made in Japan* (New York: Fontana/Collins, 1986), 79. Morita concludes by observing: "I do not believe that any amount of market research could have told us that the Sony Walkman would be successful, not to say a sensational hit that would spawn many imitators." Ibid., 82.

7. Arthur E. Morgan, "The Antioch Plan," *Engineering News-Record* 86 (January 1921), 108–11, quoted in David F. Noble, *America by Design* (New York, Oxford University Press, 1977), 201.

8. Alfred H. White, "Chemical Engineering Education in the U.S.," *Transaction of the American Institute of Chemical Engineers* 21 (1928): 85. Quoted from David F. Noble, *America by Design*, 46.

9. Ralph Frammolino, "Getting Grades for Diversity," *Los Angeles Times*, 23 February 1994. Naturally, not everyone agrees with the newly proposed accreditation scheme. Stanford and USC are not in favor. Professor Casper of Stanford is quoted by Frammolino as saying: "Lemmings run into the sea together and I don't want to do that. I don't want us all to do the same thing at the same time. That's not what has made American institutions as good as they are—and they are stunning." See also, "College Accreditation Panel Adopts Plan on Diversity," *Los Angeles Times* 24 February 1994, A3, A14.

10. For a recent review of the application of TQM in education see *The Journal for Quality and Participation* 16, no. 1 (January/ February 1993).

11. Similar observations would apply to organizations that grant accreditation or certification. Examples of such organizations would include the Registrar Accreditation Board of Milwaukee, Wisconsin (and others throughout the world), which accredits or certifies ISO 9000 auditors.

12. One could find analogies in the nonacademic world when, at the height of the real estate boom in California (1980s) and perhaps other states, applications used to be accepted for bids on houses. In most cases, customers do not apply or bid for products, except when there are product shortages.

13. Stuart I. Greenbaum observes that "Obviously, our clients are our students, past and present, and also employers of our students, past, present and future." In "TQM at Kellogg" *The Journal for Quality and Participation* 16, no. 1 (January/February 1993): 91. Although I certainly agree that universities have a responsibility to society and thus employers or parents of students, I question the wisdom of treating students (university or otherwise) as clients. As has already been mentioned, clients do not always know what is required or needed and often rely on the expertise of the supplier for advice. I believe the same should apply within a university environment. Naturally, this does not preclude the need for dialogs between faculty, students, and employers. For an excellent discussion as to the limitation of TQM in education, see William E. Matthews, "The Missing Element in Higher Education," *The Journal for Quality and Participation* 16, no. 1, 102–108.

14. Some of us wanted to always improve the course, while others always felt that the course never needed improvement. This led to some major complications regarding document control. Indeed, because some instructors did not feel comfortable with some of the changes, we had two to three different versions of the same course. The only way to identify the courses was to actually thumb through

it. We later got wiser and inserted a revision date as our control mechanism; it helped considerably.

15. The confrontation often was due to the fact that invariably the same individual always objected to one thing or another.

16. Dr. Deming in his *Quality, Productivity, and Competitive Position* (Massachusetts Institute of Technology, 1982) provides the reader with a simple formula to help determine when 100 percent inspection or no inspection would be required. The formula requires that the user know the average fraction defective (p), the cost to inspect an item ($k1$), the cost of fixing an item equipped with a defective item ($k2$), and the average cost to test one or more item to find a good one from the supply (k) where k equals $k1/(1 - p)$. Minimum total inspection cost is achieved by following the rule of no inspection if $p < k1/k2$ and 100 percent inspection if $p > k1/k2$. See Deming, chapter 13.

17. There are many reference texts available, however, I would recommend that readers wanting to learn more about the measurement system in general may benefit from the concise publication entitled the *Measurement Systems Analysis: Reference Manual*, published by the Automotive Industry Action Group (AIAG), 26200 Lahser Road, Suite 200, Southfield, Michigan 48034.

18. I am differentiating between questionnaires that are used for surveys and for which there are no right or wrong answers (fact-finding questionnaires) and questionnaires/tests (multiple choice tests, for example) used to determine a student's knowledge of a subject.

19. Many excellent software packages, such as *Statistical Package for the Social Sciences* (SPSS), SAS, BIOMED, SYSTAT (all registered trademarks) and many others, have long provided their users with various subroutines designed to test questionnaires for reliability and accuracy. A well-known program, used by psychologists to determine attitudinal scales, is Guttman Scale, which allows a test designer to verify the reproducibility and scalability of a set of items.

20. Hotels use a similar concept when they provide the house-cleaning crews with a checklist of items to be completed, dated, and initialized for each room.

21. ANSI/ASQC Q9001, 1994, paragraph 4.14.3.

22. I am aware of the fact that field service often makes recommendations to engineering outlining potential sources of (maintenance) problems. I also have learned that these recommendations are all too often ignored only to be rediscovered later (naturally, at a much higher cost).

23. *Billings Gazette*, 8 May, 1993.

24. We learned in chapter 5 that banks have to service/maintain their ATMs.

25. I once checked at a fancy hotel at around 11:30 P.M. only to find out that the room I had been assigned had not been serviced. Naturally, I was somewhat upset since it took another 15 minutes before the clerk could find me a clean room.

26. The optional fee is indeed nominal at around $1.25 per line per month. However, considering how reliable the service is, $1.25 per month multiplied by millions of telephones does provide for a substantial source of hundreds of millions of dollars in revenues.

27. E. F. Schumacher, *Small Is Beautiful* (New York: Perennial Library, Harper & Row, 1973), 243.

7   How to Proceed

The purpose of this chapter is to provide some suggestions on how to approach the implementation process. Hopefully, some of the recommendations provided herewith will minimize mistakes and simultaneously reduce stress and improve your chances of completing the task on time.

The Challenge

One of the major challenges faced by most organizations that have elected to achieve ISO 9000 registration is the challenge to induce cultural change. Although there are many ways to achieve registration (some more painful than others), the process of adapting, modifying, or otherwise aligning one's quality assurance system to the ISO model invariably leads to some form of behavioral changes. This is when stress and risk of failure are at their highest.

Among the many factors that are directly and indirectly related to implementation stress, tribal conflicts rank high. In her book, *Tribal Warfare in Organizations*, Peg C. Neuhauser explains that any organization that consists of departments is made up of tribes.[1] Each tribe has its own dialect, jargon, history, rules for appropriate behavior, and value system that, in the best of scenarios, only approximates corporate values (usually the dominant tribe). Failure to communicate the objective and purpose of achieving registration with each tribe is a sure way to either guarantee failure or reinforce the instinctive resistance to change. In turn, this will generate other problems.

As is often the case, a tribe relies on its own oral history to educate new tribal members on how to perform a set of tasks. These verbal procedures, also known as on-the-job training, are rarely documented, hence my reference to oral history. Moreover, records that would demonstrate that the oral history was passed on and understood usually are nonexistent. This inability to keep written records is directly related to the tribal tradition of transferring tribal knowledge/knowhow and rituals verbally. From an ISO 9000 perspective, the inescapable problem is that all too often these verbal procedures deviate from the written procedures. In other words, the oral history is an approximation of the written history. This does not mean that the oral history is less accurate than the written (recorded) history, but that it is different and can often be the crux of the problem as far as an ISO 9000 auditor is concerned.

Therefore, one of the challenges is to determine how much of the verbal tradition will be allowed and how much should be written (transcribed). This will generate two additional challenges: (1) the decision will have to be made by someone (or a committee) as to how much detail will need to be included in the written procedures, and (2) one must decide who will be responsible for writing the procedures (in other words, which tribe). The second challenge is easier to address than the first. I strongly urge any organization to let persons closest to the process either write the procedure or at least actively participate in the process (see point 8 on page 173). If one chooses that path, the decision as to how much detail needs to be included usually resolves itself. Consequently, to bring about changes in tribal behavior without simultaneously alienating the various tribe members, one must practice intense and repeated communication and training (one of the requirements of ISO 9001 and ISO 9002).

Where Do I Begin?
This is one of the most often asked questions. The answer depends on where your company stands along the broad spectrum of quality

assurance. Irrespective of how sophisticated your quality assurance system is, basically three options are available: (1) you can either start from your lower procedure (tier four) and work your way up to the quality manual (tier one), (2) you could reverse the process and start with the quality manual, or (3) utilize a combination of both (that is, start simultaneously from the bottom tier and the top tier, fine-tuning the system as conflict occurs.

Although all three options have advantages and disadvantages, I would recommend option two, particularly for organizations that do not have a quality manual or a well-defined quality assurance system.[2] Working on developing the first draft of your quality manual is helpful because it allows those in charge of implementation to proceed methodically through each of the clauses. The intent is not to rush toward a final version of the manual, indeed, that would be unwise since the manual's contents are likely to change several times during implementation. The ultimate objective is to ensure that all of the requirements have been addressed and are implemented, or are in the process of being implemented.

There are at least six possible scenarios.

1. You might already have a quality manual that covers more than is required by any of the ISO 9000 standards. That might appear to be an enviable situation, however, beware that auditors will have to audit whatever system you present. Consequently, although they will only be able to raise nonconformances relating to the ISO 9000 series standards, auditors can, and will, verify the effectiveness of your quality assurance system. Always remember that the primary issue is not so much how extensive and detailed your quality assurance system is, but how the documented system effectively covers all of the ISO 9001, ISO 9002, or ISO 9003 requirements.

2. The quality manual only addresses a few of the ISO 9000 requirements. In such a case, your task will be to map what is covered by the manual and address what needs to be written.

3. The quality manual is a 500-page document that contains every procedure: standard operating procedures (SOPs), calibration instructions, operating instructions, and more. My advice would be to remove

so-called tier two and tier three documents (departmental SOPs and operating or operator [how-to] instructions), and ensure that the quality manual (tier one) covers all of the appropriate ISO 9000 clauses. The rationale for suggesting this approach is that it is easier to control a 30- to 40-page document than a 400- to 500-page document. Also, if you need to distribute the manual to customers, the distribution of a 400-page manual would not be practical, especially if the manual contains specific procedures.

4. The quality manual has little if anything to do with the ISO 9000 series of quality assurance. This is unlikely to happen, but if that is the case, purchase the standards, buy a few books, and start rewriting.

5. You already have a quality assurance system that resembles the ISO 9000 model. Since you do not want to or cannot disassemble your current system, you would like to know what to do. The usual strategy is to prepare a matrix that maps the pertinent ISO paragraphs to the current quality assurance system and include the matrix in an appendix.

6. You do not have a quality manual. What luck! You can start from scratch.

How Much to Write

Unfortunately (or fortunately depending on your point of view), there are no rules defining how much needs to be written (see next section); it really depends on the type of service. Nevertheless, since the leitmotif of the 1994 updates is: "The supplier shall establish and maintain documented procedures for . . . ," procedures will have to be written, but each user will have to determine how many are required in order to effectively run the business. Too many procedures and one runs the risk of bringing business to a halt; too few, and the auditors may have some difficulty accepting that the organization is in control. There is no need to debate whether or not the maintenance of documented procedures guarantees or indicates any form of control; the standards require users to maintain such documentation. (Figure 7.1 summarizes which strategy to adopt for these scenarios).

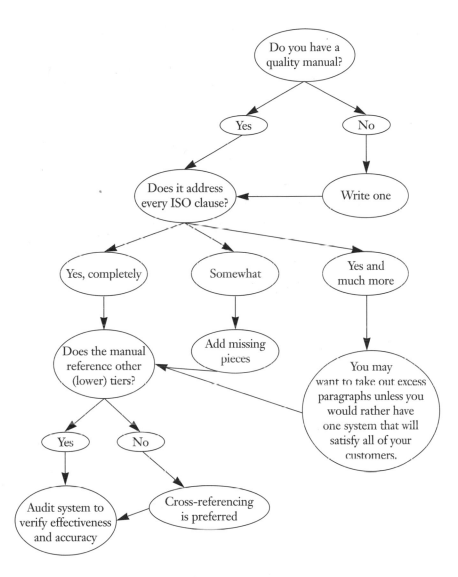

Figure 7.1. Questions to ask of your quality manual.

How Many Procedures Do I Need?

It is difficult to determine precisely how many procedures any organization will require. The number obviously will vary depending on the size of the organization and complexity of the service. Nonetheless, an estimate can be obtained by simply counting how many times reference to documented procedures are called for by the standards. Table 7.1 identifies each paragraph and subparagraph of ISO 9001 where specific references to documented procedures are made.

With the exception of a couple of paragraphs (notably 4.8 and 4.19) where documentation requirements are not phrased as a *shall* sentence, almost every clause has the words: "The supplier shall establish and maintain documented procedures. . . ." Thus, at a minimum, at least approximately 30 to 31 documented procedures will have to be identified either within the quality manual (tier one) or within lower tiers (two or three). Naturally, this does not include procedures invoked in paragraph 4.9 (work instructions) and calibration procedures called for in 4.11. No wonder many have referred to the ISO 9000 series as the documentation standards.

What Is a Procedure?

The *American Heritage Dictionary* defines a procedure as: "1. A manner of proceeding; way of performing or effecting something. 2. An act composed of steps; course of action. 3. A set of established forms or methods for conducting the affairs of a business, legislative body, or court of law."[3]

A procedure need not be a lengthy, detailed, and complex document. Before writing any procedure, consider the following universal laws of procedures.

1. Procedures have an inherent and incomprehensible tendency to mutate.

2. The more complex a procedure, the more likely it will mutate.

3. The older a procedure, the more difficult it is to recognize it.

Consequently, based on these laws, I would propose that you

1. Review your procedures on a regular and frequent basis (frequency to be determined by those most familiar with the procedure).

2. Write (if possible) simple procedures that will be easy to update.

3. Try to minimize the mutation factor by allowing flexibility.

Table 7.1. ISO 9001 references to documented procedures by paragraph.*

4.1.1 Quality policy	The supplier's management with executive responsibility shall define and document its policy for quality including objectives for quality and its commitment to quality.
4.2.1 Quality System (General)	The supplier shall establish, document and maintain a quality system as a means of ensuring that product conforms to specified requirements. The supplier shall prepare a quality manual covering the requirements of this International Standard.
4.2.2 Quality System Procedures	The supplier shall: a) prepare documented procedures consistent with requirements of this International Standard and the supplier's stated quality policy, and b) effectively implement the quality system and its documented procedures.
4.2.3 Quality Planning	The supplier shall define and document how the requirements for quality will be met.
4.3.1 Contract Review (General)	The supplier shall establish and maintain documented procedures for contract review and for the coordination of these activities.
4.4.1 Design Control (General)	The supplier shall establish and maintain documented procedures to control and verify the design of the product in order to ensure that the specified requirements are met.
4.4.2 Design and Development Planning	The supplier shall prepare plans for each design and development activity. The plan shall describe or reference these activities, and define responsibility for their implementation.
4.4.3 Organizational and Technical Interfaces	Organizational and technical interfaces between different groups which input into the design process shall be defined and the necessary information documented, transmitted and regularly reviewed.
4.4.4 Design Input	Design input requirements relating to the product, including applicable statutory and regulatory requirements, shall be identified, documented and their selection reviewed by the supplier for adequacy.
4.4.5 Design Output	Design output shall be documented and expressed in terms of requirements that can be verified and validated against design-input requirements.
4.6 Design Review	At appropriate stages of design, formal documented reviews of the design results shall be planned and conducted.
4.4.9 Design Changes	All design changes and modifications shall be identified, documented, reviewed and approved by authorized personnel before their implementation.

Table 7.1. *(continued)*

4.5.1 Document and Data Control (General)	The supplier shall establish and maintain documented procedures to control all documents and data that relate to the requirements of this International Standard including, to the extent applicable, documents of external origin such as standards and customer drawings.
4.6.1 Purchasing (General)	The supplier shall establish and maintain documented procedures to ensure that purchased product conforms to specified requirements.
4.7 Control of Customer Supplied Product	The supplier shall establish and maintain documented procedures for the control of verification, storage and maintenance of customer-supplied product provided for incorporation into the supplies or for related activities.
4.8 Product Identification and Traceability	Where appropriate, the supplier shall establish and maintain documented procedures for identifying the product by suitable means from receipt and during all stages of production, delivery and installation. Where and to the extent that, traceability is a specified requirement, the supplier shall establish and maintain documented procedures for unique identification of individual product or batches.
4.9 Process Control	Controlled conditions shall include the following: a) documented procedures defining the manner of production, installation and servicing, where the absence of such procedures could adversely affect quality.
4.10.1 Inspection and Testing (General)	The supplier shall establish and maintain documented procedures for inspection and testing activities in order to verify that the specified requirements for product are met.
4.10.2 Receiving Inspection and Testing	Verification of the specified requirements shall be in accordance with the quality plan and/or documented procedures.
4.10.3 In-process Inspection and Testing	The supplier shall: a) inspect and test product as required by the quality plan and/or documented procedures.
4.10.4 Final Inspection and Testing	The supplier shall carry out all final inspection and testing in accordance with the quality plan and/or documented procedures to complete the evidence of conformance of the finished product to the specified requirements. No product shall be dispatched until all activities specified in the quality plan and/or documented procedures are available and authorized.
4.11.1 Control of Inspection, Measuring and Test Equipment (General)	The supplier shall establish and maintain documented procedures to control, calibrate and maintain inspection, measuring and test equipment (including test software) used by the supplier to demonstrate the conformance of product to the specified requirements.

Table 7.1. (continued)

4.11.2 Control Procedures	The supplier shall: f) assess and document the validity of previous inspection and test results when inspection, measuring and test equipment is found to be out of calibration.
4.12 Inspection and Test Status	The identification of inspection and test status shall be maintained, as defined in the quality plan and/or documented procedures, throughout production, installation and servicing of the product . . .
4.13.1 Control of Nonconforming Product (General)	The supplier shall establish and maintain documented procedures to ensure that product that does not conform to specified requirements is prevented from unintended use or installation. This control shall provide for identification, documentation, evaluation, segregation (when practical), disposition of nonconforming product and for notification to the functions concerned. Repair and/or reworked product shall be reinspected in accordance with the quality plan and/or documented procedure requirements.
4.14.1 Corrective and Preventive Action (General)	The supplier shall establish and maintain documented procedures for implementing corrective and preventive action.
4.14.3 Preventive Action	The procedures for preventive action shall include: a) through d) (not listed here)
4.15.1 Handling, Storage, etc. (General)	The supplier shall establish and maintain documented procedures handling, storage, packaging, preservation and delivery of product.
4.16 Control of Quality Records	The supplier shall establish and maintain documented procedures for identification, collection, indexing, access, filing, storage, maintenance and disposition of quality records.
4.17 Internal Quality Audit	The supplier shall establish and maintain documented procedures for planning and implementing internal quality audits to verify whether quality activities and related results comply with planned arrangements and to determine the effectiveness of the quality system.
4.18 Training	The supplier shall establish and maintain documented procedures for identifying training needs and provide for the training of all personnel performing activities affecting quality.
4.19 Servicing	Where servicing is a specified requirement, the supplier shall establish and maintain documented procedures for performing, verifying and reporting that the servicing meets the specified requirements.
4.20.2 Statistical Techniques Procedures	The supplier shall establish and maintain documented procedures to implement and control the application of the statistical techniques identified.

Note: For ISO 9002, paragraph 4.4 (and all subsequent subparagraphs within 4.4) does not apply. For ISO 9003, the requirements for documentation are the same except that they apply to fewer paragraphs.

This last criteria may be achieved by viewing procedures as guidelines rather than precise documents. Naturally, there are cases where procedures must be followed to the letter in order to guarantee quality of the output. In such cases, precise, step-by-step procedures will be called for. Still, the three laws would apply.

When confronted with the task of writing procedures one is faced with two choices: (1) write detailed procedures, or (2) write generic guidelines. It is difficult to suggest which approach would best suit your needs because it all depends on the nature of your business (and hence, processes) and/or the amount of training and/or knowledge already imparted to the employees. One approach I would suggest (which may not be practical for all industries) is to first draft a general guideline (or set of guidelines) and let the users of these guidelines write in the additional missing information required to perform the task. Within a few weeks you should have a fairly good procedure that should satisfy everyone.

Writing Procedures

I am often asked: "How should we write procedures?" "How much detail should we include?" "How would the auditor look at our procedures?" The last question is perhaps the easiest to answer because a third-party auditor should only verify that the procedure is up-to-date and currently being followed. The most common task of an auditor, regarding procedures, is to ensure that they are under document control, that they are not obsolete, and that they reflect current practice. A third-party auditor should not tell you that he or she finds your procedures inadequate, yet some registrars will have auditors essentially dictate what they feel is an adequate procedure. Remember that the "I say so" registrars are more likely to have a precise idea as to how a procedure should address a particular paragraph. If you have selected a prescriptive registrar, you probably will have to spend a substantial amount of time justifying your actions.

By answering the last question, we have in essence answered the other two. Indeed, the amount of detail, format, structure, and number of procedures may depend not only on what you perceive to be adequate and sufficient to run your business, but also on which registrar you contract with. Always remember that as far as the standard is concerned, there is not a predetermined number of procedures that must be written. Moreover, documented procedures should be written "where the absence of such procedures could adversely affect quality." The decision as to what procedures might adversely affect the quality of your product is yours (or perhaps your customer), but not the registrar's. Unfortunately, too many applicants to ISO 9000 registration forsake their rights and essentially demand that the registrar tell them what is right or wrong, how much is enough, and so on.

There is little doubt that you will have to write procedures. The requirement to do so is evenly spread throughout all three standards. However, nowhere do the standards require that procedures be lengthy or detailed. They should address the requirements as specified in each standard, but do not forget the following key points (often ignored by some registrars).

1. "The design and implementation of a quality system will be influenced by the varying needs of an organization, its particular objectives, the products and services supplied and the processes and specific practices employed." (ANSI/ASQC Q9001, 1994, Introduction)

2. "It is intended that these International Standards will normally be adopted in their present form, but on occasions they may need to be tailored by adding or deleting certain quality system requirements for specific contractual situations." (ANSI/ASQC Q9001, 1994, Introduction)

3. "For the purpose of this International Standard, the range and detail of the procedures that form part of the quality system depend on the complexity of the work, the methods used, and the skills and training needed by personnel involved in carrying out the activity." (ANSI/ASQC Q9001, 1994, paragraph 4.2.2, Quality System Procedures)

These three clauses often lead to confusion and frustration on the part of the user. Let us look at some of the clauses of paragraph 4.10, Inspection and Testing.

> 4.10.1 General
> The supplier shall establish and maintain documented
> procedures for inspection and testing activities in order

to verify that the specified requirements for the product are met. The required inspection and testing, and the records to be established, shall be detailed in the quality plan or documented procedures.

4.10.2 Receiving Inspection and Testing

4.10.2.1

The supplier shall ensure that incoming product is not used or processed (except in the circumstances described in 4.10.2.3) until it has been inspected or otherwise verified as conforming to specified requirements. Verification of the specified requirements shall be in accordance with the quality plan and/or documented procedures.

4.10.2.2

In determining the amount and nature of receiving inspection, consideration shall be given to the amount of control exercised at the subcontractor's premises and the recorded evidence of conformance provided.

4.10.2.3

Where incoming product is released for urgent production purposes prior to verification, it shall be positively identified and recorded (see 4.16) in order to permit immediate recall and replacement in the event of nonconformance to specified requirements. (ANSI/ASQC Q9001, 1994, paragraph 4.10)

What are the main points required by these paragraphs? When interpreting a paragraph, it is important to consider all associated subparagraphs collectively. Thus, whereas we are told that "the supplier shall maintain documented procedures for inspection and testing activities . . ." (4.10.1), we also are told that, "in determining the amount and nature of receiving inspection, consideration shall be given to the amount of control exercised by the subcontractor's premises and the recorded evidence of conformance provided" (4.10.2.2).

This last statement complements paragraph 4.10.2.1, which states that the product may be inspected "or otherwise verified as conforming to specified requirements." Therefore, not all incoming products need to be inspected. In fact, it could be that your system relies on your sub-contractors' evidence of control (for which you should have records); consequently, you may perform very little, if any, receiving inspection. Moreover, in many industries including the service industries, the only specified requirements consist of a description of the product either by title or name and a quantity of items ordered. In such cases, no testing is performed and verification consists of a mere count and reading of the purchasing order. There is nothing wrong with these scenarios as long as the procedure(s) and their variations is/are documented either in the quality manual, quality plan, or perhaps in the receiving department.

A similar approach should be undertaken when addressing the documentation of procedures required by all other paragraphs. Still, the following question remains: "How does one determine if a procedure is required?" One fatuous argument often proposed is that an organization should have enough procedures to allow it to operate in the event that anyone should be absent from his or her post for any duration of time. Is that a reasonable proposition? Is it really possible to develop procedures for all possible job operations and, if so, is it possible to not only capture but also freeze all of the knowledge associated with that job? I do not believe such a task is possible, except in instances where the job or operation has been so specialized that a robot could perform the task. In such cases, the set of instructions might already have been automated to replace an operator who has inherited the task of maintaining the robot (potentially, another set of procedures). The standards do not expect one to develop hundreds of procedures. They recognize that training and/or knowledge acquired previously or on the job (see paragraph 4.18 of the standards) is acceptable.

The availability of documented procedures (in some cases detailed procedures) can be beneficial. A manager once told me that in the absence of the order entry clerk who was home sick with the flu, he was able to place an order using the company's computer simply because the clerk had just completed her order entry checklist (in preparation for

ISO 9000 registration). The manager conceded that the process had been tedious but achievable.

Would a third-party auditor expect to see order entry procedures and other similar procedures fully documented for each department throughout a company? Hopefully not, because that is not what the standards require. Writing and reading an order entry checklist/procedure might be relatively easy, but what about complex procedures consisting of 20 to 30 key steps and requiring special technical skills often only acquired with experience? Should these skills be documented for all to understand? I do not think so, unless you want to spend most of your life writing documents and then maintain them to ensure that they do describe current practice.

One of the obvious difficulties is that operators or supervisors who have learned to operate certain processes over the years are likely to be reluctant to document everything they know. Their position will likely be that there is little motivation for them to document their skills, besides even if they were to document their current job experience, it probably will not reflect what they will learn tomorrow and the day after tomorrow (hence the need to constantly update procedures).

We are still left with the final question: "Once it has been determined that a procedure must be developed or enhanced, how does one proceed?" If it has been determined that the procedure in question does influence the final quality of the product, as defined or perceived by the client, some form of control probably will have to be exercised. One method is to write a standardized operating procedure. Yet, when information is collected as to the official procedure, it is not uncommon to discover that two, three, or more variations of the same procedure may lead to identical final product quality. What then is the standardized procedure? It has been my experience that irrespective of the industry, the steps involved in procedures usually follow the well-known Pareto pattern. That is, 85 percent of the time the same set of steps or instructions will be followed except when (15 percent of the time) other (upstream) process variations or special customer deviations force an individual to adjust/modify or skip a subset of instructions. In such situations, my recommendation would not be to try to capture in a procedure all possible process variations generated 10 percent 15 percent of the time. Instead, focus on a description of the dominant process and explain that in special cases, the experience of the individual or supervisor is relied upon to satisfy requirements. You may conclude that these variations generated 10 percent to 15 percent of the time should be investigated under one of your corrective/preventive action procedures.

What to Do?

Achieving ISO 9000 registration need not be an unpleasant experience. If you follow the maxim: "Say what you do and make sure that you do what you say," you should experience few difficulties during the registration audit. In most cases, however, this simple rule turns out to be more difficult than anticipated because one must ensure that all of the *shall* requirements are satisfied. The following guidelines should help.

1. Recognize that the task of implementing an ISO 9001 or 9002 quality assurance system is a team effort. One person should not, nor cannot, attempt the task.

2. Obtain a 1994 copy of either ISO 9001 or ISO 9002 (ISO 9003 is not used very much for reasons stated previously). Ask yourself the following questions: "Are we doing any of this?", "Who would know?", and "Who/what do I need to help me implement this system?" The answer to these simple questions will require a few days. To facilitate the task you should

> a. Conduct a preassessment that will help you determine your current position with respect to the standard. The purpose of such gap analyses is to help the user determine how much work will be required. The simplest, but not necessarily most effective, way to conduct a preassessment is to simply rephrase each sentence of the standard into a question (some registrars issue free checklists).[4]

If you don't feel comfortable doing the preassessment, or if you believe subjectivity might interfere with your assessment (and I believe it will), you can always rely on a competent consultant—preferably one who is a certified ISO 9000 assessor.

3. Having completed tasks 1 and 2, you should now define your business objectives. This may seem an odd question to ask at this time, but I have found that firms often struggle with these issues. Yet, these are important questions to ask for they will help you address the very first paragraph of the standard, paragraph 4.1.1, Quality Policy, which states

> The supplier's management with executive responsibility shall define and document its policy for quality including objectives for quality and its commitment to quality. The quality policy shall be relevant to the supplier's organizational goals and the expectations and needs of its customers. The supplier shall ensure that this policy is understood, implemented and maintained at all levels of the organization.

When faced with the last paragraph, the natural tendency is to address the requirement by inserting an all-encompassing statement with the usual parade of cleverly interconnected buzzwords: "to be the best in our business," "to produce defect-free products," "to guarantee the highest return for our investors," "to be the best that we can be," "to strive for continuous improvement," "to empower our employees to be the best . . . ," and so on. When I read these generic statements, I often ask myself a couple of questions: "Is this a quality policy or a mission statement?" and "How do they measure their performance?" Indeed, it is relatively easy to claim that one is the best in the world, but how do you prove it? How do you measure your performance?[5]

A mission statement is *not* a quality policy. As explained in chapter 4, the quality policy is a subset that should complement the (global) mission statement. The following mission statement, formulated by Pat Riley, basketball coach of the New York Knicks, is as good an example of a mission statement as I have read in recent months.[6]

- Our culture is hardworking.

- We focus on defense.

- Our defense is aggressive.

- Our aggressiveness is domination driven.

Although Coach Riley does not specify what the Knicks' quality policy is, he does explain how he once instituted the Career Best Effort (CBE) with the Los Angeles Lakers. The CBE consisted of a set of 15 individual statistics used to compare a player against opposing players at similar positions. Measurement is of the essence in the fiercely competitive world of professional sports. Similarly, I would propose that in industry, as in professional sports, a policy that cannot be quantitatively verified is likely to be weak.

I also would recommend that after you have written your statement or resuscitated an old one, ask yourself if it indeed addresses the intent of paragraph 4.1.1. If answered affirmatively, you should question how you will monitor the effectiveness of the policy. In other words, which parameters would you need to monitor to measure the policy's effectiveness.

For example, if you are a distributor, your business objective(s) might be

Purpose: To distribute the right (state product[s] to our customers as rapidly as possible and in a cost-effective manner.

This brief statement would require defining at least three terms.

1. How will you measure the distribution of "right" products. What parameter(s) would you monitor. You also should consider which statistical technique would be best suited to effectively monitor the parameter(s).

2. What does "as rapidly as possible" mean: within 24, 48, or 72 hours? Rapidity may be a function of the type of customer or urgency of the order or a combination of other factors. This should be defined.

3. How would you measure a "cost-effective manner"? This may require you to investigate your various processing costs. Although that is not (yet) a requirement of any of the ISO 9000 standards, it is a very good idea. Besides, many customers require their suppliers to monitor their cost of quality.

After you have specified your (business) purpose and defined how you will monitor/measure it, you should have little difficulty formulating your quality policy.

4. Write the first draft of the quality manual as quickly as possible. I do not mean to suggest that the writing of the quality manual should be rushed, but that you should not delay the process (a common error). Use the format/structure of the standard to help guide you in your efforts. If you do not know how your organization currently addresses any one of the clauses simply paraphrase the standard and brainstorm whether or not the clause is pertinent to your type of service and if so, how you will address it. If the clause is not pertinent, and you have verified your conclusion with others, you still must justify your decision in writing. Please note that there are only a few paragraphs that may not be applicable—4.6.4.1 (Supplier Verification at Sub-contractors), 4.6.4.2 (Customer Verification of Sub-contracted Product), 4.7 (Control of Customer Supplied Product), 4.8 (Product Identification and Traceability), and 4.19 (Servicing).

5. You must next determine how the quality assurance system described in your quality manual will be subject to document control. This means, among other things that *all* documents that pertain to the quality system must be reviewed and approved by authorized personnel prior to issue. Moreover, any change to documents must also be approved by the same authority who performed the original review and approval.

It is important to address the document control issue early on because the tendency is to first generate documents only to realize later that each generated document that pertains to the quality assurance system must be controlled.

6. Do not assume that you will have to write hundreds of procedures. The best strategy to adopt is to use/rely/refer to as much as possible on your current system. For many organizations, some form of a system that parallels the 9001 or 9002 should be in place already. However, the system will likely be outdated and will need to be updated.

7. Determine who will write what and by when. Circulate procedures and/or documents for review. Repeat the review cycle two or three times until you have a satisfactory, but not necessarily perfect, draft. Do not spend too much time searching for the best sentence or word. That is not important at this stage. What is important is that you have an accurate draft that has the support of all parties.

8. The next task is to decide how many documented procedures will be needed. This is a difficult task. There are at least two major types of procedures: (a) standard operating procedures or guidelines designed to address the ISO clauses (but that allow for some latitude because employees have been properly trained) and (b) detailed operating/assembly (how-to) procedures typified by clause 4.9, Process Control or 4.15, Shipping, Handling, and Packaging. The first type of procedure should be relatively easy to develop. Since you will need procedures for almost every one of the ISO 9001, ISO 9002, or ISO 9003 clauses, you will need (at a minimum) approximately 17 to 20 procedures or guidelines (guidelines recognize that the operator has received training, has knowledge, and thus allows more flexibility). Determining how many of the second type of procedures are required is more difficult. Deciding on how much detail/information to include in these procedures is even more difficult. The right answer to these questions cannot be provided by a consultant, nor can it be provided by a registrar. It can only be determined by you, the local expert in your industry. In doing so, you should try to adhere to the following guidelines.

    a. Avoid writing detailed procedures.

    b. Whenever possible, rely on the people closest to the task to write the needed procedures.

    c. Avoid writing procedures that read like job descriptions. For departmental procedures, try to emphasize who your internal customers are, the department's value-added functions, and the output(s).

    d. Remember that anything written can and likely will be audited.

9. Within a few weeks after you have genuinely started implementation, begin planning the internal audit procedures. Start conducting and documenting your internal audits as soon as possible. This will allow you to: (a) rehearse your audit skills, (b) review the implementation process and simultaneously help resolve problems as they occur, and (c) allow everyone (auditors and auditees) to understand the purpose and process of an internal audit. I also suggest that at least one individual be trained in how to conduct internal audits. (*Note:* This does not mean that the individual(s) must participate in a lead assessor course.) For the first six to eight months, you may wish to schedule internal audits about eight to 10 weeks apart. The frequency should be reduced later.

10. Do not wait until you have reached what you think is perfection. After your second or third audit, call several registrars, get to know them, and select the one you feel is the most compatible (see Selecting a Registrar). Do not worry if the registrar does not seem to specialize in your particular area of manufacturing. Third-party ISO 9000 should not be confused with second-party audit where second-party auditors are more likely to tell their suppliers how to perform certain tasks. Moreover, although the ISO 9000 series originally was designed for the manufacturing world, the models were not designed for any particular industry. Therefore, I would propose that auditing to a generic standard does not demand auditors with special technical skills! Remember, third-party auditors essentially audit how your quality assurance system functions and whether or not trained people operate your processes. Auditors should *not* evaluate or question the technical competency of your system and processes.[7] Nevertheless, if you feel you must have a registrar or an auditor who has some technical expertise in your particular industry, by all means, hire their services. Be advised, however, that this will not necessarily facilitate your audit.

11. Schedule your third-party audit. Address nonconformances (if any), and obtain certification.

Selecting a Registrar

Selecting a registrar can be tricky because the selection process depends on many parameters, some of which may be intangible (such as personal preference). I have seen consultants produce a fancy decision matrix designed to supposedly help the user select the best registrar. I don't believe a matrix can substitute for common sense. If you export solely to the United Kingdom, you might want to consider a British registrar. If you export to several European countries, the selection process becomes more complicated because bilateral and multilateral agreements (between registrars) are not formalized. Strange as it may sound, you may want to select a non-EEC registrar or perhaps an approved American registrar. This may eliminate, or temporarily defuse, the current recognition bickering among European registrars. The reader should realize that ISO 9000 registration is big business and since the standard is an international one, the new theme of the political economy of quality is bound to emerge sooner or later.

Registrars come in a broad variety of profiles. At one end of the spectrum are registrars/auditors for whom ISO stands for: "I Say sO!" At the other end of the spectrum stand registrars for whom ISO means: "I Say shOw me!" As you might suspect, the "I say so" registrar is not likely to conduct a third-party audit from the same perspective as the "I say show me" registrar. "I say so" registrars are more likely to have a definite point of view on each and every one of the clauses. As far as they are concerned, there is but one way to interpret the clause, and they know that way. The "I say show me" registrars are not likely to be so affirmative and opinionated. Naturally, both are convinced they are correct in their interpretation of the standards.

As for auditors, they too come in a wide variety of types. However, in the case of auditors, things can get more complicated when one considers that there are at least two broad categories of auditors: industry specialists and generalists (each category having its own variety of psychological profiles). Combining the auditor dimension with the registrar dimension, one obtains the graph in Figure 7.2.

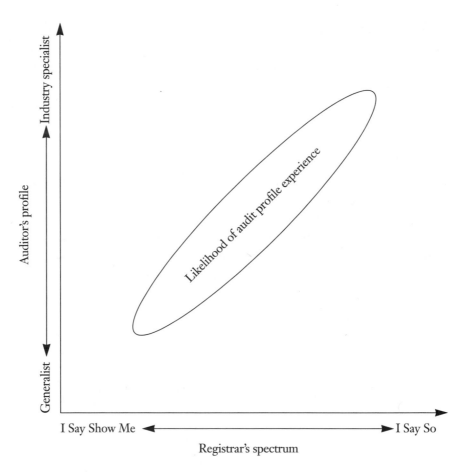

Figure 7.2. Registrar auditor space.

Of all the possible permutations along the likelihood of audit ellipse, I will focus on the two extremes: (1) Industry specialist coupled with the "I say so" registrar (type I), and (2) the generalist coupled with the "I say show me" registrar (type II). (*Note:* A third type often preferred by some registrars, combines the best of both worlds by teaming a generalist [lead auditor] with an industry specialist [auditor] who usually focuses on the process control and inspection paragraphs.) Although both types of auditors are likely to address the same issues, they will approach their role differently.

The typical type I profile would produce an audit whereby the auditor is more likely to be looking for industry-specific applications of each clause. In some cases, the registrar may even provide the auditor with a well-defined list of industry-specific questions to be appended to the ISO 9001, ISO 9002, or ISO 9003 checklist. This may appear to be beneficial to the customer, however, it must be remembered that the list of industry specific questions is only one registrar's interpretation of what should be implemented in order to properly satisfy a specific clause. This approach goes beyond the purpose of an ISO 9000 audit.

Much as the type I counterpart, the typical type II profile looks for evidence that all *shall* clauses have been effectively implemented. However, unlike the industry specialist, the generalist is less likely to have no predetermined ideas (or opinions) on how a clause must be implemented. The choice as to which profile best suits your needs is naturally yours.

In most cases, price differential should not be the decisive factor. Whatever you do, I would suggest that you contact at least three registrars. Get to know them and try to assess their auditing philosophy (in other words, profile). This is probably the most important criteria. The basic question you should ask yourself is: "Can I work with these people?" Or, better yet, since you are the customer and the registrars are the suppliers, why not practice your ISO 9000 skills and apply your supplier selection skills. The last thing you want to do is sign up with a registrar who does not share your interpretation of the standard. However, please don't get carried away. I have seen companies interview as many as nine registrars and ask all sorts of cleverly designed questions that had little to do with the important issues of registrar assessment. Actually, the difficulty is not likely to directly involve the registrar, but the auditors selected by the registrar to conduct the audit. If possible, try to have at least one dialog with the lead auditor. Finally, recognize that if you are genuinely interested in achieving registration, you eventually will become registered. Always remember that as of late 1993, nearly 2000 firms had already achieved some form of ISO 9000 registration. If they can, why can't you?

Conclusion

The implementation of a quality assurance system that will conform to the requirements of ISO 9001, ISO 9002, or ISO 9003, is a team effort. Even for small firms (in other words, less than 25 employees), the process must include as many individuals as possible. The more people are involved in the quality assurance system, the more likely the system will reflect current practices and successfully address each of the requirements. My final suggestion is that you start as soon as possible and do not be afraid to make mistakes. However, do recognize that you probably will have to revisit processes and procedures and modify, adjust, and fine-tune in an attempt to constantly improve, simplify, or consolidate processes. The system that you are about to (re)develop must always be tested for its efficiency and effectiveness. There is no need to implement a documented structure that may read very well, but has little to do with reality, or, worse yet, generates frustration everywhere. Always recognize that the purpose of internal audits and management reviews is not only to verify that a company is indeed doing what it says, but also to encourage its people to continuously improve the system's overall effectiveness. This can be achieved only by carefully listening to the internal customers—each of the individuals who has to live with the system on a daily basis.

Notes

1. Peg C. Neuhauser, *Tribal Warfare in Organizations* (Cambridge, Mass.: Ballinger Publishing Company, 1988).

2. The author and an associate have developed a window-driven software package (ISOFT) designed to help users interpret the 1994 standards and write a quality manual. Although not specifically written for the service industry, the software provides numerous comments, examples, and cut-and-paste features designed to help users prepare the first draft of a quality manual.

3. *American Heritage Dictionary* 2d ed., s.v. procedure.

4. I find the use of checklists (which consist of "yes," "no," or "N/A" answers) extremely limiting. There is more to implementation than a simple yes or no answer.

5. William E. Matthews observes that one of the traps of the generic vision/mission statement is that since it satisfies nobody, it infuriates nobody and thus the mission can be "conveniently put aside and forgotten except as a page (or two) to be incorporated in all official publications." W. E. Matthews, "The Missing Element in Higher Education," *The Journal for Quality and Participation* 10, no. 6 (January/February 1993): 103.

6. Pat Riley, "The Winner Within," *Success* (September 1993): 39.

7. This may not be the case for certain manufacturers of so-called regulated products for which the CE mark is required by members of the European community. In such cases, a notified body with expertise in the particular product will audit the product and the associated processes.

8   Where Is the ISO 9000 Series Heading?

The generic nature of the ISO 9000 series is such that it can be applied to just about any process within any industry. Whether it should or should not be applied to all industries remains questionable. This chapter explores whether or not the ISO 9000 series is for everyone and concludes with some observations regarding the future of the series.

Some Unexplored Advantages of Obtaining ISO 9000 Registration

From time to time, I have wondered why insurance companies do not encourage their clients to register their quality assurance system to one of the ISO 9000 standards. The basic premise would be that firms that achieve ISO 9000 registration would offer a lower risk and thus deserve some discount. Naturally, I do not know whether or not the premise is correct; the hypothesis is well worth verifying.[1]

Banks also could request firms that are not solvent or are on the verge of bankruptcy to develop and implement an ISO 9000 registration plan before granting additional loans. The exercise could be beneficial only to all interested parties.

Is ISO 9000 for Everyone?

One of the reasons for the rapid growth in ISO 9000 registration in the United States is that as firms achieve ISO 9000 registration, they often require their supplier to get registered. The process cascades downwards until eventually small firms of half a dozen or less employees are forced to consider ISO 9000 registration. There are a variety of reasons why a firm would require its suppliers to achieve ISO 9000 registration. My purpose is not to review the reasons, but to ask if the cascading process is wise. The following scenario illustrates this point.

As an increasing number of oil companies (high-order firms) register their refineries to ISO 9002, they could cascade the registration process down to their retailers. Gas stations (low-order firms) could achieve ISO 9000 registration. However, one must ask why and what would be the benefits? For the majority of gas stations, especially those that only pump gasoline, I seriously doubt there is any value in achieving ISO 9000 registration. As a customer, I am not sure I would see the benefits. After all, the specifications for the gasoline have been set by the supplier: low octane (85–88) or high octane (91–92). The product comes either as leaded, unleaded, or diesel. The pumps, which are calibrated at a certain frequency by state agencies, appear to deliver the correct quantity. The price is adjusted every week (usually to match the station across the street). Finally, if I want to clean my windshield—a service within a service rarely provided nowadays—I usually have all of the necessary ingredients and tools at my disposal. What else would I need that ISO 9000 registration could provide?

I believe there is a threshold below which a service would not gain anything by achieving registration. Since it is unlikely that motorists will ever demand that their gas station achieve ISO 9000 registration, I doubt that the phenomenon will occur soon.

Nonetheless, there is a possible application if the gas station doubles as a convenience store that offers car wash, food, and other services. In such cases, where a multitude of services are offered, registration may not be such a silly idea after all. Still, I do not envision customers lining up at the counter inquiring as to when their favorite gas station will be "ISO registered." Clean facilities and fast service are their primary concerns.

The same could be said of dry cleaners and a host of other low-order services (barber shops, pet grooming, pet food supply stores, tanning salons, and so on). This does not mean that, in most cases, the application of the ISO 9000 series to these services is ill-suited, for it is not. In fact, if a dry cleaner or a gas station were to begin advertising that it had achieved ISO 9002 or ISO 9003 registration, and if customers could notice a significant improvement in the service, it is likely that others within the industry would soon apply for registration.

I can think of other services that could benefit from ISO 9002 registration, but are not likely to ever consider it. The lawn mower dealer where I first took my lawn mower for repair could certainly improve his service image. After a four-week wait I had no choice but to retrieve my lawn mower and take it to another dealer whose facilities did not look any more promising, but who at least promised to have it repaired within seven to 10 days (*Note:* I think he actually did it in 12 days; still that is better than four weeks.)

Similarly, despite talk in September 1993 about TQM within the federal government, I do not foresee federal agencies, such as the IRS, or state agencies, such as the state highway patrol, rushing toward ISO 9000 certification. Indeed, let us examine the possibility of applying one of the ISO 9000 standards to the state highway patrol (basically an enforcing agency responsible for inspection, verification, and control) of your local state. What would be the difficulties?

To begin with, let us ask one very important question: "Who is the customer?" In fact, one can even go further and ask if the state highway patrol has customers in the ISO 9000 sense of the word. I believe that is one of the primary (unrecognized) difficulties faced by anyone who tries to implement a quality assurance program within any governmental (and hence monopolistic) agency. I am not suggesting that officials within the state or federal agencies are not aware of the fact that they have customers. Since many state and federal officials are likely to have attended one or more seminars on TQM, one can assume that the notion of internal and external customers is understood. Still, difficulties abound, as the following brief anecdote will illustrate.

On a flight to Washington, D.C., I happened to be sitting next to an official from the Bureau of Soil Conservancy (I no longer recall the exact title of his office). One of the functions of the bureau is to ensure that farmers throughout the United States do not overplow their fields and thus increase the chances of serious loss of topsoil via eolian (wind) or runoff erosion. Our conversation drifted to the subject of quality and TQM in particular. When I asked the individual, "Who are your customers?" his reply was: "Congress and field services *(our internal customers)*." After a brief pause, he added, "Of course, our field staff is close to the farmers . . . I suppose that farmers are our customers." I believe the gentleman's answer to be revealing because the idea of farmers as customers only occurred to him last. Congress was/is his first customer.

Of course, one could argue that farmers can perhaps influence congresspeople, who in turn may influence the bureau. Nevertheless, I would propose that Congress was mentioned first because it has more clout (budgetwise) as an entity than the millions of individual farmers. Thus, although the intellectually correct answer to my question is "farmers," the fact remains that Congress is the ultimate customer. If Congress wants the bureau to be ISO 9001 or ISO 9002 registered, the bureau will achieve registration. If farmers want the Bureau to achieve ISO 9001 or ISO 9002 registration, they probably will have to wait a long time.

Returning to the state highway patrol, when a patrolperson, who has an enforcement monopoly on interstate highways, stops me for exceeding the speed limit do I become a customer? Do I willingly purchase the traffic violation? Can I negotiate the fee? What would be the contract review phases? Certainly, I could challenge the citation, but that is not always practical, particularly if I am ticketed 1000 miles from home.

In this, and similar cases, although the agency (state highway patrol) provides a variety of services to society (which in some states seem to focus on rigorously enforcing the speed limit), these services are not purchased on the market. This does not mean that the state highway patrol agencies do not have to satisfy certain requirements—they do. However, in this case the requirements are not set by motorists, but are linked to various federal laws and/or highway funds.

Still, suppose one could argue that there is a customer supplier relationship. Other difficulties emerge. If the state patrol attempted to achieve ISO 9002 (or would it be ISO 9003?) certification, it would have great difficulty explaining how patrol persons enforce the enforcement process. Everyone knows that if the highway patrol really wanted to strictly enforce the 55 mph or 65 mph speed limit, they would constantly stop motorists. Fortunately, most state patrol officers allow for an unspecified upper limit (which varies from state to state). In the state of Washington, known for its less than lenient enforcement of the speed limit, the unspecified and unofficial upper limit seems to be around +5 to 8 mph. In other words, in a 55 mph zone you may safely proceed at around 60 to 63 mph and not be stopped. In a 65 mph zone, you may push the limit to around 70 to 73 mph. As an auditor, one would like to know how and why these deviations from procedures, which are laws, are implemented. The why is relatively easy to explain. Most patrol officers would probably argue that there are so many violators, they simply cannot ticket everyone. And yet, within the manufacturing world, some experts would say, "If you can't maintain the specs, change them." A wonderful idea, but unfortunately neither the state patrol nor the millions of drivers set the speed limit—the federal government sets speed limits on interstate highways and the state patrols are left with the task of enforcing them.[2]

How each state enforces the law, or deviations from the law, is more difficult to explain and may have something to do with yet another clause of the standards—Control of Inspection, Measuring, and Test Equipment. If the state patrol was ISO 9002 registered, motorists who are pulled over for speeding could ask some pertinent questions such as: "Excuse me, officer, but when was your radar last calibrated?", "Could I see your calibration records?", or, better yet, "Are you sure I was going 74 mph? What is the accuracy of your radar?" Come to think of it, I believe it might be a good idea to require all state highway patrol to be ISO 9002 registered. But who will be empowered to do the requiring, drivers or state agencies?

Based on these scenarios, one can conclude that after an individual is recognized as a customer, she or he must have enough clout to force a supplier to achieve ISO 9000 registration. If either of these conditions are not satisfied, then one can assume that a supplier is unlikely to ever be forced to consider ISO 9000 registration unless pressured to do so because of some real or perceived/imaginary loss in market share. In other words, the larger the customer base, the less likely a firm is to achieve ISO 9000 registration. Thus, firms who rely on thousands, tens of thousands, or even millions of customers for their economic well being are unlikely to ever be forced to consider ISO 9000 registration simply because each customer contributes an infinitesimal percentage of the company's total sales. Similarly, organizations that have a large market share also are unlikely to voluntarily seek ISO 9000 registration unless they have significant exposure in Europe and/or are requested to achieve registration.

Where Is the ISO 9000 Series Heading?

Is the ISO 9000 series guaranteed long-term success or is it headed for oblivion? It is unlikely that the series will be headed for oblivion soon. Based on the current sustained interest in the ISO 9000 series, particularly from the various organizations associated with the monitoring, accreditation, and regulation of the ISO 9000 series, one can safely conclude that ISO 9000 is too big a business to disappear soon. But, what is meant by soon? Will the ISO 9000 series last another decade? It depends on how many firms will be required (as opposed to need) to be registered. Preliminary evidence indicates that more and more customers are routinely requiring their suppliers to achieve ISO 9000 registration to reduce or eliminate the current cost of conducting second party (in other words, customer) audits. If one assumes that there are approximately 350,000 manufacturing and nonmanufacturing firms that could require ISO 9000 registration and that only 15 percent of them (50,000 to 55,000 firms) will eventually be required to achieve registration, how long would it take to register all 55,000 firms? Assume that the top 20 registrars can perform, on average, a demanding 120 registrations per year. At a rate of approximately 2500 registrations per year it would take over 20 years to register all firms.[3] Since a firm is not likely to want to wait more than a few weeks to achieve registration, what must happen? Either more registrars will have to be formed (53 currently formed), more auditors will need to be trained (which is happening), or less firms will become registered and the registration process will simply slowly fade away. Regardless of which scenario occurs, one thing is certain, the ISO 9000 phenomenon is very likely to be around for the next three to five years. By then (1997 to 1999) the process will have to be revised and new predictions will no doubt be forecast.

Finally, one would hope that the various committees in charge of updating the ISO 9000 series resist the temptation of transforming the standards into a series of increasingly prescriptive documents. Chapter 2 explained that the standards were influenced by Mil-Q-9858 and other military standards. I should clarify that these comments are not a criticism of the Mil-Q-9858 document, which has aged rather well, but at the bureaucracy that surrounds its official enforcement. Indeed, as Ryan Bradley explains in an unpublished paper.[4]

> In the areas of quality standards and management, DoD needs to shift emphasis from dictating quality programs and measuring procedural compliance with military standards, to a focus on processes related to products (services, supplies, software, and technical data) that are provided under a contract. *Different types of acquisitions and industries will have different approaches.* Improved quality in design of processes and products is the key to higher quality in new acquisitions, while reprocurements need to get the best out of existing technical data. A cooperative effort between program offices, industry, and contract administration offices is needed to recognize new quality system models and find more efficient and economical means to deliver products that meet program need.
>
> Despite the significant contribution made to the field of quality, the military standards have themselves become *costly to administer* and an *impediment* to the integration of military and commercial industries. DoD and defense prime contractor practices have emphasized surveillance of procedures and documentation to show compliance with an increasingly restrictive interpretation of the military standards. *A focus on detailed requirements, audits, and documentation has inhibited*

innovation and limited resources that might otherwise be
available to develop more capable and efficient processes. . . .
Contractor and Government contract quality assurance
practices related to the standards need to change.

The reference to administrative costs mentioned by Bradley cannot be ignored. The cost associated with issuing and monitoring standards (in other words, bureaucracy) can quickly become staggering and, if not monitored, lead to ludicrous situations as demonstrated by the following examples.

In 1907, the U.S. Army issued a *Signal Corps Specification, No. 486* entitled: "Advertisement and Specification for a Heavier-Than-Air Flying Machine." The document consisted of one page. On October 26, 1973, the federal government issued specification LLL-T-1332A. The five-and-a-half-page specification referenced six other specifications and two military standards: MIL-STD-105–*Sampling Procedures and Tables for Inspection by Attributes* and MIL-STD-129–*Marking for Shipment and Storage.* The scope of the specification reads as follows: "This specification covers both round and flat hardwood toothpicks." We have come a long way.

The concerns expressed by Bradley are shared by many businesspeople who must deal daily with various federal regulatory agencies. Reviewing the role of the Food and Drug Administration, ex-CEO W. Hunter Simpson notes:

> If our country is to remain competitive in the global business community, our country's regulatory agencies must change their perspective. Granted, regulation is needed in a complex society. But regulation needs a coat of common sense. When our regulatory agencies encourage their inspectors to come out shooting before they understand the nature of the target, then American business is doomed. Competition rather than over-regulation should be America's weeding agent. . . . Our regulatory agencies are not paid to be policemen. They are in business to protect public welfare.[5]

Of course, one would hope that ISO 9000 audits are not likely to be conducted with the same outlook as audits conducted by regulatory agencies. My hope is that the concerns expressed by Simpson will never be expressed by clients of the ISO 9000 registration process.

Similarly, when I express a hope that the ISO 9000 series does not become too prescriptive, I am not focusing so much on the standard, but on the emerging bureaucracy of registrars, accreditation agencies, course approval societies, auditor certification programs, and so on. The real danger may be associated with the army of interpreters who might lose sight of the standards' purpose and intent, which is to provide its vast array of users with a model of quality assurance. Let us hope the enforcer attitudes described by Bradley are not rediscovered by the ISO 9000 community of auditors or, worse yet, isolated committee experts.[6]

Reasons for Concerns—Some Comments Regarding ISO 9000-1

Upon reviewing 9000-1, *Quality Management and Quality Assurance Standards—Guidelines for Selection and Use,* one notices that the document's pagination has increased from seven to 17 pages. Although the scope is essentially the same, the amount of guidance has increased significantly from the 1987 edition. The Introduction section wisely reassures the reader that "The standards in the ISO 9000 family describe what elements quality systems should encompass but not *how* a specific organization implements these elements. It is not the purpose of these standards to enforce uniformity of quality systems." (ANSI/ASQC 9000-1, emphasis added). The standard then proceeds to offer numerous suggestions that go beyond the general intent of the standard's title. For example, after offering some opinions as to how a quality system should be evaluated, audited, and documented (4.9, Evaluating Quality Systems, and 5.0, The Roles of Documentation), contributors to the standard inform us that

> The ISO 9000 family is intended to be used in four situations:
>
> a) guidance for quality management;
>
> b) contractual, between first and second parties;

c) second party approval or registration; and

d) third party certification or registration.

The supplier's organization should install and maintain a quality system designed to cover all the situations (among those listed under a, b, c, and d) the organization meets.

Moreover, we are told that, "For situation a) this system will strengthen its own competitiveness to fulfill the requirements for product quality in a cost effective way."

The reader is thus told, without the support of any substantive proof whatsoever, that the ISO 9000 family can only increase one's competitiveness. Such self-serving comments should raise concerns. Indeed, not only are we told that the standards can be used in all situations, but the implication is that in view of the obvious economic and competitive rewards imparted by ISO 9000 registration, anyone in his or her right mind will surely see the advantages in seeking and achieving ISO 9000 registration. Although one cannot deny that achieving some form of ISO 9000 registration can bring about (for an indeterminate period of time) certain competitive/marketing advantages, it is still much too early to determine the long-term benefits.

Of particular concern to this author is that references to other standards are now called for. Indeed, perhaps one of the most significant new additions to the 9000-1 standard is section 7 entitled, Selection and Use of International Standards on Quality, in which several new standards are introduced as "guidance standard." In view of this new development, the obvious questions are: "How many more guidelines will be produced by the various ISO technical committees over the next few years?" and "How long before these guidelines become incorporated within the ISO 9001, ISO 9002 and ISO 9003 standards?" (a phenomenon that has already occurred with the 1994 edition). Finally, "How will registrars interpret the incorporation of additional guidelines within ISO 9001, ISO 9002, and ISO 9003?" "Will they (registrars) treat the guidelines as official parts of the standards, and, if so, what will be the consequences for the eventual customer, in other words, the applicant to ISO 9000 registration?"

Will ISO Become ISOlated?

I first heard the suggested play on words when I was visiting a client in Oregon who had been assigned the task of implementing ISO at his plant. The individual in question had surrounded himself with ISO-related literature; this had led one of his co-workers to point out that he had become ISOlated. It occurred to me that the analogy was perhaps very relevant. Could it be that the many ISO 9000 committees, sub-committees, working groups, and technical committees (in other words, the community of experts) were becoming ISOlated from their ultimate customers? Attending meetings and reviewing the voluminous amount of memos and technical notes produced by the many committees, I had observed that the isolation process already was under way. The task of representing the ultimate customer is most difficult. The few delegates, rarely exceeding 20 individuals from perhaps as many countries, cannot possibly represent the opinions of millions of users. An argument could be made that since these delegates are experts in their field, they do know what is required. True as this may be, such arguments represent a dangerous attitude, as the following quotation illustrates.[7]

> In the audit function, there are examples of registration being granted before adequate assessment and imple-mentation have been achieved. There is a need to define audit as a base term so that others, such as those in occupational health and the environment (where the monitoring process, and the inspection of measurement results, are also called audits) are not confused by the multiple meanings of the term. We must determine if there is a need for clarification. *We, the experts, have a good understanding but the message must get to the broad client base.* A series of simple brochures is envisaged to create this understanding.

The reader should have noted the reference to experts having to con-vey the message to the client base (in other words, nonexperts). Also, note that simple brochures will have to be created to enlighten the broad base of client. One would hope that the various ISO committees do not adopt such sanctimonious attitudes. Unfortunately, there is good reason to believe that such sentiments, which can only lead to alienation from the so-called "broad base of clients," are not uncommon; certainly, other examples could be cited. Indeed, one of the emerging themes from the last international gathering in Budapest, Hungary, seems to be the reference to the "ISO 9000 family" of standards and guidelines. Despite objections from various members, the apparent intent is to generate more guidelines and eventually integrate all these guidelines in a holistic fashion. For example, one of the intents for the next series of revisions is to give more importance to the ISO 9004-1 document (*Quality Management and Quality System Elements*).[8] Consequently, as guidelines are generated, the various committees must find ways to ensure that the public at large will adopt these guidelines by whatever means possible. Naturally, all of this is done in the sacrosanct name of quality; therefore, how could it possibly be challenged? Moreover, the delegates who contribute to these standards usually approve most of them. I would simply ask the reader to consider the following question: "Do these delegates truly represent the millions of users who will now be impacted by the new standards?"

I will conclude by suggesting that the following observations made by Michael Scrage are worth considering: "Creating new standards is not like developing new products. Your competitive edge comes not from what you keep secret and proprietary, but from what you make open and accessible." Relating to the well-known success of Microsoft, Scrage notes that[9]

> Microsoft really isn't in the software business, it's in the standards business. Microsoft succeeds not because it writes the best code but because it sets the best standards. . . . Microsoft's goal was emphatically not the maximization of revenue or even market share; it was creating relationships with customers, software developers and microprocessor firms such as Intel to give as many good reasons as possible to support—strategically, financially and technically—Microsoft's operating systems. These networks of relationships . . . are what make a standard something more than a product. The standard is not the product of a company, it's the byproduct of these networks.

I believe that in order to avoid alienation, the various ISO 9000 committees should begin to develop the type of network relationships mentioned by Scrage. That is certainly good advice for all to follow.

Conclusion

Unlike the manufacturing, processing/assembly world where requirements for ISO 9000 registration may be mandated by European directives for regulated products or other motivations, the service industry is not yet required to achieve registration.[10] Consequently, the motivation to achieve registration is not as pressing. The purpose of this book has been to demonstrate that, with some thoughtful applications and adaptations, the ISO 9000 series of standards can be applied easily to most, if not all, service industries. The applications to monopolistic industries (cable companies, public utilities, phone companies) or industries that do not perceive themselves as an industry (education) is more tentative and even questionable. Yet, even in these cases, the limitations or constraints applied to only a few of the clauses.

In the Preface, the question was asked as to whether the application of ISO 9001, ISO 9002, and ISO 9003 standards to the service industry would make sense. Several chapters later, I believe one can conclude by stating that, if smartly applied, the ISO 9000 series can be of benefit to many services. A smart application of the standards does not mean that an entire series of guidelines would have to be written for each sector of the service industry. I firmly believe that with a minimum of guidance, users of the ISO 9000 series can successfully apply the standards to their industry. I would certainly hope that the service industry can learn from some of the mistakes made by the manufacturing, processing, assembling sector. For example, one of the classic mistakes is to view the standards as government regulations/requirements or assume that they are specifications. When viewed from that perspective, the natural tendency is to ask: "What must I specifically do to satisfy the requirements?" This question, or similar ones, are common from people who are first faced with the task of implementing the standards. This is understandable but unfortunate because, unlike mathematics, the implementation of the ISO 9000 series is not, nor can it ever be, an exact science. Yet, to some, that is precisely what was annoying about the (1987) standards; they were not precise enough; there was too much room for interpretation. To them, an inexact, poorly specified world is unbearable. To others, the motto would be: "The fewer rules, the better." As far as the ISO 9000 standards are concerned, I would side with the "fewer is better" faction; generic standards written for all cannot be prescriptive for the very reasons outlined in chapter 3. A sensible perspective should always be maintained. Professor Hitoshi Kume of the University of Tokyo summarized it best when he stated that.[11]

> The motivation for improvement does not exist in standards-regulated activities. Improvement occurs when people are constantly on the lookout for problems, are dissatisfied with the status quo, and have sufficient energy and vitality to improve it. This depends very greatly on individual attitudes and cannot be elicited by standards-based management alone.

Professor Kume's comments are wise. One of the purposes of this book has been to occasionally challenge the status quo and offer in the process a critical review of how the ISO 9001, ISO 9002, or ISO 9003 standards can be successfully applied to the service sector. I hope to have achieved these objectives to your satisfaction and thus help you reach a more informed decision and ease your task. The final challenge is yours.

Notes

1. I have recently learned that some insurance companies are very interested in pursuing ISO 9000 registration.

2. I realize that, in theory, there should be no distinction between taxpayers and the federal (or any other) government, but there is. I also realize that if enough taxpayers wanted to change the speed limit it could perhaps be done, but the efforts would be enormous.

3. If we assume further that each audit would consist of only 1.5 auditors per audit team (a conservative estimate), it appears that the ISO 9000 auditing market in the United States could absorb 3750 to 4000 auditors.

4. Ryan Bradley, "A New Look at DoD Quality Management and Quality System Standards." Washington, D.C. (July 4, 1993): 1, 2. Emphasis added.

5. W. Hunter Simpson, "Puzzling FDA Probe Unfair to Physio-Control," *The Puget Sound Business Journal* (September 17–23, 1993): 11. The valuable functions performed by the FDA must be recognized. For an interesting, if dated, look at the limited powers of the FDA in enforcing regulation see Selig Greenberg, *The Quality of Mercy* (New York: Atheneum, 1971), chapter 7.

6. Already, articles such as Dick Schaaf's, "The Case Against ISO 9000," are gaining some attention. See *Training Magazine* (September 1993): 5–10. In the United Kingdom, where the BS 5750/ISO 9000 series has been applied ever since the mid-1980s, users have begun to ask some important questions. I. E. Burrows in his "Never Mind the Width Feel the Quality—Ship Years of Ship Management Quality Assurance," concludes his thoughtful analysis of the registration process by concluding: "The author is extremely concerned that if care is not taken QA will become an end in itself. Things will be done not because they are right but because they suit QA. Sensibly used, QA should complement the operation not dictate it." Paper presented to the The Institute of Marine Engineers, London, February 2, 1993.

7. ISO/TC 176 N195, dated 1993-10-25, p. 3. Emphasis added.

8. One of the memos specifically refers to concerns relating to "insufficient prominence of the 9004-1 Guideline document as a precursor to the establishment of the selected Program Model." The memo concludes by stating, "This will hopefully change with eventual issue of the 1996 Revisions which will likely be substantial, hence the much wider concept now envisioned for 9004-1." CAC/ISO/TC176, SC2/WG12 WD ISO 9004-1.

9. Michael Schrage, "How the U.S. Won Round One in the Battle Over Standards," *Los Angeles Times*, 24 February 1994.

10. Besides the examples already mentioned (courier service), some services that operate overseas have been required to achieve registration in order to obtain contracts.

11. Quoted in *ISO 9000 News* 2, no. 6 (November/December 1993): 6.

Appendix A Sample Quality Manual

The following sample manual is based on ideas or practices derived from half a dozen consulting firms with which the author has been associated throughout the years. Four of the firms are major players in the TQM, corporate culture change, and other related activities. The other two are engineering consulting firms. Ironically, none of these firms have (to my knowledge) a quality manual, and a couple of them would have some difficulties implementing the very concept they preach. All of them have similar processes, yet none of them implement any of the procedures described in this manual. In most cases, parts of the procedures are implemented. One would have to search across firms to uncover the procedures as described herewith.

Since an increasing number of firms are relying on software to monitor their processes, documents, and document control requirements as specified by the ISO 9000 series of standards, it would appear logical for the fictitious Himalayas Consulting Group to also rely on a computerized system to manage its documentation and procedures. Although several documents (or files) are referenced throughout the manual, I have not included this second tier of documentation. The reader will no doubt be aware of the increasing number of computerized databases available (some of which appear to be good). I leave it to the computer experts to decide how to structure their local area networks and format the required data bases.

A software package (ISOFT) has been developed by the author and an associate. The software was developed for two reasons: to help individuals better understand the standards' requirements and to help users develop, with minimum effort, a first draft of their quality manual that would conform to the basic requirements of the ISO standards.

Himalayas Consulting Group
Quality Manual

Preface

The quality assurance manual of HCG is approved by the president and CEO of HCG.

Signed: *Oliver J. Cadish, President and CEO*

Version: 8/20/94   Last Update: 1/13/94 (see ARCHIVE file)

Contents

Quality Manual of the Himalayas Consulting Group

0.1 Purpose
This manual addresses the requirements stated in the ISO 9001 (1994) standard entitled: *Quality System—Model for Quality Assurance in Design, Development, Production, Installation and Servicing.*

0.2 Scope
The content of this manual applies to the Himalayas Consulting Group (HCG) located at 1515 N.E. 15th Avenue, Seattle, Washington 98008.

0.3 Document Control
The quality manual is electronically stored and can be accessed via our local area network. The electronic file is the only master copy. The file has a write protect status and can only be accessed and modified by the company's president or one of his or her delegates. The file is backed up daily and can be read and printed by any HCG employee. The manual's contents is reviewed twice a year. Updates, approved by the president, are inserted by one of his or her delegates. Records of all updates identifying the nature of the change, date of the change, and other pertinent information are automatically stored in an archive file. Outdated copies of the manual are automatically saved prior to updating the manual (see Document Control).

Copies of the manual distributed to clients are not subject to the above requirements and are therefore labeled "uncontrolled."

Reference: MIS programs ARCHIVE, SAVE, BACKUP, and QMANUAL

0.4 Definitions
Product: Within the context of HCG, the term *product* can either mean: consultancy or training services as they relate to the field of quality sciences and management (see 0.5, Types of Services). Service also is meant to include all subsequent reports produced as a by-product of consultancy or training.

Process: Either the consultancy or training process. By extension the term *process* can also mean the process of developing course material or seminar/workshop presentations as well as the process of report generation.

Nonconformity: There are two major types of nonconformities: (1) nonconformities caused by ambiguities in the contract, which lead to unexpected results, and (2) nonconformities in the form of inaccuracies (for example, typographical or spelling errors) found in reports.

Measuring instrument: A test or survey used to either assess someone's knowledge of a subject, measure socioeconomic or psychological dimensions, or collect statistics.

0.5 Types of Services

HCG was founded in 1985. It consists of a staff of six consultants, a librarian, a manager in charge of the management information system and computer network, a financial manager, two full-time assistants, and one part-time administrative assistant. HCG specializes in providing consultancy and training services in the field of quality assurance. HCG consultancy services include, but are not limited to, the following areas:

- TQM implementation and training
- Process optimization techniques, such as design of experiment, statistical process control, and other related techniques
- Just in time inventory
- ISO 9000 registration including: preassessment, document review, internal audit training, and implementation plan

References: Marketing brochures

1.0 Management Responsibility

1.1 Quality Policy

HCG designs each consultancy assignment to best suit its clients' unique and particular needs. As facilitator, our primary objective is to ensure that our clients' needs and expectations and objectives have been clearly defined, mutually agreed upon, and achievable. Our secondary objective is to rely on the vast experience of our associates to assist and guide our clients to reach their goals in an efficient and effective manner.

This quality policy is conveyed to every associate and employee who, in turn, is expected to practice it on a daily basis. Employees are encouraged to suggest improvements to the policy.

1.2 Organization

1.2.1 Responsibility and Authority

HCG's interface with its clients is broken down into five major activities: (1) preliminary or precontract phase, (2) contract proposal, (3) external (in other words, client) verification/approval, (4) implementation, and (5) report generation.

Activity	*Responsibility/Authority*
Precontract phase	President
Contract proposal	Lead consultant
External verification	Client/Lead consultant
Implementation	Lead consultant
Report generation	Consultant/Support staff
Document review	Librarian
Computer systems	MIS manager
Customer support	All staff

Customer dissatisfaction relating to any of the above activities are the responsibility of the lead consultant. With input and approval from the client, the lead consultant is responsible for initiating, recommending, implementing, and monitoring the effectiveness of corrective actions. Records of all corrective actions are maintained with the customer file.

(See Corrective and Preventive Action paragraphs).

1.2.2 Resources

Our current staff of consultants can adequately satisfy our clients' needs. Should additional resources be needed, HCG will either hire full-time or part-time consultants (see Assessment of Subcontractors).

All consultants have a masters degree or higher level of education and at least five years of experience in their field of expertise (see Training).

Although all HCG consultants are certified ISO auditors, internal quality audits are led by an outside lead auditor (see Quality Audits).

1.2.3 Management Representative

The responsibility and authority to oversee the implementation and effectiveness of this quality system is rotated once a year. The president assigns an internal consultant who is responsible for (1) ensuring that the current system conforms with the ISO 9001 model and (2) reporting (at least) biannually to management and staff the performance and effectiveness of the quality system (see Management Review and Internal Audits).

1.3 Management Review

The quality system is reviewed (at least) biannually by management. The purpose of these reviews is to monitor the suitability and effectiveness of the quality assurance system vis-à-vis HCG's quality policy. Any HCG employee can suggest improvement to the system via electronic mail. Suggestions are reviewed on a weekly basis for merit. If approved by the president or his or her delegate, they are inserted in the manual.

Computerized records of all reviews are maintained by the management representative in charge of quality assurance system maintenance. All records are maintained in a central computer file for a period of one year after which time they are archived for a period of seven years (see Quality Records).

2.0 Quality System

2.1 General

The present quality manual addresses all of the requirements required of the ISO 9001 standard.

2.2 Quality System Procedures

Procedures designed to satisfy the requirement of the ISO 9001 standard are identified in this manual.

2.3 Quality Planning

Requirements specified in this particular clause of ISO 9001 either do not apply or do not translate very well to HCG. Nevertheless, for each contract/project, HCG relies on two techniques to monitor client satisfaction: (1) periodic meetings with the client to assess whether or not objectives are met and (2) questionnaires (see form 1012). Special customer requests exceeding the criteria specified in form 1012 are identified in a separate quality plan prepared in cooperation with the client.

Reference: File 1012 in questionnaire folder

3.0 Contract Review

3.1 General

The contract review phase consists of two phases: precontract and contract proposal/review.

Precontract

Responsibility: HCG President

This phase consists of one or more initial contacts with a potential client. The purpose of this initial phase is to assess, formulate, and clarify the clients' requirements and determine whether or not HCG is capable of satisfying said requirements. If HCG determines that it can satisfy the client's need, a formal proposal is offered. Otherwise, the customer's file is closed.

Reference: Proposal folder

3.2 Proposal/Review

Once accepted a proposal is assigned a lead consultant. The lead consultant is responsible for clarifying any ambiguities raised during the precontract phase and to formulate a formal and detailed proposal complete with estimated milestones. All proposals, which must follow guidelines set in the Proposal Guidelines document, are reviewed by the president or one of his or her delegates.

3.3 Amendment to Contract and Records

The proposal is reviewed by the client for final approval. Any change to the proposal must be approved by both parties.

3.4 Records

Records of all correspondence and revisions are maintained in a computer file.

Reference: File maintenance procedure in Doc control folder; Proposal guidelines in proposal folder

4.0 Design Control

4.1 General
HCG designs consultancy assignments, seminars, training sessions, and workshops. The design phases are controlled by a series of guidelines that ensure the following activities take place.

4.2 Design and Development Planning
Within each contract is included a consultancy plan. Depending on the nature of the mission, the plan describes/identifies one or more of the following:

- The objectives and deliverables of the mission
- The project team which consists of the project leader and associates
- The responsibilities of each team member
- Preliminary GANTT chart and milestones
- Frequency of audits
- Operational variables used to assess progress

Changes that may affect anyone of the above items are reviewed by the client and project leader and, when mutually agreed upon, are recorded accordingly in the updated consultancy plan.

4.3 Organizational and Technical Interfaces
Since most assignments rarely exceed two to three consultants, the need for technical interface is not really pertinent to HCG. Nevertheless, should the need for technical expertise between various experts be required, these activities are defined within the consultancy plan.

4.4 Design Input
Within HCG, design input requirements will vary depending as to the nature of the assignment: consultancy, training, seminars, workshop, audit, preassessment, and so on. For each one of these activities, input parameters/requirements are negotiated with the client during the contract review phase. Input requirements are identified in the Deliverable section of the consultancy plan.

4.5 Design Output

At HCG, design output usually consists of the following:

For training: tests/questionnaires, surveys and/or interviews designed to verify on the job application of techniques

For workshops: either evaluation questionnaires and/or workshop assignments

For consultancy: Periodic interviews/survey of client's satisfaction (form 1012)

For seminars: Surveys

In most cases the client does not participate in the development of so-called design output. However, in cases where the client wishes to have particular topics or items inserted in lectures or assignments, these materials are, upon review by the project leader or consultant in charge, invariably inserted within the presentation.

4.6 Design Review

There are two types of design reviews: standardized presentation and customized presentation. Standardized presentations consist of seminar, training, or workshop materials (in other words, transparencies, course notes, and so on). In such cases, the client is encouraged to review the material and determine if it will satisfy his or her need. If modifications are needed, a customized presentation is prepared.

Customized presentations also can be reviewed by the customer prior to final printing. Changes must be approved by both the client's representative and the lead consultant/project leader. Records of all approved changes are kept with the appropriate design file.

4.7 Design Verification/Validation

Within HCG, verification and validation of the design can only be performed during presentation of the material. For training and workshop assignments, verification/validation consists of administering a survey designed by the consultant to measure the effectiveness of the material. Should the survey reveal deficiencies in the presentation, design changes are inserted.

4.8 Design Changes

All designed changes are approved by the consultant in charge of the particular design function.

References: Consultancy plan folder

5.0 Document and Data Control

5.1 General

HCG relies on a computerized database to control, via hierarchical passwords issued to employees, all of its quality assurance documents relating to this manual.

5.2 Document Approval and Issue

Computerized or hard copy documents relating to the quality assurance system are approved either by the president, the consultant in charge on the project, or the director of the management information system. In all cases, computerized files are the master file. Since a master file of all pertinent files/documents is automatically updated whenever any file is modified and since users only have access to the latest updated files, no invalid or obsolete copies are available. Printed copies are only valid the day they are printed.

5.3 Document Change

Changes to any document must be approved by the person responsible for the document(s). Changes are automatically archived in the archive file of the appropriate folder.

Reference: PASSWORD folder

6.0 Purchasing

6.1 General

HCG does not purchase product that must conform to particular specifications. Besides clerical support material, which is not subject to any particular set of requirements, products purchased by HCG only need to satisfy standardized industry requirements.

6.2 Evaluation of Subcontractors

HCG does not usually rely on subcontractors to perform its consultancy/training assignments. If assignments are subcontracted, HCG relies on a small pool of individuals who have been recommended.

Prior to assigning any job to a subcontractor, HCG first interviews the selected candidate to determine whether or not special training will be required.

Once retained, the subcontractor becomes HCG certified and his or her name is retained on file (see Approved Subcontractors file).

6.3 Purchasing Data

With the exception of software and books, HCG does not purchase product that is incorporated in the final service. For software and books, the usual information is captured by the purchasing order.

Prior to release, the purchasing order is verified for inaccuracies by the person placing the order.

6.4 Verification of Purchased Product

6.4.1 Supplier Verification at Subcontractor

Given the scope and nature of HCG's services, this paragraph is not applicable. Should the need arise or an application found, it will be addressed.

6.4.2 Customer Verification of Subcontracted Service

Services are rarely subcontracted. However, should any part of a consultancy assignment be subcontracted, the client will be informed of the decision and will be given the option to approve the subcontractor.

7.0 Control of Customer-Supplied Product

If a client wishes to submit to HCG a particular set of materials to be incorporated within HCG's presentation, the lead consultant will review the material to determine its suitability. Depending on the nature of the information, legal council may be sought to protect both parties. Addendums will be inserted in the contract to address such cases.

8.0 Product Identification and Traceability

Identification and traceability is not a particular requirement of HCG's clients. Documents are identified within computerized folders by client's name, project title, and date of issue.

9.0 Process Control

The manufacturing process control requirements relating to production, installation, and servicing as required by the ISO 9001 standard (subparagraphs a–g) are, for the most part, not applicable to consultancy/training services.

The production and control of consultancy services are determined within the design control and are specified in the consultancy plan. The delivery of services specified in paragraph 0.5 is the product installation. These installations require no set of procedures as they rely on the individual training and experience. Nonetheless, video and written materials are available as reference materials in the library (see Training).

Besides the use of flip charts, overhead projectors, books or supporting material, and video equipment, no special equipment requiring special approval is used during any of the production and installation phases.

Servicing consists of the consulting support (phone, mail, electronic mail, or fax) provided throughout the life cycle of a project and even after the project is terminated (see Servicing).

All materials prepared for presentation or training must follow the general guidelines set in the presentation guidelines folder. Prior to release, all materials are reviewed by the librarian for conformance assessment.

References: Presentation guidelines folder
Presentation video

10.0 Inspection and Testing

10.1 General

Inspection activities are performed by the lead consultant and the librarian.

10.2 Receiving Inspection and Testing

10.2.1 Testing inspection is not applicable to HCG processes. Receiving inspections are performed during the precontract, contract review, and design control phases. Since HCG does not include incoming products in its processes, the receiving inspection consists of verifying that customer requirements are adequately defined and translated into deliverables.

10.2.2 This paragraph is not applicable.

10.2.3 This paragraph is not applicable.

10.3 In-process Inspection and Testing

Whenever an assignment must be customized to a particular set of client requirements, the client and the lead consultant are in frequent communication to ensure that the deliverables meet the customer requirements as specified in the consultancy plan. Such activities, however, do not result in a formal in-process inspection. Such activities are performed during final inspection prior to releasing the product.

10.4 Final Inspection and Testing

Whenever surveys, questionnaires, or tests must be customized, they are tested for adequacy (see 4.11). Final inspection consists of reviewing with the client the final product (for example, workshop material, course content, seminar presentation) to ensure that it meets objectives/deliverables stated in the consultancy plan.

No product is released unless officially approved by the client. Adjustments and corrections are reviewed by both parties. Such approvals may be waived by the client. The final release of a document or product consists of the final draft approved/signed by the lead consultant.

10.5 Inspection and Test Records

Release of the final document or set of documents by the lead consultant constitutes the inspection record.

11.0 Control of Inspection, Measuring, and Test Equipment

11.1 General

HCG does not use instruments/equipment hardware. HCG's instruments consists of soft measuring tools, such as tests, questionnaires, or surveys. As with hardware, these instruments need to be verified for accuracy. Since national standards are unavailable, calibration techniques do not apply. If required, HCG relies on statistical techniques designed by psychometricians and statisticians to measure the repeatability and reproducibility of some instruments. Data control is done via routine statistical procedures found in most commercial statistical packages.

11.2 Control Procedures

Control procedures as specified in paragraph 4.11.2 a–i of ISO 9001 not only do not apply, but are not required by our clients.

Reference: Statistical package

12.0 Inspection and Test Status

Inspection status does not extend beyond requirements specified in paragraph 4.10.

13.0 Control of Nonconforming Product

13.1 General

Nonconforming product consists principally of either (1) presentation material that serves the intended purpose as specified in the consultancy plan, or (2) presentation material that contains errors (in other words, typographical errors). The first type of nonconformity is essentially nonexistent thanks to our in-process and final inspection processes. Should nonconformity occur it is handled as per paragraph 13.2 The second type of nonconformity is also handled as per 13.2.

13.2 Nonconforming Product Review and Disposition

a) The lead consultant is responsible for the review and disposition of all nonconformity relating to the consultancy plan as well as verifying the accuracy of all reports.

b) The secretarial staff is responsible for verifying spelling and correct formatting of reports.

Nonconformities relating to paragraph a can either be rewritten or accepted as such. Nonconformities relating to paragraph b must be corrected and resubmitted. In both cases, corrections are verified by the appropriate authority prior to final release. In both cases, records of the so-called nonconformity need not be maintained.

14.0 Corrective and Preventive Action

14.1 General
HCG always strives to improve any of its processes via its process of biweekly continuous improvement staff meetings.

14.2 Corrective Action
The purpose of these meetings is fourfold.

1. To review internal and external customer complaints

2. To investigate the cause(s) of complaints/nonconformity

3. To determine what corrective action may need to be implemented

4. To monitor effectiveness of corrective action

Reference: Minutes from meetings

14.3 Preventive Action
Preventive action is the responsibility of all HCG employees. Any opportunity to detect or otherwise eliminate potential causes of non-conformities are processed via the continuous improvement meetings. Solutions and/or suggestions approved by consensus, are first tested for effectiveness prior to being formally incorporated within the system.

15.0 Handling, Storage Packaging, Preservation, and Delivery

15.1 General
Procedures for this paragraph are covered in sections 15.2–15.6 of this manual.

15.2 Handling
Since the delivered products are not handled, this paragraph does not apply to the type of services provided by HCG.

15.3 Storage
Documents are stored in electronic media (in other words, diskettes or computer mass storage). Besides file back up and storage of diskettes and other related magnetic storage equipment in an air conditioned environment, no additional special storage requirements are provided. Should a need for additional storage procedures be determined, they shall be developed as needed (see MIS BACKUP procedures).

15.4 Packaging
No special packaging material, beyond the use of standard cardboard boxes and peanuts, is required for the delivery of product.

15.5 Preservation
Product does not need to be preserved.

15.6 Delivery
HCG relies on the service of an ISO 9002 registered courier service for the delivery of all its documents.

16.0 Control of Quality Records
Quality records pertaining to this quality assurance system are fully computerized. All aspects relating to identification, collection, indexing, accessing, filing, of said records are specified in MIS procedure FILE MAINTENANCE.

Computerized records are stored in hard disks, diskettes, or backup tapes. Unless otherwise specified (in the retention field), all computer records are archived for seven years on CD ROM.

Reference: MIS FILE MAINTENANCE

17.0 Internal Quality Audits
The quality assurance system herewith described is audited twice a year by HCG internal staff with the assistance of a third party. The auditing is performed by personnel independent of those having direct responsibility for the activity being audited.

Results of the audits are documented in the AUDIT folder and distributed to the appropriate manager via E-mail. Unless otherwise mutually agreed upon, the manager is expected to propose corrective actions within 21 working days. The effectiveness of the corrective action is verified during follow-up audits.

Reference: AUDIT folder

18.0 Training
Consultants working at HCG are selected on the basis of their education (masters degree or doctorate) and years of experience (five or more years). The support staff is selected based on a particular set of skills that

emphasize computer literacy. The identification of training needs is the responsibility of both management and the staff. Records of training is maintained by the finance manager.

19.0 Servicing

Although servicing is not a specified requirement of our customers, HCG does service its expertise long after an engagement is terminated. Consequently, even after completion of a mission, consultants are expected to answer phone inquiries not only from clients but also from ex-clients.

20.0 Statistical Techniques

20.1 Identification of Need

When the need to verify statistical process capability arise, HCG will implement meaningful and effective statistical control.

20.2 Procedures

Not applicable until 20.1 becomes effective.

Appendix B   The ISO 9000 Series and the Software Industry

Starting in 1992, the ISO 9000 series began to slowly penetrate the software industry. Originally initiated by the British with their TickIT program, the status of the ISO 9000 series within the software industry is still uncertain.

There are several reasons why the software development community at large is expressing some skepticism vis-à-vis the ISO 9000 series. The only ISO 9000 models available for the software industry are ISO 9001 and ISO 9000-3 entitled *Quality Management and Quality Assurance Standards Part 3: Guidelines for the Application of ISO 9001 to the Development, Supply and Maintenance of Software.* Published in 1992, the ISO 9000-3 guidelines, although concise, suffer from some drawbacks. For example, the guidelines already are outdated since they rely on the 1987 version of the ISO 9001 standard, which was updated in 1994. Also, it is evident that the contributors to the ISO 9000-3 guidelines were influenced by various other standards written some years ago for the development of large software projects. Although there is certainly nothing wrong with large projects (except for their complexity, which is never easy to manage), the classic waterfall model, suggested by the ISO 9000-3 guidelines, does not take into consideration software methodologies and tools developed in recent years.

Another concern is that there are several other competing software engineering models each claiming, or implying, that their model and methodology is at least as good, if not better than the ISO 9001 and 9000-3 documents. Examples would include the Capability and Maturity Model (CMM) developed by Carnegie Mellon's Software Engineering Institute (SEI); the Software Quality Systems Registration proposal (unreleased as of early 1994) representing the Registrar Accreditation Board (RAB) in Milwaukee, Wisconsin; the *Modelling a Software Quality Handbook* (MSQH) published by the Icelandic Council for Standardization; and the many military standards such as MIL-STD-973 *Configuration Management*. All is not lost, however. SEI is currently establishing dialogs with an ISO 9000 software committee to explore how the two models can better complement each other. (MSQH can be purchased from the Icelandic Council for Standardization, Iontaeknistofun Islands, Keldnaholti, IS-112 Reykjavik, Iceland).

SEI's Capability and Maturity Model

It is significant to note that SEI is sponsored by the U.S. Department of Defense. This explains the impressive pagination of the CMM document (approximately 500 pages as opposed to a mere 18 pages for ISO 9000-3). The CMM project originated in November 1986 when the federal government began to realize that a model was needed to evaluate the capability of its software contractors. By early 1993, SEI had released CMM v1.1.

The CMM for software "is a framework that describes the key elements of an effective software process."[1] Among software development firms, CMM identifies five levels of maturity (influenced by a blend of Crosby's and Juran's philosophies on quality management).

1. The *initial level*, characterized by unpredictable processes

2. The *repeatable level*, characterized by planning and tracking of software processes

3. The *defined level*, where standard and consistent processes exist

4. The *manages level*, where firms have developed predictable processes that operate within measurable limits

5. The *optimizing level*, where firms continuously improve the capability of their processes

The disturbing statistics are that according to an SEI survey, 74 percent of all software firms are at level 1, 19 percent at level 2, and a mere 7 percent at level 3.[2] Such statistics seem to indicate that there are quite a few dubious practitioners of software development, or that the CMM is perhaps too demanding and hence unachievable (at least as far as levels four and five are concerned).

A comparison of the CMM model to the ISO 9001/ISO 9000-3 (1987) model–guideline was undertaken by Mark Paulk of SEI and others. Based on Paulk's analysis, CMM and ISO match well except for clauses 4.7, Purchaser Supplied Product and 4.15, Handling, Storage, Packaging, and Delivery, which are not adequately addressed by CMM. The CMM is viewed as a superior model in the following areas.

• Process change management

• Technology change management

• Software quality management

• Quantitative process management

• Integrated software management

• Organization process definition

• Organization process focus

The ISO model (defined as ISO 9001 plus ISO 9000-3) is described as being fully adequate for only four categories: peer reviews, software product engineering, software configuration management, and software quality assurance. Based on his analysis, Paulk concludes that "a Level 1 organization according to the CMM could be certified as compliant with ISO 9001. That organization would, however, have significant process strengths at Level 2 and noticeable strengths at Level 3."[3]

I am not sure I share Paulk's optimism regarding the likelihood of having Level 1 organizations achieve ISO 9001 registration. Indeed, from an ISO 9000 perspective, the 1994 updates to ISO 9001—coupled with ISO 9000-3—although not as specific as CMM's Key Process Areas, Common Features, and Key Practices, cut across at least the first three or four levels of the CMM model. Consequently, I believe that one could have a (CMM) Level 3 organization and still not comply technically with all of the ISO 9001 requirements. However, this might point out a deficiency in the ISO 9000-3 model rather than vice versa.

The ISO 9000-3 Guidelines

Much in the same spirit as the ISO 9001 standards, the opening paragraphs of the guidelines recognize that: "Contracts between two parties for software product development may occur in many variations. In certain cases of two-party contracts, these guidelines might not be applicable even if 'tailored.' It is therefore important to determine the adequacy of the application of this part of ISO 9000 to the contract."[4]

The scope of the ISO 9000-3 guidelines specifies that the guidelines are "intended to provide guidance where a contract between two parties requires the demonstration of a supplier's capability to develop, supply, and maintain software products." After defining some key terms (see glossary in Appendix D) the guidelines provide the reader with a Quality System Framework summarized in Table B.1.

Some Limitations of ISO 9000-3

The ISO 9000-3 guidelines do not address all aspects of software quality assurance. Figure B.1 illustrates some of the limitations of the standard. Indeed, if one is to consider the traditional waterfall methodology, it is evident that ISO 9000-3 focuses only on some of the key phases of the complete process.[5] Nevertheless, the emphasis on configuration management ensures that from a management point of view, the ISO 9000-3 guidelines do cover the complete cycle.

Although ISO 9000-3 does provide brief definitions for some key terms and/or concepts such as verification and validation, many terms are not defined. For example, despite the importance placed on configuration management and the repeated reference to methods and tools, these terms are not defined. The following definitions are provided in the hope that they might help the reader better interpret the ISO 9000-3 guidelines.

Table B.1. ISO 9000-3 major headings with brief paragraph description. Italicized items are paragraph summaries by the author. (Source: ISO 9000-3).

Quality System—Framework	*5.4.1 General*
4.1 Management responsibility	*5.4.2 Development plan*
4.1.1 Quality policy	*5.4.2.1 Phases*
4.1.1.2 Organization	*(Various development phases may have to be*
4.1.1.2.1 Responsibility and authority	*planned.)*
4.1.1.2.2 Verification resources and personnel	*5.4.2.2 Management*
	(How will the project be managed?
4.1.1.2.3 Management representative	*Scheduling, progress control, organiza-*
	tional responsibilities, technical
4.1.1.2.4 Management review	*interfaces?)*
4.1.2 *Purchaser's management respon-sibility*	*5.4.2.3 Development methods and tools*
(Purchaser should cooperate with the sup-	*(Which method, practice and/or convention,*
plier to provide all necessary information in	*tools, and techniques will be used?*
a timely manner and resolve pending items.)	*5.4.3 Progress control*
4.1.3 Joint reviews	*(Progress review should be planned to*
(Should cover: verification results,	*ensure effective execution of development*
acceptance test results, conformance to	*plans.)*
requirements.)	*5.4.4 Input to development phases*
4.2 Quality system	*(Input to development phase should be*
4.2.1 General	*defined and documented.)*
4.2.2 Quality system documentation	*5.4.5 Output from development phases*
4.2.3 Quality plan	*(Ensure that output requirements*
4.3 Internal quality system audits	*are defined and documented, meet require-*
4.4 Corrective action	*ments, including regulatory requirements.)*
5.0 *Quality system—Life-cycle activities*	*5.4.6 Verification of each phase*
5.1 General	*(Verify, via measurable goals, record keep-*
5.2 Contract review	*ing and configuration control, that outputs*
5.2.1 General	*meet input requirements.)*
(More detailed than 9001)	*5.5 Quality planning*
5.2.2 Contract items on quality	*(Who reviews, approved, updates the qual-*
5.3 Purchaser's requirements specification	*ity plan?)*
(Customer requirements should be complete	*5.5.1 General*
and unambiguous and subject to document	*5.5.2 Quality plan content*
control.)	*(What quality metrics do you have in place?*
5.3.2 Mutual cooperation	*What test plans have been identified? Who*
(Cooperation between customer and supplier	*is responsible for configuration manage-*
should focus on definition of terms, record-	*ment? etc.)*
ing of reviews, etc.)	*5.6 Design and Implementation*
5.4 Development planning	*5.6.1 General*
(Key part of ISO 9000-3. Objectives must	*5.6.2 Design*
be defined, various phases identified, sched-	*(Very generic guidelines relating to good*
uling of resources and time, approval, etc.)	*design practices.)*

Table B.1. *(continued)*

5.6.3 Implementation
(Specific to development activities such as programming language, variable naming convention, amount of commentary, programming rules.)

5.6.4 Reviews
(Design review should be conducted and recorded).

5.7 Testing and validation
(May be a combination of validation, field testing, and acceptance testing).

5.7.1 General

5.7.2 Test planning
(Types of tests [functional, performance, usability, etc.]; test cases [data] and expected results, user documentation, training required, special environment, etc.)

5.7.3 Testing
(Recording of test results, corrective action routed to those responsible for change, retesting after patches are inserted, etc.)

5.7.4 Validation
(Validation of the software product as a complete product.)

5.7.5 Field testing
(Where testing under field conditions is required.)

5.8 Acceptance

5.8.1 General

5.8.2 Acceptance test planning
(To be determined with the customer.)

5.9 Replication, delivery, and installation

5.9.1 Replication
(This section often is subcontracted. Nevertheless, several items should be considered, such as custody of master and back-up copies.)

5.9.2 Delivery
(Verification of correctness and copies of software being delivered.)

5.9.3 Installation
(Who is responsible for what during installation.)

5.10 Maintenance
(When maintenance is required, what procedures are available for problem resolution, interface modification, functional expension, etc.)

5.10.2 Maintenance plan
(Scope of maintenance, support organization, records, etc.)

5.10.3 Identification of the initial product status

5.10.4 Support organization

5.10.5 Types of maintenance activities
(All changes should be made according to the same procedures, as far as possible. All changes should be documented in accordance with document control).

5.10.6 Maintenance records and reports
(Items to consider would be: list of requests for assistance, who is responsible for responding to requests, ranking of corrective actions, statistical data for failure occurrences, etc.)

5.10.7 Release procedures
(Need to consider such activities as: ground rules to determine where localized "patches" may be incorporated, types of releases, method to inform customer of future changes, method to confirm that changes do not introduce other problems, and record keeping for identifying nature of change and location for multiple products.)

6.0 Quality system—Supporting activities

6.1 Configuration management
(Traceability of previous releases, updating of software, etc.)

Table B.1. *(continued)*

6.1.2 Configuration management plan *(Organization, and activities to be brought under configuration control should be defined. Tools and techniques used in support of configuration management should be defined.)* **6.1.3 Configuration management activities** ***6.1.3.1 Configuration identification and traceability*** *(Traceability would include replication and delivery as well as interfaces with other software items.)* ***6.1.3.2 Change control*** *(Procedure for review, approval, effect, traceability, and authorization of change shall be maintained.)* ***6.1.3.3 Configuration status report*** *(Change reports will be maintained as per procedure.)* **6.2 Document control** *(Same as ISO 9001)* **6.2.2 *Types of documents*** *(Includes documents produced as a result of the following activities: development, verification, documentation for purchaser, and maintenance of product.)* **6.2.3 Document approval and issues** *(Same as ISO 9001)* **6.2.4 Document changes** *(Same as ISO 9001)* **6.3 Quality Records** *(Same as ISO 9001)* **6.4 *Measurement*** ***6.4.1 Product measurement*** *(Although no universal measures of software quality currently exists, the supplier is*	*expected to develop a minimum set of software [product] metrics such as field failures and code errors per x units of codes. These metrics should not only be collected, but also analyzed as to their effectiveness and used to implement corrective action.)* ***6.4.2 Process measurement*** *(Metrics should defined and used to assess process development and delivery capabilities [i.e., effectiveness to meet milestones and schedule].)* ***6.5 Rules, practices, and conventions*** *(What rules, practices, and conventions will be used to ensure that the quality assurance system will be effective.)* ***6.6 Tools and techniques*** *(Not specific as to which tools or techniques should be used except that they should be effective for management's purpose and product development.)* **6.7 Purchasing** **6.7.1 General** **6.7.2 Assessment of subcontractors** *(Same as ISO 9001)* **6.7.3 Validation of purchased product** *(Key concept: Validation of subcontracted work.)* ***6.8 Included software product*** *(Similar of purchaser supplied product but extends also to third party software product which **may** have to be included in the product. Key words: Validation, storage, protection, and maintenance.)* **6.9 Training** *(More extensive than ISO 9001)*

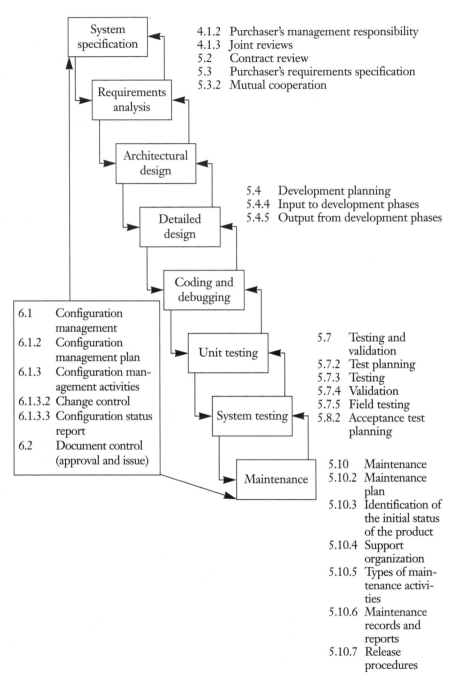

Figure B.1. Extensions of the waterfall life cycle and relation to ISO 9000-3.

Configuration management: "Configuration management is the practice of handling changes systematically
so that a system can maintain its integrity over time.
Another name for it is 'change control.' It includes
techniques for evaluation proposed changes, tracking
changes, and keeping copies of the system as it existed at
various points in time."[6]

Methodology: "A step-by-step 'battle plan,' or cook-
book, for achieving some desired result." Life cycle is a
synonym for methodology. Method is a step-by-step
technical approach for performing one or more of the
major activities identified in an overall methodology.
Structured analysis is a method for carrying out the
analysis phase of a project, while object-oriented design
is a method for performing the design phase."[7]

One of the noticeable drawbacks of the ISO 9000-3 guidelines
(hopefully to be corrected in future updates) is that contributors to the
guidelines have not taken into consideration newer methodologies such
as the Incremental and Spiral Models of the Modern Waterfall or the
Spiral Life Cycle proposed by Boehm. This last model incorporates the
prototyping life cycle first proposed by Bernard Boar in 1984 as a means
to determine user requirements.[8] As Yourden explains

Prototyping is widely praised as an effective way of
exploring alternative human interfaces for a system, for
example, for exploring different input formats, display
screens, and output reports. And it may be the *only* way
of eliciting requirements from a user who is unsure of
the very nature of the system he or she wants built.[9]

Another observation worth noting is that, surprisingly, nothing is
said in ISO 9000-3 about software code changes control or software code
changes using version-control tools. (For example, see Steve McConnell,
Code Complete, p. 533). The closest ISO 9000-3 comes to mentioning
anything about code is in 5.6.3, Implementation and 5.6.4, Reviews.
Under subparagraph b of 5.6.3, one can read that "Implementation

methodologies: the supplier should use appropriate implementation methods and tools to satisfy purchaser requirements."

ISO 9000-3's occasional reference to the use of tools (5.4.2.3, Development Methods and Tools, and 5.6.3, Implementation) should be relatively easy to satisfy given the plethora of programming, debugging, and testing tools now available. My programmer friends tell me that source-code control tools and source-code editors are available to analyze code and report on the complexity and quality of subroutines. Debugging tools, known as source-code comparators, can keep track of all programming modifications. Software design tools, such as computer assisted software engineering (CASE) or hierarchy input process output (HIPO), have now been in use for a few years. (see Yourdan, pp. 136–138 for description of limitations. See also McConnell, chapters 20 and 26).

Similarly, although several references are made to the need to develop measurements (see paragraph 6.4, Measurement), the guidelines can only state that "There are currently no universally accepted measures of software quality. However, at a minimum, some metrics should be used which represent reported field failures and/or defects from the customer's viewpoint" (6.4.1, Product Measurement). Yet, over the past few years various authors have suggested numerous metrics relating to software development. Table B.2 lists a few examples provided by Steve McConnell and Edward Yourdan.

Finally, one should note that although the ISO 9000-3 guidelines attempt to implicitly differentiate between external and internal quality requirements, essentially no guidelines are provided. McConnell identifies the following external and internal software quality characteristics.

External	*Internal*
Correctness	Maintainability
Usability	Flexibility
Efficiency	Portability
Reliability (MTBF)	Reusability
Integrity	Readability
Adaptability	Testability
Accuracy	Understandability
Robustness	

Table B.2. Some examples of software metrics.

Lines of codes
Number of defects
Defects per thousand lines of code
Defects per module
Number of global variables
Hours to complete a project
Mean time to repair a defect (MTTR)
Tests passed on first attempt
Error leakage (analysis errors that slip through to the design phase or design errors that slip through to the coding phase, and so on).
Cumulative software defects discovered during each version or release of a system
Defects discovered per person-hour of review effort
Customer responsiveness metrics
• Timeliness of responses to customer problems
• Quality of responses to customers
• Timeliness of solutions to customers
• Quality of solutions

Source: Steve McConnell, *Code Complete*, Section 22.4, and Edward Yourdan, *Decline & Fall of the American Programmer*, chapter 7.

Should ISO 9001/ISO 9000-3 Registration Be Required for All Software Development Firms?

The question as to whether or not all software projects should be subject to some sort of management and document control has been asked by many. Edward G. Cale in "Quality Issues for End-User Developed Software" comments that

> One of the overriding concerns caused by the trend towards end-user computing has been the potential decrease in quality and control as individuals with little or no formal information systems training have increasingly taken

responsibility for developing and implementing systems of their own making.

Not the least of these control risks is inadequate testing and documentation of the system once developed.[10]

Cale relies on Richard Ball's 1987 classification scheme (published in *Computer World*), which suggests a sliding scale of documentation standards as one progresses from Class A to Class C applications (see Table B.3).

To verify Ball's classification scheme, Cale developed a questionnaire that was submitted to 52 information and noninformation managers working in 25 firms within the Boston, Massachusetts, area. A summary of some of Cale's findings is presented in Table B.4.

Noting that Ball's classification scheme "does appear to touch on factors which the questionnaire respondents felt relevant to testing and documentation policy," Cale concludes that, "In general, the respondents were reluctant to require formal testing and documentation in the case of systems which are developed and used by the same individual,

Table B.3. Documentation requirements by type of organization.

	Class A	Class B	Class C

Data attributes	–Personal
	–Nonstrategic
	–Low volume
	–Independent
		–Departmental
		–High volume
		–Use by other
		  programmers
			–Strategic or
			  sensitive
			–Used to update
			  corporate database

Application attributes	–Personal
	–Stand alone
	–Low complexity
		–Corporate
		–Used by more
		  one person
			–Complex
			–Updates corporate
			  database

Project attributes	–One to five
	  work days
	–No formal project
	  management
	  warranted
		–Six to 20 work days
		–Some project
		  management
		  warranted
			–21 to 40 work days
			–Formal project
			  management
			  warranted

Source: Cale, "Quality Issues for End-User Developed Software," *The Journal of Systems Management* (January 1994): 37.

Table B.4. Cale's survey.

1. Does your organization maintain a policy, either written or unwritten, at the corporate or departmental level, on the testing and documentation of end-user developed systems?

	Policy		
	Written	Unwritten	None
Document	14%	31%	55%
Test	9%	28%	63%

2. How would you agree with the following statement: "Lack of testing (or documentation) of end-user developed applications is a potential serious problem."

	St Agree	Agree	Undecided	Disagree	St Disagree
Document	74%	15%	11%		
Test	60%	25%	15%		

3. How would you agree with the following statement: "My organization provides adequate support (time, people, guidance) for the (testing/documentation) of end-user developed applications."

	St Agree	Agree	Undecided	Disagree	St Disagree
Document	9%	12%	26%	38%	15%
Test	6%	8%	25%	42%	19%

particularly when outputs from the application do not impact beyond the developer. On the other hand, should such a development effort, however restricted, involve much more than one or two days of effort, most felt it should be tested anyway."[11]

Conclusion

Review of the survey in Table B.4 indicates that one should not assume that the ISO 9001/ISO 9000-3 standards are valid or valuable for all software project development. Based on the evidence provided by Cale, a reasonable argument probably could be made suggesting that, for small projects involving one to three programmers, producing small (2K–64K) programs, many of the configuration management requirements of ISO 9000-3 might be of little assistance and might hinder a project (nevertheless, ISO 9000-3 might still be a requirement if the software, no matter how small, ends up in a so-called regulated product).

However, as the number of programmers increases, the potential communication interaction between programmers increases at the rate of $0.5 \times n!/(n - 2!)$—that is when configuration management becomes important.

One would think that given the multitude of tools available on the market today, the issues surrounding the overall quality of software design, development, and maintenance sketched by the ISO 9000-3 guidelines would be a relatively easy task to achieve. Unfortunately, such is not the case. The author's experience with firms involved with software development has led him to conclude that although the technology and methodology has been available for quite a few years, the discipline to use these tools and manage software projects is still not what it should be. In too many cases, the approach seems to have changed very little from a decade ago when I had a brief part-time career as a programmer. In those days, one of the favored approaches was to begin writing code as soon as possible and then find out what you were supposed to do. Of course, that is an exaggeration because we actually did listen to what the customer wanted, but invariably we would somehow redefine what we thought was a better way of satisfying the customer's requests. Naturally, we always had to spend some time trying to convince the customer that the tables we had produced were exactly what were ordered. The fact is we often did not have all of the requirements and the customer was often not completely clear as to what she or he wanted. Naturally, we always tried to clarify customer requirements, but when the delivery date approached and we discovered that either we were still missing some requirements or the numbers did not make sense, we had little choice but to guesstimate some of the requirements. There is little doubt that, for some of our larger projects, the discipline required by the ISO 9000-3 guidelines would have helped us produce better software in less time.

Notes

1. Mark C. Paulk, Bill Curtis, Mary Beth Chrissis, and Charles V. Weber, "Capability Maturity Model for Software, Version 1.1," Software Engineering Institute, Carnegie Mellon University (February 1993): O7.

2. See "An Analysis of SEI Software Process Assessment Result" Software Engineering Institute presentation of August 1993. For a discussion on SPICE (Software Process Improvement and Capability Determination) see, "On the Horizon: An International Standard for Software Process Improvement," *Bridge*, (1993): 27–30.

3. Mark C. Paulk, "ISO 9001 and the Capability Maturity Model for Software," (Carnegie Mellon Institute, 1993), 14–15.

4. ISO 9000-3 *Guidelines for the Application of ISO 9001 to the Development, Supply and Maintenance of Software*, Introduction.

5. Steve McConnell notes that the waterfall software development model places too much emphasis on inefficient unit testing. Steve McConnell, *Code Complete* (Redmond, Wash.: Microsoft Press, 1993), 593. See also Edward Yourdon, *Decline and Fall of the American Programmer* (Englewood Cliffs, N.J.: Yourdon Press, Prentice Hall Building, 1992), 94–96.

6. McConnell, *Code Complete*, 530.

7. Yourdon, *Decline and Fall*, 94.

8. Ibid., 103.

9. Ibid., 104.

10. Edward C. Cale, "Quality Issues for End-User Development Software," *Journal of Systems Management* (January 1994): 36–39.

11. Ibid., 38.

Appendix C ISO 9001 or ISO 9002 and the Construction Industry

In 1993 the consulting engineering and construction industries began to look into the applicability and relevancy of the ISO 9000 series to their industries. As has been shown in previous chapters, engineering consulting firms already have begun to adapt and implement the ISO 9001 to their needs (some are already registered). Although the application of ISO 9001 to engineering consulting firms is straightforward, contractors seem to experience greater difficulties interpreting the standards and questioning their relevancy to their business. Yet, several conversations with consulting and project engineers have revealed that implementation of a quality assurance that would conform to the principles outlined in the ISO 9002 standard (of particular relevance to contractors) is logical. This is not to say that the industry has no quality assurance guidelines to follow for, as we shall soon see, such guidelines do exist. Unfortunately, the construction industry is (like all industries) subject to the same laws of human nature, which basically state that although everyone recognizes the value of quality assurance, no one wants to spend the time practicing its fundamental principles.

Some Examples of Quality Assurance in the Engineering Construction Industry

Without having performed any detailed research on the subject, I have come to find out that a few quality assurance guidelines for the engineering and construction industry have been available for the past 10 to 12 years. In my library, I have at least three documents that directly relate to the ISO 9000 series: (1) *Quality Assurance for Consulting Engineers*, (2) *Guidelines for Development of Architect/Engineering Quality Control Manual*, and (3) *The REDICHECK Interdisciplinary Coordination*.

The *Quality Assurance for Consulting Engineers: ACEC Guidelines to Practice*, volume V, number 2 document was first published by the American Consulting Engineers Council in 1986. A review of chapters 2, 4, 5, 6, and 7 revealed that there is some overlap with the ISO 9000 series; the mapping is far from being complete, however. A cursory analysis of the document indicates that the only ISO 9001 paragraphs addressed, with various degrees of completeness, appear to be 4.1, 4.3, 4.4, 4.5, and 4.18. However, Appendix A of the ACEC guidelines lists over 30 documents that collectively would appear to address other ISO 9001 or ISO 9002 paragraphs. A selected list of document titles is included in Table C.1.

Table C.1. Selected documents.

1910-1 *Standard Form of Agreement Between Owner and Engineer for Professional Services—1984*; 52 pages

1910-8 *Standard General Conditions of the Construction Contract—1983*; 33 pages

1919-8B *Change Order—1983*; 2 pages

1910-8-D *Certificate of Substantial Completion—1983*; 2 pages

1910-8-F *Work Directive Change—1983*; 2 pages

1910-9-C *Focus on Shop Drawings—1985*; 18 pages

1910-10 *Standard Form of Agreement Between Engineer and Architect—1985*; 15 pages

---

The Guidelines for Development of Architect/Engineer Quality Control Manual, published in 1982 by the National Society of Professional Engineers, was prepared "in response to the request of design professionals for a guide to office practices and procedures that will enable them to render their services in a more efficient manner and with greater quality control." A review of the table of contents (listed in Table C.2) gives a flavor of the document's overall emphasis.

The last document, *REDICHECK Interdisciplinary Coordination* (February 1992), was developed by William T. Nigro who explains

> The focus of the REDICHECK system is the interface
> of disciplines. If the design office does not discover and
> correct interdisciplinary errors and omissions during
> the preparation of contract documents or during a final
> quality assurance review, the contractor almost assuredly
> will, and at the most inopportune time.[1]

The REDICHECK system thus ensures that interdisciplinary reviews required of all construction projects is undertaken so as to minimize design errors and/or omissions.

Table C.2. Table of contents from the *Architect/Engineer Quality Control Manual*.

General Management Considerations for Quality Control
Section A   Preproposal Project Scope Evaluation
Section B   Proper Contractual Agreements
Section C   Project Manager & Design Team System
Section D   Written Project Program
Section E   Design Budget and Time Schedule
Section F   Project Phases and Reviews
Section G   Project Scheduling and Control
Section H   Checking Procedures
Section I   Construction Contract Administration

Since the industry can rely on several guidelines that collectively cover most of the requirements of ISO 9002, one would think that the application of an ISO 9001 or ISO 9002 quality assurance system should be a minor task. Unfortunately, as was already stated, such is not the case. Indeed, a conversation with Nigro revealed that although many guidelines are available, and even though some firms will claim that they follow a certain guideline, reality paints a different picture. This explains why owners will keep on hiring engineering consultants to ensure that they will get what was promised. The problem is no doubt partially due to the fact that the guidelines are strictly voluntary. Perhaps the adoption of the ISO 9000 series to construction could bring about some form of minimum industry standard recognized by all.

Note

1. William T. Nigro, *REDICHECK Interdisciplinary Coordination* (Peachtree City, Ga.: The REDICHECK Firm, 1987), 1.

Appendix D   Glossary

Accuracy   "The accuracy of an instrument is the extent to which the average of a long series of repeat measurements made by the instrument on a single unit of product differs from the true value. This difference is usually due to a systematic error in the measurement process. In this case, the instrument is said to be "out of calibration." J. M. Juran and Frank M. Gryna, Jr. *Quality Planning and Analysis*. New York: McGraw-Hill, 1980, 390. ISO reference: paragraph 4.11.2 a).

Appropriate   "Suitable for a particular person, condition, occasion, or place; proper, fitting. From Latin *appropriatus*, to make one's own." *The American Heritage Dictionary*. 2d ed. Houghton Mifflin, 1991. Appropriate does not mean appropriate to the registrar or third-party auditor. The word is used throughout the standard.

Calibration   "The process of comparing one standard against a higher-order standard of greater accuracy is called calibration. The ability to relate measurement results back to the primary reference standard is called traceability of the standard." J. M. Juran and Frank M. Gryna, Jr. *Quality Planning and Analysis*. New York: McGraw-Hill, 1980, 390. ISO reference: 4.11.1, 4.11.2 b, c.

Capability   ". . . competence, based on tested performance, to achieve measurable results." Frank M. Gryna, Jr., in J. M. Juran and Frank M. Gryna, *Juran's Quality Control Handbook*. 4th ed. New York: McGraw-Hill, 1988, 15–16. *See also* Process Capability. This definition favors the statistical definition of the word *capability*. Frank Gryna uses it as part of his definition of process capability. ISO reference: 4.3.2, "capability to meet contract"; 4.9 g) "ensure continuing process capability"; 4.11.1 "measurement capability."

Contract   "1. An agreement between two or more parties, esp. one that is written and enforceable by law." The *American Heritage Dictionary*. 2nd ed. Houghton Mifflin Company, 1991. ISO reference: 4.3.

Control   As with the word *quality*, the word *control* is much used and abused and can lead to some confusion, particularly when used in a bilingual or trilingual environment. For example, it is interesting to note that in French, the word *control* is translated as *maîtrise* (or mastering). Thus statistical process control is translated as maîtrise statistique des procédés. To add to the confusion, the English translation for the French word *contrôle* is *inspection*. If you are statistically inclined, control might imply statistical control (in other words, a process is in statistical control when it is stable and its variation is due to random error).

As far as the ISO standards are concerned, the word *control* is used in more than one context and can have several meanings. In paragraph 4.5, Document Control, control means that documents are formally or officially reviewed prior to being issued or changed and eventually approved and released. In paragraphs 4.11 and 4.20, Statistical Techniques, the standard alludes to control in the statistical sense of the word (actually, the standards refer to measurement and process capability). In all other cases, the meaning of the word control is defined in the General paragraph. For example in paragraph 4.9, Process Control, controlled conditions consist of six conditions specified in subparagraphs a–g. In other instances, as in paragraph 4.11.1, where the words *control of equipment* are used, the meaning must be inferred from reading subsequent paragraphs (*see also* Measurement Capability). The word *control* also is used in paragraph 4.15.4, Packaging: "The supplier shall control packing, packaging and marking process . . ." and, 4.15.5, Preservation: ". . . (when) product is under the supplier's control." In 4.15.4, the intent is to demonstrate effective operation of the processes. In 4.15.5, control implies responsibility.

Design Change   "A well-established engineering change procedure must govern all the issued and released engineering documents, such as layouts, drawings, specifications, part lists, and assembly instructions, as well as an agreed schedule for incorporation of the change concerned." D. J. Leech and B. T. Turner, *Engineering Design for Profit*. New York: John Wiley & Sons, 1985, 260.

Design Control   "The problem of the control of design becomes one of: forecasting costs, allocating resources (costs) to each project, setting the program for each project so that the drawings will be delivered on time, monitoring the use of resources by each project, and monitoring the course of each project against its program." D. J. Leech and B. T. Turner, *Engineering Design for Profit*. New York, John Wiley & Sons, 1985, 133.

Design Input   "Design input is the design definition phase, or the design requirements definition phase, in which the design's physical and performance features or characteristics are defined. The design input is typically configured in the form of a description of all pertinent design requirements, such as physical, functional, environmental, safety, and regulatory requirements. This phase also includes the identification of components that require development and/or analysis." *Federal Register*, 58: 224 (23 November, 1993): 61961. For medical devices, labeling requirements are an important element of design input (for example, safety needs of the user, environmental conditions in which the device will be used, reliability, safeguards against misuse, and/or servicing). ISO 9001 reference: 4.4.4.

Design Output   "Design output means the results of a design effort at each design phase and at the end of the total design effort. The total finished design output consists of the device, its packaging and labeling, and the associated specifications and drawings and the production and quality system specifications and procedures. . . ." *Federal Register*, 58: 224, 61979. This definition is specifically written for the medical device industry, but should apply to most other industries. ISO 9001 reference: 4.4.6.

Design Review   "Design reviews are one way of providing a communication forum for the specialist concerned with a particular design effort." "A design review is a formal synergistic, documented, and systematic study of design by users and specialists who are not directly associated with realizing the design." D. J. Leech and B. T. Turner, *Engineering Design for Profit.* New York: John Wiley & Sons, 1985, 274, 279. Each one of the definitions of design change, control, and review favor the engineering definition of design. For example, in the service sector, design activities also are performed daily, however, they do not necessarily result in the production of drawings, but rather draft documents or a variety of information using a host of media. ISO 9001 reference: 4.4.5.

Design Validation   *See* Validation.

Design Verification   *See* Verification.

Document   "1. A written or printed paper bearing the original, official, or legal form of something, and which can be used to furnish decisive evidence of information." *The American Heritage Dictionary.* 2d ed. New York: Houghton Mifflin, 1991. ISO reference: throughout.

Effective—An effective action is an action that produces an intended or desired result or intention. The word effective is used in paragraph 4.1.3, Management Review, "to ensure suitability and effectiveness (of the quality system); in paragraph 4.14.2, Corrective Action, as in "the effective handling of customer complaints," and again in paragraphs 4.16 and 4.17, Internal Audit, "to determine the effectiveness of the quality system." Third-party auditors, do not really want to audit a quality assurance system that is not effective (in other words, a system that does not match reality). An effective quality assurance system, from an ISO 9000 point of view, is a living system that addresses all of the standards' paragraphs.

Efficient   *Roget's Thesaurus* uses the word *efficient* as a synonym to effective. Yet, efficiency denotes minimum energy or expense or unnecessary effort. Thus, an efficient quality assurance system should not have any redundancy. I suppose some of us who are familiar with the 1987 version of the ISO 9000 series would argue that the 1987 was, in some respect, a more efficient series than the 1994 edition.

Measurement capability   See comment for paragraph 4.11 in body of text.

Precision   "The precision of an instrument is the extent to which the instrument repeats its results when making repeat measurements on the same unit of product. The scatter of these measurements may be designated as sigma (e), meaning the standard deviation of measurement error. The lower the value of sigma (e) the more 'precise' is the instrument." J. M. Juran and Frank M. Gryna, Jr. *Quality Planning and Analysis.* New York: McGraw-Hill, 1980, 390. ISO reference: paragraph 4.11.2 a.

Procedure   "1. A manner of proceeding; way of performing or effecting something. 2. An act composed of steps; course of action. 3. A set of established forms or methods for conducting the affairs of a business, legislative body, or court of law." *The American Heritage Dictionary.* 2d ed. Houghton Mifflin, 1991. ISO reference: throughout the standard, particularly in association with the word *documented* as in "documented procedures."

Process Capability   "Process capability is a measure of the inherent uniformity of the process." J. M. Juran and Frank M. Gryna, Jr., *Quality Planning and Analysis.* New York, McGraw-Hill, 1980, 272. "Process capability is the measured, inherent reproducibility of the product turned out by a process." Frank M. Gryna, Jr., in J.M. Juran and Frank M. Gryna, *Juran's Quality Control Handbook.* 4th ed. New York: McGraw-Hill, 1988, 15. *See also* Capability. ISO reference: 4.9 g and 4.20.1. *See also* Validation.

Product   "The result of activities or processes; product includes 'hardware,' 'software,' 'processed material,' and 'service' or a combination thereof and shall apply to 'intended product' only." [ISO 9001, 2 and 3, paragraph 3.2.] Referred throughout the standards.

It is important to note the reference to *intended product* (in other words, product ordered by the customer). Nevertheless, since the term *product* is used in different context, it can mean different things. In paragraph 4.6.1, Purchasing General, the reference is to "purchased product" that is, product purchased by the supplier. Naturally, the reference to product is not meant to apply to office supplies but rather to ingredients, raw materials, components, subcomponents, subassemblies, software, and so on, which is to be incorporated within the product to be delivered to the customer.

In paragraph 4.6.4.2, Customer Verification of Subcontracted Product, the term *product* now refers to subcontracted product (in other words, subassemblies, components, and so on).

In 4.7, Control of Customer-Supplied Product, the term applies to any hardware, software, processed materials, or service provided by the customer and incorporated into the supplies (in other words, the final product).

In 4.10.2, Receiving Inspection and Testing, product is all incoming products to be used or otherwise incorporated in the fabrication, creation, assembly of the final product. Examples could include: dies (manufacturing), documents (blueprints, design requirements, training materials), and tools (software tools, cutting tools, and so on).

Quality The standard does not define the term *quality* despite the fact that the term is occasionally used rather obtusely in several sentences. In 4.6.4.2 one reads about "effective control of quality" and in 4.9 (Process Control), one is told that

> Controlled conditions shall include the following:
>
> a) documented procedures defining the manner of production, installation and servicing, where the absence of such procedures could adversely affect quality;

For a definition of quality one can turn to the ISO 8402 document where quality is defined as "Totality of characteristics of an entity that bear on its ability to satisfy stated and implied needs." [ISO 8402-1994, 2.1]. The appended seven notes proceed to further define what is and is not meant by quality. It is evident that as far as the standard is concerned, the term *quality* is meant to mean much more than stated or implied needs as expressed or otherwise documented by a customer, clarified or modified by the supplier, and formalized in a mutually acceptable contract. Quality explicitly and implicitly encompasses quality of design, contract review, subcontractors and/or vendors, raw materials, subcomponents, subassemblies, process control, manufacturing, installation, servicing, inspection, testing, handling, storage, packaging, shipping, delivery, and other activities. Consequently, quality means quality of the system as a whole and all of its interrelated parts.

Quality Plan   "A document setting out the specific quality practices, resources and sequence of activities relevant to a particular product, service, contract or project." [ISO 8401-1986, 3.9]. ISO reference: 4.2.3 a). In some cases, a quality plan may have to be written to address particular customer requirements (for example, tighter tolerances, tighter acceptance sampling) In most cases, these special or additional requirements are written in the contract and thus may constitute the plan.

Quality Record   Any record called for by any of the paragraphs of ISO 9001, ISO 9002, or ISO 9003 requirements, (for example, inspection records, test records, nonconformity records, calibration, and so on). *See* Records. The need for quality records is invariably called for in the standards by referencing paragraph 4.16, Control of Quality Records.

Record   "1. To set down for preservation in writing or other permanent form. 2. To register or indicate. 3. To register (sound) in permanent form by mechanical or electrical means for reproduction." *The American Heritage Dictionary*. 2d ed. New York: Houghton Mifflin, 1991. A record should not be confused with a document; therefore, one does not need to subject records to document control procedures.

Servicing   "1. To make fit for use; adjust, repair, or maintain." *The American Heritage Dictionary*. 2d ed. New York: Houghton Mifflin, 1991. Servicing also can apply to the service sector. For example, a consulting firm may have to service its reports or engineering drawings by answering phone requests or sending consultants in the field to provide further assistance and/or interpretation. ISO reference: 4.9, 4.11.1, 4.12, 4.19.

Specifications   "A detailed and exact statement of particulars, esp. a statement prescribing materials, dimensions and workmanship for something to be built, installed, or manufactured." *The American Heritage Dictionary*. 2d ed. Houghton Mifflin, 1991. I find this definition more eloquent than the one provided by the ISO 8402 document where specification is concisely defined as: "The document that prescribes the requirements with which the product or service has to conform." [Definition 3.22] ISO reference: throughout the standard as in "meet specified requirements."

Subcontractors   The entities to whom work is subcontracted.

Suitable   "Appropriate to a given purpose or occasion." *The American Heritage Dictionary.* 2d ed. New York: Houghton Mifflin, 1991. Often used as synonymous to *appropriate*.

Supplier   In ISO 9000 parlance, the user of the standard, not to be confused with your suppliers that are referred to in ISO as subcontractors.

Validation   With respect to a device or product, validation means "establishing and documenting evidence that the device is fit for its intended use. With respect to a process, 'validation' means establishing and documenting evidence that the process will consistently produce a result or product meeting its predetermined specifications and quality attributes." *Federal Register* 58: 224 (23 November 1993): 61979. "In some instances, validation, field testing, and acceptance testing may be one and the same activity." ISO 9000-3, *Quality Management and Quality Assurance Standards—Part 3: Guidelines for the application of ISO 9001 to the Development, Supply, and Maintenance of Software.* Paragraph 5.7.1. ISO 9001 reference: paragraph 4.4.8.

Verification   "Confirming and documenting with valid, objective evidence, that specific requirements have been met. Verification includes the process of examining the results of an activity to determine conformity with the stated specifications for that activity and ensuring that the device is adequate for its intended use." *Federal Register* 58: 224 (23 November, 1993): 61979. ISO 9001 reference: paragraph 4.4.7.

Bibliography

Abler, Ronald, John S. Adams, and Peter Gould. *Spatial Organization: The Geographer's View of the World.* Englewood Cliffs, N.J.: Prentice-Hall, 1971.

Albrecht, Karl, and Ron Zemke. *Service America.* New York: Warner Books, 1985.

Automotive Industry Action Group (AIAG). *Measurement Systems Analysis: Reference Manual,* Southfield, Mich.: Automative Industry Groups, 19.

Averitt, Robert T. *The Dual Economy: The Dynamics of American Industry Structure.* New York: W. W. Norton & Company, 1968.

Bemowski, Karen. "Trailblazers in Reinventing Government." *Quality Progress* (December 1993): 37–42.

Bradley, Ryan. "A New Look at DoD Quality Management and Quality System Standards." Washington, D.C., July 4, 1993.

Brigham, Steven E. "TQM: Lessons We Can Learn from Industry." *Change* (May/June 1993): 42–48.

Burney, Robert. "TQM in a Surgery Center." *Quality Progress* (January 1994): 97–100.

Burrows, I. E. "Never Mind the Width Feel the Quality—Ship Years of Ship Management Quality Assurance." *The Institute of Marine Engineers* (February 2, 1993).

Charters, David. "U.S. Postal Service Delivers Total Quality." *Quality Digest* (June 1993): 25–31.

Coonley, Howard. "The International Standards Movement." In *National Standards in a Modern Economy*, edited by Dickson Reck. New York: Harper & Brothers, 1954.

Crosby, Philip B. *Quality Without Tears*. New York: Penguin Group, Plume Book, 1984.

De Bono, Edward. *Surpetition: Going Beyond Competition*. New York: HarperBusiness, 1992.

Deming, W. Edwards. *Quality, Productivity, and Competitive Position*. Cambridge, Mass.: Massachusetts Institute of Technology, Center for Advanced Engineering Studies, 1982.

Dixon, John R. *Design Engineering: Inventiveness, Analysis, and Decision Making*. New York: McGraw-Hill Book Company, 1966.

Drucker, Peter F. *Innovation and Entrepreneurship: Practice and Principles*. New York: Harper & Row, 1986.

Durand, I. G., D. W. Marquardt, R. W. Peach, and J. C. Pyle, "Updating the ISO 9000 Quality Standards: Responding to Marketplace Needs." *Quality Progress* (July 1993): 23–28.

Dwyer, Kevin. "Cool-Hand Luke," *Washington CEO* (June/July 1991): 12–14.

Edgerton, Russell. "The Re-examination of Faculty Priorities." *Change* (July/August 1993): 10–25.

Entin, David H. "Boston: Less than Meets the Eye." *Change* (May/June 1993): 28–31.

Ewell, Peter T. "Total Quality & Academic Practice: The Idea We've Been Waiting for?" *Change* (May/June 1993): 49–55.

Feigenbaum, Armand V. *Total Quality Control*. New York: McGraw-Hill, 1983.

Goldberg, Stephanie B. "The Quest for TQM." *The ABA Journal* (November 1993): 52–58.

Goodman, John, Arlene Malech, and Colin Adamson. "Don't Fix the Product, Fix the Customer." *The Quality Review* (Fall 1988): 8–11.

Greenbaum, Stuart I. "TQM at Kellogg." *The Journal for Quality and Participation* 16, no. 1 (1993): 91.

Greenberg, Selig. *The Quality of Mercy*. New York: Atheneum, 1971.

Harrington, Donald C. "The Relationship of Quality Surveillance to Various Health Care Delivery Systems." *Quality Assurance of Medical Care*, Conference U.S. Department of Health, Education, and Welfare, February 1973.

Harris, R. Lee. *The Customer Is King*. Milwaukee, Wis.: ASQC Quality Press, 1991.

Horowitz, Jacques H. *The Quality of Service, Towards the Conquest of the Customer.* Paris: InterEditions, 1987.

Ishikawa, Kaoru. *What Is Total Quality Control?* (Englewood Cliffs, N.J.: Prentice-Hall, 1985).

Kacker, Raghu N. "Quality Planning for Service Industries." *Quality Progress* (August 1988): 39–42.

Kanter, Rosabeth Moss. *The Change Masters*. New York: Simon and Schuster Touchstone Book, 1988.

King, Carol A. "A Framework for a Service Quality Assurance System." *Quality Progress* (September 1987): 27–32.

Lamprecht, James. *ISO 9000: Preparing for Certification*. New York: Marcel Dekker, 1992.

———. *Implementing the ISO 9000 Series*. New York: Marcel Dekker, 1993.

Lash, Linda M. *The Complete Guide to Customer Service*. New York: John Wiley & Sons, 1989.

Liswood, Laura A. *Servicing Them Right*. New York: Harper Business, 1990.

Leech, D. J., and B. T. Turner. *Engineering Design for Profit*. New York, John Wiley & Sons, 1985.

Matthews, W. E. "The Missing Element in Higher Education." *The Journal for Quality and Participation* 10, no. 6 (January/February 1993): 103.

McConnell, Steve. *Code Complete*. Redmond, Wash.: Microsoft Press, 1993.

McKnight, John. "Professionalized Service and Disabling Help." In *Disabling Profession*. London: Marion Boyars Publishers, 1977, 69–92; distributed by Kampmann & Co.

Morita, Akio. *Made in Japan*. Glasgow: William Collins Sons & Co., 1986.

Morrow, Mark. "Companies Find Savings with ISO 9000." *Quality Digest* (November 1993): 20.

Neuhauser, Peg C. *Tribal Warfare in Organizations*. Cambridge: Mass.: Ballinger Publishing Co., 1988.

Noble, David F. *America by Design*. New York: Oxford University Press, 1977.

Osborne, David, and Ted Gaebler. *Reinventing Government*. Reading, Mass.: Penguin Group, Plume Book, 1993.

Paich, Milo R. "Making Service Quality Look Easy." *Training* (February 1992): 32–35.

Papanek, Victor. *Design for the Real World*. Chicago: Academy Chicago Publishers, 1992.

Peach, Robert W. *The ISO 9000 Handbook*. Fairfax, Va.: CEEM Information Services, 1992.

Peric, T. S. "Government in Action: A Look Inside the Federal Quality Institute." *Quality Digest* (June 1993): 34–37.

Petroski, Henry. *To Engineer Is Human*. New York: Vintage Books, 1992.

Phaneuf, Marie C. "Quality Assurance—A Nursing View." *Quality Assurance of Medical Care.* Conference U.S. Department of Health, Education, and Welfare (February 1973): 347–361.

Riley, Pat. "The Winner Within." *Success* (September 1993): 39.

Rooney, E. M. "A Proposed Quality System Specification for the National Health Service." *Journal of the Institute of Quality Assurance* 14, no. 2 (1988): 45–49.

Rosenfeld, L. S. "Standards for Assessing Quality of Care." *Quality Assurance of Medical Care.* Regional Medical Programs Service, U.S. Department of Health, Education, and Welfare (January 1973): 9–34.

Schaaf, Dick. "The Case Against ISO 9000." *Training Magazine* (September 1993): 5–10.

Schumacher, E. F. *Small Is Beautiful: Economics As If People Mattered.* New York: Harper & Row, Perennial Library, 1973.

Simpson, W. Hunter. "Puzzling FDA Probe Unfair to Physio-Control." *The Puget Sound Business Journal* (September 17–23, 1993): 11.

Sittig, J. "Defining Quality Costs." *Quality Engineering* 28 (July/August 1964): 103–111.

Souza, Anthony R. de, and J. Brady Foust. *World Space-Economy.* Columbus, Ohio: Charles E. Merrill Publishing, 1979.

Stebbing, Lionel. *Quality Management in the Service Industry.* New York: Ellis Horwood, 1990.

Stratton, Brad. "How the Federal Government Is Reinventing Itself." *Quality Progress* (December 1993): 21–34.

Tribus, Myron. "Quality Management in Education." *The Journal for Quality and Participation* 16, no. 1 (January/February 1993): 12–21.

Van Rossem, F. "Piggybacking on ISO 9000." *ISO 9000 News* 2, no. 6, (November/December 1993): 7–8.

Walker, H. Kenneth. "The Problem-Oriented Medical Record in Medical Audit. *Quality Assurance of Medical Care.* Conference U.S. Department of Health, Education, and Welfare (February 1973): 215–220.

Wallace, Thomas F. *Customer Driven Strategy*. Essex Junction, Vt.: Oliver Wright Publications, 1992.

Willingham, Ron. *Hey! I'm the Customer*. New York: Prentice Hall, 1992.

Yourdon, Edward. *Decline and Fall of the American Programmer*. Englewood Cliffs, N.J.: Yourdon Press, 1992.

Zeithaml, Valarie A., A. Parasuraman, and Leonard L. Berry. *Delivering Quality Service*. New York: The Free Press, 1990.

Zimmerman, Charles D., and John W. Enell. "Service Industries." In J. M. Juran, *Juran's Quality Control Handbook*. New York, McGraw-Hill, 1988.

Index